QUEER ANCIENT WAYS

Fig. 1. Hieronymus Bosch, *Ship of Fools* (1490–1500)

First published in 2018 by punctum books, Earth, Milky Way.
https://punctumbooks.com

Part of chapter 1 was published as "Below Either/Or: Rereading Femininity and
Monstrosity inside *Enuma Elish*," *Feminist Theology* 26, no.2 (2018): 115–32, reproduced with permission of Sage Publishing. Part of chapter 4 was published
as "The (De)Coloniality of Conceptual Inequivalence: Reinterpreting *Ometeotl*
within Nahua *Tlacuiloliztli*," in *Decolonial Readings of Latin American Literature
and Culture,* eds. Juan Ramos and Tara Daly, 39–55 (New York: Palgrave Mac-
millan, 2016), reproduced with permission of Palgrave Mcmillan.

ISBN-13: 978-1-947447-93-6 (print)
ISBN-13: 978-1-947447-94-3 (ePDF)

LCCN: 2018963381
Library of Congress Cataloging Data is available from the Library of Congress

Book design: Vincent W.J. van Gerven Oei
Cover image: Line drawing of the statue Coatlicue Mayor, National Museum of
Anthropology, Mexico City. Wikimedia Commons.

HIC SVNT MONSTRA

QUEER ANCIENT WAYS

A DECOLONIAL EXPLORATION
BY ZAIRONG XIANG

Contents

獻給爸爸媽媽：感謝你們教導我，與眾不同是珍貴且值得驕傲的品質，並抗拒世俗的壓力，遷就寵溺你們另類的兒子

Preface

[...] *o mar é-se como o aberto de um livro aberto e esse aberto*
é o livro que ao mar reverte e o mar converte pois de mar se
trata do mar que bate sua nata de escuma se eu lhe disser que
o mar começa você dirá que ele cessa se eu lhe disser que ele
avança você dirá que ele cansa se eu lhe disser que ele fala você
dirá que ele cala e tudo será o mar e nada será o mar [...]
— Haroldo de Campos, *Galáxias*[1]

When, where, and how do the earth, the sea, the world, the universe, the cosmos, and the galaxy begin? Creation myths all over the world have their own ways of explaining this inexplicable mystery. So it is inevitable that a book about creation myths should deal with its own beginnings.

But there is no single beginning. Genesis is always already generative; *it* will always have been *many,* a plurality of geneses. Every beginning is already entrenched in other forms of beginning, continuity, and (pre-)existence. *Queer Ancient Ways: A Decolonial Exploration* also has its own messy geneses. Like every instance when someone proclaims, "I have done all these solely

---

1   Haroldo de Campos, *Galáxias* [1963–1976] (São Paolo: Editora 34, 2004). This poem has no beginning or ending and is presented in an interactive format. For an English version that preserves this format, see Haroldo de Campos, *Galáxias,* trans. Odile Cisneros with Suzanne Jill Levine, http://www.artsrn.ualberta.ca/galaxias/index.html.

by myself," it is a big lie. Even the biblical God Elohim was plural when "he" is said to have created the world into being. This book is about original myths but also about debunking the myth of origin that lies behind one of the most influential ideas concerning creation: *creatio ex nihilo,* creation out of nothingness.

I am not sure about when, where, and how this unexpected journey through the lands surrounded by rivers (Mesopotamia) and by waters (Cemanahuac, Mesoamerica's Nahua name) began.[2] Therefore, "beginnings." We will start over twice with Part I: The Waters and Part II: The Earth, with Part O: Nulla in between.

This book has not been created *ex nihilo.* It has been enlightened by colonized people who resist colonial imposition and elimination in diverse ways; animated by scholarly labors that excavate, retell, and reinterpret old myths; and populated by its protagonists, the goddesses. There are watery goddesses, earthly goddesses, heavenly goddesses, malicious goddesses, benevolent goddesses, life-generating goddesses, destructive goddesses. Goddesses who refuse to be feminized, sometimes by taking up the male gender, sometimes by transcending such binaries; goddesses who wear the face of an animal or the body of a serpent; goddesses who, if we looked at them closely, would defy our rationale for calling them "goddesses" in the first place. Collectively, these are goddesses who announce from time immemorial the possibilities of the total abolition of the dual and dull gender system of colonial hetero-modernity.

The main protagonists of the book are Tiamat, co-creatrix of heaven and earth in *Enuma Elish,* the *Babylonian Epic of Creation,* and Coatlicue, the Nahua creatrix of the sun, the moon, and the myriads of stars. These are no individual beings. They

---

2   Nahuatl is the official language of the Aztec Empire and also the lingua franca of the Mexican valley before the Spanish *Conquista*. I change the word's morphology according to the linguistic rules of Nahuatl, by dropping the suffix *-tl,* which is normally a marker of a substantive, to make it into an adjective and a noun meaning the speakers of Nahuatl. "Nahua(tl)" is a more inclusive concept than the more commonly known but empire-related "Aztec."

have existed since forever, way before an essentialist ontology could fix things in their places and before the colonial/modern gender dualism could aggressively claim its universality, implanting the belief that male–female, god–goddess, friend–fiend are dichotomies that have always been there, way before the invention of *creatio ex nihilo,* by which one could pretend to be self-generated, to be "without a mother." As divine beings, these old deities are literally entangled with stars and oceans, heavens and earths, not to mention forms belonging to the allegedly "opposite sex" and other possible embodiments.

Tiamat, the Babylonian primordial goddess is first and foremost the salt-water sea, commingled with Apsu, the often masculinized fresh-water sea, hidden underneath the etymological and epistemological layers of the most discussed sentence of the Judeo-Christian Bible, found in Genesis 1:1–2: "When God began to create heaven and earth, and the earth then was welter and waste and darkness over the deep [*tehom*] and God's breath hovering over the waters, God said, 'Let there be light.'"[3] This mysterious *tehom*[4] lurking behind the blinding *light* has a deeper history involving other watery deities in Mesopotamia. This is the topic of Part I: The Waters. Water flows and circulates. Tiamat will speak from the distant past to contemporary queer struggles, from creation battles with a masculinist superpower embodied by the self-righteous Marduk to a new (or newly remembered) *tehomophilia* that speaks in the language of a future-oriented queer apophasis.[5]

Part II: The Earth jumps forward several thousand years, bringing us to the land surrounded by water, Cemanahuac, to something that has not been successfully erased by European

---

3 Robert Alter, *Genesis: Translation and Commentary* (London: W.W. Norton & Company Inc., 1996).

4 *Tehom* is "the deep" upon whose (sur)face, the spirit of God was moving before "he" created heaven and earth.

5 *Tehomophilia* is a word coined by feminist theologian Catherine Keller. I will discuss this concept with Keller's work in both Part I and Part O. See Catherine Keller, *Face of the Deep: A Theology of Becoming* (London: Routledge, 2003).

conquest, something that resists the temporal demarcation of "before" and "after" the *Conquista de América*. Coatlicue, the earth goddess who is also the mother of the sun (Huitzilopochtli), the moon (Coyolxauhqui), and the stars (Centzonhuitznahuac), is represented and present in/as the colossal Coatlicue Mayor statue, which still stands in a central hall of Mexico's National Museum of Anthropology, a temple, albeit secular, with its own distinct aura. She (? — and this is a big question mark) is firmly linked to the Nahua earth that stretches far beyond what we, under the influence of modern science, habitually refer to under that term.

The Coatlicue Mayor statue also has an underside, forever hidden from the uninitiated viewer. There lies Tlaltecuhtli, a motherly lord of the earth who generates life and at the same time brings death. Tlaltecuhtli is said to be a goddess in many modern retellings of "her" story, yet bears the name of a lord, *tecuhtli*. She also occasionally wears a face of Tlaloc, the rain deity who falls from above like the fertilizing rain, whose name shares the same earthly root *tlal-* (from *tlalli,* "earth") as Tlaltecuhtli. At the same time, Tlaltecuhtli used to swim in the primordial sea, where the often male-identified deities Quetzalcoatl (or the plumed-serpent) and Tezcatlipoca (or the smoking-mirror) tear "her" apart to create a new cosmic era.

Just as Marduk is credited with the same act of creation by cutting Tiamat in two in a primordial sea, is the combat between the masculinized duo Quetzalcoatl-Tezcatlipoca and the feminized Tlaltecuhtli a struggle between order and chaos, good and evil, gods and monsters, which scholarly studies of mythology would call *Chaoskampf*? Or is this ocean at the dawn of a new creation of the Nahua cosmos a remote relative, or even incarnation, of the older Mesopotamian Tiamat? We shall try to address these over-determining and seemingly straightforward questions in the chapters to come.

Over the past few years, these deities have been guiding me on my journeys in different parts of the world to learn and try to understand different ways of seeing and constructing the world. But why Babylonian and Nahua mythologies? There is no univocal reason for this selection, but, at the same time, the four deities that we will encounter in what follows — Tiamat, Apsu, Coatlicue, and Tlaltecuhtli — share some remarkable similarities as regards their shared colonial history of Western modernity starting with the *Conquista,* while uncompromisingly refusing the categorical grids of modern rationality this has brought, whether these entail the categorizing of gender and sexuality, or some more generally self-righteous "order."

Queer Ancient Ways is as much about the reception of these ancient divine beings, about how they have been seen through colonial/modern eyes, as it is, more importantly and perhaps also more intriguingly, about how they have resisted that gaze. In that resistance, I wish to show throughout this book, lies something we could learn from, something that enables us to think otherwise, to think *anold.*

The power of colonial history is strongly felt in my own education. My studies in China and Europe have been more Sinocentric and Eurocentric than I might previously have wanted to admit. My "cross-cultural" or "comparative" self-presentation was primarily a narcissistic affiliation with these two cultures and their languages only. This book is therefore also a scholarly effort to remedy this limitation, an attempt to extend my narrow view of the world outside my first and second "homes."

While studying Nahua writings, José Rabasa coined the term "elsewheres" in order to "understand spaces and temporalities that define a world that remains exterior to the spatio-temporal location of any given observer."[6] I am the "elsewhere" of Mesopotamian and Mesoamerican myths, cultures, and languages as much as they are mine. The two geographical and cultural

---

6   José Rabasa, *Tell Me the Story of How I Conquered You:* Elsewheres *and Ethnosuicide in the Colonial Mesoamerican World* (Austin: University of Texas Press, 2011), 1.

constructs — ancient Babylonian and Nahua mythologies — are remote from me in terms of discipline, temporality, and epistemology. Rabasa further points out that by intuiting the *elsewhere*, "[one] disrupts the assurance that [the] invasion of the West has imposed a singular world and history."[7] That colonial linkage, although pretending to be singular, has not been successful. Mine is perhaps, in this regard, different from Rabasa's, who suggests that his own project of learning from *elsewhere* is "inevitably grounded in Western thought."[8] Neither grounded exclusively in Western thought, nor speaking from a non-Western *elsewhere,* I opt for a "decolonial exploration." By "decolonial," I mean first and foremost the necessity of learning to learn from these *elsewheres.* This seemingly redundant formulation is necessary. It involves, as we will see, a double process of unlearning and relearning.[9]

Speaking from the locus of a Chinese native trained in European modern languages, feminisms, and queer theories, I experience and empathize with the sufferings of non-European subjects and cultures damaged by an aggressive Eurocentrism manifest in the form of not only territorial but also epistemic colonialism, the latter less visible than the former while largely dominating academia, as a form of what Portuguese sociologist Boaventura de Sousa Santos calls "epistemicide."[10]

The "decolonial exploration" presented here conjures a critique of the modern reception history of the two ancient mythologies and cultures discussed in this book, and more importantly an engagement with learning to learn from them. For some, such an endeavor may give rise to concerns about the risk

---

7   Ibid., 207n4.
8   Ibid.
9   See Madina Tlostanova and Walter Mignolo, *Learning to Unlearn: Decolonial Reflections from Eurasia and the Americas* (Columbus: Ohio State University Press, 2012), and Bulan Lahiri, "In Conversation: Speaking to Spivak," *The Hindu,* February 5, 2011, http://www.thehindu.com/books/In-Conversation-Speaking-to-Spivak/article15130635.ece.
10 Boaventura de Sousa Santos, *Epistemologies of the South: Justice against Epistemicide* (New York: Routledge, 2016).

of "appropriating" and therefore "exploiting" so-called native cultures. I would respond by citing an analogy made by Rabasa:

> [I]n the "same way" that Europe remains Europe after the incorporation of Mesoamerica (Chocolate, cacao, cochineal, silver, gold, but also the concepts of the "noble savage," cannibalism, wildness, the New World, America) into its systems of thought and everyday life, Mesoamerica remains Mesoamerica after the incorporation of European life-forms. The processes of appropriation, expropriation, and exappropriation [*sic*] involve a two-way street."[11]

Meanwhile, I contend that neither Europe nor Mesoamerica, nor China for that matter, has remained the same after modern global colonialism. Mesoamerica would not be possible without the concept of "America," invented after Christopher Columbus's "discovery" of a continent that had hitherto known itself by different geographical and cosmological demarcations. For the Nahuas, the world where they lived is called Cemanahuac, meaning "what is entirely surrounded by water."[12] The Andeans, in their own understanding, were living in Tawantinsuyu, not South, let alone *Latin* America.[13]

Today, we dwell in a world that has survived but is profoundly structured by the trauma of the Western colonialism of the past six hundred years, starting from the *Conquista de América.* The seemingly unrelated Babylonian and Nahua mythologies are implicated in the global history of colonial/modern scrutiny and knowledge production.

---

11 Rabasa, *Tell Me the Story of How I Conquered You,* 11.

12 Miguel León-Portilla, *La filosofía nahuatl: Estudiada en sus fuentes* (Mexico D.F.: Universidad Nacional Autonoma de México, 1956), 69: "lo que enteramente está circundado por el agua." All translations to English from non-English sources, unless stated otherwise, are mine.

13 See Edmundo O'Gorman, *La invención de América: El universalismo de la cultura occidental* (México D.F.: Universidad Nacional Autónoma de México, 1958).

If the critique of the Eurocentric worldview in general and the coloniality of (heteronormative) gendering in particular is the first step in the decolonization of knowledge, a serious engagement with local cultures and cosmologies is the second. These "first" and "second" steps intersect and are not to be understood as sequential, but, as Bolivian feminist Silvia Rivera Cuscanqui succinctly puts it, "there can be no discourse of decolonization, no theory of decolonization, without a decolonizing practice."[14] The book therefore intends to weave complex negotiations between learning and unlearning, criticism, and commitment.

Investigating colonial/modern scholarly receptions of "goddesses" and other divine figures in Babylonian and Nahua creation myths means first to expose the ways in which they have consistently been gendered (as feminine). The feminization of the Babylonian (co)creatrix Tiamat and the Nahua creator-figures Tlaltecuhtli and Coatlicue is complicit with their monstrification in a manner that is not supported, and in some cases actively discouraged, by the texts themselves. This complicity tells us less about the mythologies themselves than about the dualistic system of gender and sexuality within which they have been studied, underpinned by a consistent tendency in colonial/modern thought to insist on unbridgeable categorical differences.

Queer Ancient Ways, meanwhile, advocates a profound unlearning of colonial/modern categories that have functioned, from the dawn of European colonialism in the 16th century to the present, to keep in obscurity the forms and theories of embodiment and queerness of the most ancient of sources. This is done simultaneously through a decolonial exercise in learning-to-learn from non-Western and non-modern cosmologies,

---

14 Silvia Rivera Cusicanqui, "*Ch'ixinakax utxiwa:* A Reflection on the Practices and Discourses of Decolonization," *South Atlantic Quarterly* 111, no. 1 (2012): 95–109, at 100.

which helps us to approach a rich queer imaginary that has been all but lost to modern thought.

Through a commitment to methodological experimentation with cross-references from critical traditions in English, Spanish, French, Chinese, and Nahuatl, this book departs from the overreliance of much queer theory on European (post)modern thought. That is to say, much more than a *queering* of the non-Western and non-modern, *Queer Ancient Ways* constitutes a decolonial and transdisciplinary engagement with ancient cosmologies and ways of thought, which are in the process themselves revealed as theoretical sources of and for the queer imagination.

This book therefore does not prioritize "theories" over "primary sources," but seeks to treat its objects of study as living, dynamic ways of knowing from which we as outsiders dwelling in their *elsewhere(s)* need to learn to learn from. The structure of the book is intended to support the development of a theory that can adequately accommodate the simultaneous fluidity and fixity of these creation myths. This queer/decolonial "learning-to-learn" involves a thorough restructuring of the very form in which thinking is undertaken. Instead of a linear, straightforward progression, the book is organized as a kind of "speculum," or according to what I call elsewhere the *yinyang* transdualism of "either…and."[15]

Yinyang transdualism is, in particular, the motivation for the two-chapter structure of each of Parts I and II. As *yin* has the tendency to descend and solidify while *yang* has the tendency to ascend and vaporize, the physical placement of these chapter pairings suggests a dynamic, generative, and erotic mingling, with *yin* and *yang* embracing each other. In each of the two-chapter parts, the first, *yin* chapter deals with concrete politics of specific (feminine) figures. The second, *yang* chapter questions the essentializing gender identifications of the deities taken for granted in the first chapter through a thorough con-

---

15 Zairong Xiang, "Transdualism: Towards a Materio-discursive Embodiment," *TSQ: Transgender Studies Quarterly* 5, no.3 (2018): 425–42.

textualization and close reading of and within their respective cosmologies. The *yang* chapters therefore perform a reading through which the deities' queerness can emerge. However, the *yang* chapter does not cancel out the earlier *yin* chapter; endorsing the queerness of Tiamat-Apsu does not require sacrificing Tiamat's motherhood and femininity. The interplay between the two oppositional yet complementary chapters leads to the emergence of new queer theories that neither pin down gender fluidity, nor abandon political accountability. They are mingled but not merged. This concurrence does not lead to the obliteration of their respective features, melting them into a synthetic grey. Rather, they resemble the rainbow, the radiant queerness of light whose ensemble leads to an "either…and" of mutually transforming black and white, illustrated by the *taiji* symbol.[16] This converging *yinyang* is intuited in the fusing water(s) of Tiamat-Apsu which is/are at once *one* and *many,* echoing the Nahua duality principle *ometeotl.*

Chapter 1. Tiamat's Anger: Feminization and Monstrification inside/outside the *Enuma Elish*

This chapter takes the femininity of Babylonian goddess Tiamat for granted and sets out to show how the feminized Tiamat has been monstrified in both modern reception and in the epic *Enuma Elish* itself. A close analysis of several instances of Tiamat's anger reinstates her motherliness against the stunning distortions it has undergone in the reception history. Without associating motherliness with benevolence or monstrosity, the chapter concludes that in *Enuma Elish,* Tiamat's motherliness and monstrosity do not oppose each other (as the feminist critique would have it) nor run together (as the misogynist receptions would like).

---

16   Ibid.

Chapter 2. Queer Divine Waters

The salt-water and sweet-water deities Tiamat and Apsu (often reduced to the heterosexual couple of the "fertility myth") have constantly intermingled. Contextualized in the *longue durée* of the personification of watery beings and their (gendered) transformations from the Sumerian *Nammu* to the Biblical *tehom,* the queerness hinted at in the ancient texts has remained unattended to in the reception history. This chapter will explore the queer deification embodied by the ancient waters for a contemporary queer politics urgently in need of a theory of porosity and passivity that is unclean, non-identitarian, and un/differentiating.

Part O: Nulla is one long section uninterrupted by chapter divisions. Situated between the two buttressing parts of the book on the Babylonian *Water* (Part I) and the Nahua *Earth* (Part II), this long section, deliberately named *Nulla,* aims to debunk the theo-political concept of *creatio ex nihilo* (creation out of nothingness). It provides an analysis of this concept's decisive influence on colonialism and coloniality and its persistence in the scholarly reception of mythologies and even queer theory. This chapter shows the interweaving of colonial logic with *creatio ex nihilo,* which historically and discursively links the seemingly unrelated Mesopotamia with Mesoamerica inside their creation myths and outside, through their receptions.

Chapter 3. The Strange Case of Tlaltecuhtli

Part II moves from the land in the middle of rivers (Mesopotamia) to the land "surrounded by water," Cemanahuac. The first chapter of this part examines the coercive translation of the Nahua name Tlaltecuhtli as "goddess of the earth," which denies the semantic signification of *tecuhtli,* Nahuatl for "lord," not "goddess." Through a discussion of the particular *tlacuilolli* writing/painting system of Nahuatl alongside a survey of the debate on the grammatology of non-alphabetic writing, especially in terms of the Western reception of Chinese writing, this chapter shows that Nahua *tlacuilolli,* which is congruent with Nahua cosmo-philosophy, allows a "gender transgression" of a rather queer motherly lord of the earth: Tlaltecuhtli Tonantzin (Lord of the Earth, Our Benevolent Mother).

Chapter 4. Coatlicue Mayor: Or, Other Ways of Rereading the World

This last chapter studies *tlacuilolli,* the writing/painting system of the Nahuas. It develops a decolonization of the concept of writing and argues that *tlacuilolli* is not confined to the book format. By focusing specifically on the Coatlicue Mayor statue and its synchronic linkage with the Calendar Stone through a rereading of the duality principle *ometeotl* and the complex temporality of the Nahuas, this chapter understands the Coatlicue Mayor statue within and as both the Nahua cosmo-philosophy written/painted/sculpted and as a divine presence itself, rather than a secular artistic representation of an allegedly decapitated "goddess." Learning from *tlacuilolli* as a textual and visual system that conveys queerness without domesticating it, this last chapter concludes with a reflection on the decolonial and queer strategies and significance of the Nahua cosmo-philosophical *elsewheres,* embodied by the underside of the Coatlicue Mayor statue, where Tlaltecuhtli resides.

PART I

—

THE WATERS

1

Below Either/Or: Rereading Femininity and Monstrosity inside *Enuma Elish*

Was aus Liebe getan wird, geschieht immer jenseits von Gut und Böse.
— Friedrich Nietzsche, *Jenseits von Gut und Böse*[1]

Is it possible to separate fresh water from salt water after they have mixed? The Babylonians seem to be ambiguous about this. Their creation myth, written in cuneiform and known as *Enuma Elish*,[2] opens its world with two mingling waters, the salt water Tiamat and the sweet water Apsu:

---

1   "What is done out of love always takes place beyond good and evil." Friedrich Nietzsche, *Beyond Good and Evil*, trans. Helen Zimmern (Madison: Cricket House Books, 2012), "Apophthegms and Interludes," no. 153.

2   Unless otherwise noted, all quotes of *Enuma Elish* are taken from the English translation by Stephanie Dalley, *Myths from Mesopotamia: Creation, The Flood, Gilgamesh, and Others* (Oxford: Oxford University Press, 2008), 233–77. As the research mainly concerns the first pages of the epic, I will not provide pagination for the sake of clarity. I have also consulted other versions of translations in English and French. When there are discrepancies on the translation of key words, I will refer to the other translations. I am not versed in either the cuneiform script or the Akkadian language in which *Enuma Elish* was written. Since I am mainly concerned with its modern reception history rather than its archaeological aspect of the "original" version (a concept in contestation as well), I have consulted as many translated versions and dictionaries/encyclopaedias as possible.

> When skies above were not yet named
> Nor earth below pronounced by name,
> Apsu, the first one, their begetter
> And maker Tiamat, who bore them all,
> Had mixed their waters together,
> [....]
> Then gods were born within them

Although neither the skies nor the earth are named, the primordial waters do have names, Apsu and Tiamat. If we stop here and look back to their linguistic roots, it is not difficult to find out that *apsu* means (sweet) water/sea, similar to *tiamat*.[3] In the Babylonian Epic of Creation, *Enuma Elish,* they are "begetter" and "maker" of the new generations of gods: "gods were born *within them*." The newly born gods "would meet together/And disturb Tiamat / [... and] stirred up Tiamat's belly."

While "Tiamat became mute before them / However grievous their behavior to her, / However bad their ways, she would indulge them," Apsu cannot bear the noise anymore: "Apsu made his voice heard / And spoke to Tiamat in a loud voice / [...] 'I shall abolish their ways and disperse them!'" Knowing Apsu's intention of murder,

> She [Tiamat] was furious and shouted at her lover;
> She shouted dreadfully and was beside herself with rage,
> But then suppressed the evil in her belly.
>> "How could we allow what we ourselves created to perish?
>> Even though their ways are so grievous, we should bear
>> it patiently."

Now we learn that Apsu and Tiamat are lovers, referred to respectively as "he" and "she." Apsu is certainly upset by Tiamat's anger and reluctance to act. He goes to his "vizier," Mummu, who "replied and counseled Apsu / [...] Apsu was pleased with

---

3   David Toshio Tsumura, *The Earth and the Waters in Genesis 1 and 2: A Linguistic Investigation* (Sheffield: Sheffield Academic Press, 1989), 60–62.

him, his face lit up / At the evil he was planning for the gods his sons. / (Vizier) Mummu hugged him, / Sat on his lap and kissed him rapturously." Although men kissing each other might have been a common practice in Ancient Near East, this explicit homoerotic encounter at least unsettles the "heterosexual" coupledom of Tiamat and Apsu. Mummu only appears here in Dalley's translation from which we quote. However, in many other translations, Tiamat first appears as "Mummu-Tiamat."[4] For example, the British Museum's 1921 version of *The Seven Tablets of Creation* has the first lines translated as "Apsu, the oldest of beings, their progenitor, / 'Mummu' Tiamat, who bare [*sic*] each and all of / them."[5]

In the Sumerian creation myth, which is in an ancestral relationship with the Babylonian one (somehow like the inheritance of ancient Greece for ancient Rome), we have the primordial ocean, (the) *apsu,*[6] whose personification in that even older myth is a feminine figure, the primordial mother goddess Nammu, whose "name is usually written with the sign *engur* which was also used to write Apsu. In ancient times she personified

---

4   See E.A. Wallis Budge, *The Babylonian Legends of the Creation and the Fight between Bel and the Dragon (As Told by Assyrian Tablets from Nineveh)* (London: The British Museum, 1921); Philippe Talon, *The Standard Babylonian Creation Myth Enūma Eliš* (Helsinki: Neo-Assyrian Text Corpus Project, 2005).

5   Budge, *The Babylonian Legends of the Creation and the Fight between Bel and the Dragon*, 32.

6   As we said earlier, *apsu* also means "fresh water." In the Sumerian mythology, the *apsu* (or *abzu*) is personified by Nammu, the primordial goddess, while in the Babylonian mythology, the apsu conflates with Apsu the deity. In order to make this clear, I will use "the *apsu*" to refer to the Sumerian sea and "Apsu" to refer to the personification of the primordial sea in *Enuma Elish* in order to retain the pun between the *apsu* (sea) and Apsu the primordial "father." In the case of *Enuma Elish,* as we will analyze in Chapter 2, Apsu the deity and "the *apsu*," the primordial sea "he" personifies, are ambiguously run together, which is itself an interesting issue to explore. So occasionally I will also refer to the Babylonian Apsu as (the) Apsu, suggesting that there is a double meaning of it with or without the parenthesized "the."

the [*apsu*] as the source of water and hence fertility in lower Mesopotamia."[7]

In Part I: The Waters, we will dedicate two chapters to study the primordial water deities of the Babylonian Epic of Creation *Enuma Elish*. In this chapter, we will closely investigate Tiamat, through a critique of the receptions that have touched upon her/ it from the 19th century to today, drawing upon studies in mythology and feminist theology. We shall see how Tiamat, through her scholarly reception, has become stabilized as a recognizable female monster, allegedly symbolizing the order-menacing chaos. We will then analyze a particular issue concerning Tiamat, i.e., her/its monstrosity, by examining the complex interplay between monstrosity, femininity, and motherhood, as constructed inside and outside the epic. The last section of this chapter will further complicate and negotiate the issue of motherhood and monstrosity through a rereading of Tiamat's battle with Marduk in *Enuma Elish* against its various receptions.

I beg the reader to bear in mind that the whole creation story, often too quickly simplified as the so-called battle against chaos, happens inside Tiamat (and Apsu). Adherent to this "withinness" of Tiamat(-Apsu) and the epic's narrative, I propose an immanent feminist rereading beyond, or more precisely, *below* the logic of either/or,[8] which will pave way for by uncovering or recovering the "queerness" of these ancient divine figures in the subsequent chapter.

---

7   Gwendolyn Leick, *A Dictionary of Ancient Near Eastern Mythology* (London: Routledge, 1991), 124.

8   This chapter tries to re-read *Enuma Elish* in a way that does not reproduce the logic of either/or. I choose to address this attempt through a slightly awkward phrasing: "below either/or," to avoid the transcendental (or the "either/or-ness") of the more obvious and common phrasing, "beyond either/or," which still operates in a logic of succession that "goes *beyond*."

1.1 Tiamat Is Not Born a Woman:
Enuma Elish and Its Modern Receptions

Enuma Elish, also known as the Babylonian Epic of Creation, is one of the best-known creation myths of Ancient Mesopotamia. The epic became extremely important with the rise of Babylon as a ruling state in the second millennium BCE. However, the accessible versions of the myth are the tablets on which the epic was written in cuneiform from a later period. We also know that the epic was recited every year on the New Year's Festival in Babylon in the month of April.[9]

The epic begins with the primordial world. Two primordial waters, Apsu, the fresh water, the "husband," and Tiamat, the sea water, the "wife," mingle together and within them, several generations of gods are born. Scholars of Mesopotamian studies already have different opinions about how many "waters" there are at the outset of the epic, because in the original epic, "Tiamat" is written as Mummu-Tiamat. Who is this Mummu? Is it an adjacent title or a third figure that personifies one type of primordial waters? No clear answer can be given. Alexander Heidel considers Mummu to be "the personified fog or mist rising from the waters of Apsu and Tiamat and hovering over them [which in] mythological language [...] could easily be called the 'son' of the two primeval deities."[10] It is necessary to bear in mind that Apsu's "vizier" who appears later and who counsels him is also called Mummu, which may or may not be the same Mummu as in Mummu-Tiamat.

1.1.1 The Creation Story in Enuma Elish.
The mingling primordial waters, personified as Apsu and Tiamat (and perhaps also Mummu), give birth to several generations of gods, the most important line among them being the

---

9 See Takayoshi Oshima, "The Babylonian God Marduk," in *The Babylonian World,* ed. Gwendolyn Leick, 348–60 (New York: Routledge, 2007).

10 Alexander Heidel, "The Meaning of *Mummu* in Akkadian Literature," *Journal of Near Eastern Studies* 7, no. 2 (1948): 98–105, at 104.

patrilineage Anshar–Anu–Ea (Ea later gives birth to Marduk, the patron god of *Enuma Elish* and the Babylonian state). The story goes that the newly born gods are restless and produce a great disturbance that "stirred up Tiamat's belly." The behavior of the young gods is particularly annoying for Apsu, perhaps because, to a large extent, Apsu has already become part of Tiamat after their mingling. Apsu, incited by his vizier Mummu, suggests to Tiamat to kill the young gods. He shouts to Tiamat: "Their ways have become very grievous to me. / By day I cannot rest, by night I cannot sleep. / I shall abolish their ways and disperse them!" Tiamat becomes angry with Apsu and says: "How could we allow what we ourselves created to perish? / Even though their ways are so grievous, we should bear it patiently."

Apsu is upset, and Mummu "did not agree with the counsel of his / earth mother"[11] either. Thus Mummu comforts Apsu, hugs him and kisses him. Their plans of infanticide are overheard by Ea, the most intelligent among the young gods. He casts a spell on Apsu, makes him sleep, "[takes] away his [Apsu's] mantle of radiance and put[s] it on / himself," and finally kills Apsu and chains the vizier Mummu. Ea builds his residence and "rested quietly inside his private / quarters" which he "named […] Apsu." The British Museum translation of *The Seven Tablets of Creation* suggests that "Ea overcame both his adversaries [Apsu and Mummu] and divided Apsu into chambers and laid fetters upon him."[12] Here we have a conflation between Apsu the personified deity and "the Apsu" as the primordial ocean. Such a rhetorical device or "pun" is also found in Genesis between *'adam* the human being, "Adam" the name of the first created

---

11 This might be a translation error for nowhere else is Tiamat, the personification of the salt water sea, represented as an *earth* mother. This slippage might slightly hint at an unchecked universal belief that the earth is feminine, a topic that will be discussed at length in Part II: The Earth.

12 Budge, *The Babylonian Legends of the Creation and the Fight between Bel and the Dragon,* 34.

human, and the soil *'adamah* from which God created the human (human/humus).[13]

Marduk is born to Ea and Damkina (a goddess we only encounter briefly here) in their newly constructed dwelling built inside (the) Apsu: "And inside Apsu, Marduk was created; / Inside pure Apsu, Marduk was born." With the birth of Marduk, Apsu as the primordial "father" becomes obsolete in the epic. Marduk (also referred to as "Bel" or "Bel-Marduk") is said to be very powerful from the start, and he is called "superior in every way." The epic continues with a detailed description of Marduk's attributes and how the nurse "reared him [and] filled him with / awesomeness." Almost in the same manner as today's parents might instruct their lads on how to play with aggression in order to become a man, Anu, his grandfather (i.e., the "begetter" of Ea) spoils him with weaponry: "Anu created the four winds and gave them birth, / Put them in his [Marduk's] hand, 'My son [*sic*], let them/play!'" With the winds in his hand, Marduk "fashioned dust and made the whirlwind carry it; / He made the flood-wave and stirred up Tiamat." Again, Tiamat does not react, but "heaved restlessly day / and night." This time, however, it is the other gods who cannot bear the noise of young Marduk stirring up Tiamat's belly.[14] They provoke Tiamat by accusation and agitation:

> "Because they slew Apsu your lover and
> You did not go to his side but sat mute,
> He has created the four, fearful winds
> To stir up your belly on purpose, and we simply cannot
>   sleep!
> Was your lover Apsu not in your heart?
> And (vizier) Mummu who was captured? No wonder you
>   sit alone!

---

13 Scott B. Noegel, ed., *Puns and Pundits: Word Play in the Hebrew Bible and Ancient Near Eastern Literature* (Bethesda: CDL Press, 2000), 8n7.

14 Similar to the Apsu/(the) Apsu conflation, "Tiamat's belly" somehow suggests the watery space inside which all generations of gods are still living. We will come back to this "queer space" in the next chapter.

> Are you not a mother? You heave restlessly
> But what about us, who cannot rest? Don't you love us?
> [...]
> Remove the yoke of [sic] us restless ones, and let us sleep!
> [...]"
> Tiamat listened, and the speech pleased her.

These cruel words seem to be sufficient. Tiamat agrees to take action, gathering great weapons and venomous monster-snakes, together with other monsters such as a great-lion, mad-dog, scorpion-man, centaur, and so on. She also makes a previously unmentioned figure called Qingu her consort and the supreme leader of the assembly, giving him the "tablet of destinies." Ea, the father of Marduk, is afraid because he knows that the power of Tiamat is beyond him, but nevertheless downplays it, showing that since time immemorial misogyny has served to rhetorically restore masculine self-esteem:

> Ea went, he searched for Tiamat's strategy,
> But then stayed silent and turned back.
> He entered into the presence of the ruler Anshar,
> In supplication he addressed him.
>> "My father, Tiamat's action were too much for me.
>> [...]
>> Her strength is mighty, she is completely terrifying.
>> [...]
>> I feared her should, and I turned back.
>> But Father, you must not relax, you must send someone
>>   else to her.
>> However strong a woman's strength, it is not equal to a
>>   man's.

Anshar, Anu's father and Ea's great-grandfather, asks his great great-grandson Marduk for help. Marduk agrees to take action and wage war against Tiamat, on the condition that all the gods worship him as the supreme one. He "made a net to encircle Tiamat within it," and introduces evil winds that "advanced behind him [Marduk] to make turmoil inside / Tiamat." Then we hear another speech of Marduk, addressing Tiamat:

> Why are you so friendly on the surface
> When your depths conspire to muster a battle force?
> Just because the sons were noisy (and) disrespectful to their
>   fathers,
> Should you, who gave them birth, reject compassion?
> […]
> Stand forth, and you and I shall do single combat!

Marduk cunningly transforms the conflict between him and the other irritated gods who seek help from Tiamat into a generational conflict between the homogenized "sons" and their homogenized "fathers," accusing Tiamat the mother of not protecting the sons. Marduk thus abuses Tiamat's previous indulgence of the naughty disturbances in her belly, the first time by the newly born gods who annoyed Apsu and the second time by Marduk himself. These words finally manage to antagonize Tiamat: "When Tiamat heard this, / She went wild, she lost her temper. / Tiamat screamed aloud in a passion." A cosmic combat between Marduk and Tiamat begins. In the end, Tiamat and her allies are destroyed by Marduk, who "sliced her in half like a fish for drying; / Half of her he put up to roof the sky." Marduk is thus said to have created the world using the dead body of Tiamat.

> He places her head, heaped up [   ]
> Opened up springs: water gushed out.
> He opened the Euphrates and the Tigris from her eyes,
> Closed her nostrils, [   ]
> He piled up clear-cut mountains from her udder.[15]

---

15 The brackets in this particular quote are original indicating the missing part of the tablets. See Dalley, *Myths from Mesopotamia,* 257.

He created the shrine for the gods over (the) Apsu and proclaimed: "I hereby name it home of great / gods. We shall make it the centre of religion." Then he creates human beings from the blood of Qingu "who started the war, / He who incited Tiamat and gathered an army!"[16] The rest of the tablets give an account of Marduk's other creations, such as the vegetation. The epic ends with a statement: "In remembrance of the song of Marduk / Who defeated Tiamat and took the kingship."

As we have seen, *Enuma Elish* is a complex creation myth that entails generational and gendered conflicts. There are several puzzles, like the mysterious Mummu, the free jump between proper names and concepts, especially those of Apsu and Tiamat, the strange space inside which the gods are living. The watery spaces of Tiamat and Apsu seem to be inseparable. So how can Marduk possibly slaughter Tiamat if he is inside Tiamat to cause turbulences hardly bearable for the other gods and Tiamat herself? And, we may ask, where in fact is the boundary between Apsu and the Apsu, and (the) Apsu and Tiamat?

Investigations of *Enuma Elish* seem to have two major concerns. Philologists of ancient Mesopotamian languages tend to focus on the linguistic functions and possible translations of different words and the puns they generate, such as the meaning of Mummu or Marduk.[17] Mythologists on the other hand read the combat between Marduk and Tiamat as a cosmogony, the so-called *Chaoskampf par excellence.* Our focus will be on the

---

16   This is another ungrounded accusation, for Qingu does not incite Tiamat to war but is merely a representative chosen by her to possess the "tablets of destinies." The victim is turned into a perpetrator. We will come back to this in Chapter 2, rather unexpectedly, with the inculpation of homosexuals, the victims of AIDS, for spreading the disease during the AIDS epidemic.

17   See Heidel, "The Meaning of *Mummu* in Akkadian Literature"; Victor Avigdor Hurowitz, "Alliterative Allusions, Rebus Writing, and Paronomastic Punishment: Some Aspects of Word Play in Akkadian Literature," in *Puns and Pundits: Word Play in the Hebrew Bible and Ancient Near Eastern Literature,* ed. Scott B. Noegel (Bethesda: CDL Press, 2000), 63–113; Piotr Michalowski, "Presence at the Creation," in *Lingering over Words: Studies in Ancient Near Eastern Literature in Honor of William L. Moran,* ed. P. Steinkeller (Atlanta: Scholars Press, 1990), 381–96.

second group of scholars, with a particular focus on the gender politics in the readings that have produced the interpretation of *Chaoskampf* for *Enuma Elish* and its "order versus chaos" dichotomy. It will be our claim that on closer inspection, this interpretation no longer seems convincing.

1.1.2 Representing Tiamat in Scholarship

The tablets of *Enuma Elish* were first published as *The Chaldean Account of Genesis* by George Smith (1876), followed by several excavations made at the sites of Nineveh, Ashur, and Kish by British, German, and American archaeologists at the end of the 19th century and beginning of the 20th century.[18] Since its discovery, innumerable scholars from archaeology, biblical studies, literature, philosophy, and the history of science have been fascinated with the epic. We will select some studies from the late 19th century to our time, which, despite their disciplinary differences, all seem to have agreed on one thing, namely that Tiamat *is* a dangerous chaos monster seeking to oppose Marduk, the righteous representative of order.

In 1893, George A. Barton published an article entitled "Tiamat," which introduces the Babylonian figure while drawing possible parallels with the biblical serpent Leviathan and other mythical figures in Mesopotamia. He identifies Tiamat as "a female dragon, queen of a hideous host, who are hostile to the gods, and with whom Marduk fights, conquers them, cuts their leader [i.e., Tiamat] in two, and of one part of her body [Marduk] makes heaven, of the other the earth."[19] Toward the end of the article, Tiamat is alleged to have "opposed creation,

---

18 The late 19th and early 20th century are an interesting historical moment, especially if we take into consideration Edward Said's seminal book *Orientalism* (London: Routledge & Kegan Paul, 1978) and other works on the crises of gender, sexuality, science, and religion in late Victorian England and *fin-de-siècle* Europe, such as Elaine Showalter, *Sexual Anarchy: Gender and Culture at the Fin de Siècle* (London: Bloomsbury, 1991). We will discuss these in the next chapter and in Part O.

19 George A Barton, "Tiamat," *Journal of American Oriental Society* 15 (1893): 1–27, at 12.

at every step resisted God, tempted and *seduced* man" and the author believes that she/it was "the popular personification of hideousness, *arrogance* and evil."²⁰ Barton's quite unfounded but nevertheless passionate accusation seems to have had a lasting influence on *Enuma Elish's* reception ever since.

One year later, an article entitled "The Babylonian Account of Creation" by W. Muss-Arnolt (1894) compares *Enuma El-ish* with the biblical book of Genesis, stating in the language of Christian theology: "Light and Darkness, chaos and order, are ever struggling one against another."²¹ The author believes that the "victory of light and order is described [...] in the fight between Bel-Merodach [Marduk], the principle of light, and Tia-mat, the principle of darkness, represented as the dragon, the wicked serpent."²² After the establishment of a dichotomous antagonism between Tiamat and Marduk, the author argues that "the victory of Marduk over Tiamat [... is] order over anarchy."²³

Some years later, Ross Murison analyzes the figure of the snake in the Bible by drawing a comparison with the great mythological snake figures in other cultures. In order to support his claim that "[e]vil has thus always taken a definite form, preferably that of a serpent," he adds a footnote describing Tiamat as "a dragon of most hideous aspect."²⁴

By 1905, when Murison's article is published, a full transcription and translation of *Enuma Elish* is not yet available. The classical study by Leonard W. King is able to translate the following lines of the epic only very fragmentarily: "(Thus) were established and [were ... the great gods (?)]. / But T[iamat and Apsu] were (still) in confusion [...], / They were troubled and [...] /

20 Ibid., 27, emphasis mine.
21 W. Muss-Arnolt, "The Babylonian Account of Creation," *The Biblical World* 3, no. 1 (1894): 17–27, at 19.
22 Ibid.
23 Ibid., 20.
24 Ross G. Murison, "The Serpent in the Old Testament," *The American Journal of Semitic Languages and Literatures* 21, no. 2 (1905): 115–30, at 128n35.

In disorder (?) … […]."²⁵ Although several lines after Apsu's suggestion to Tiamat to kill the gods, we clearly read: "When Tiamat [heard] these words, / She raged and cried aloud […]. / [She …] grievously […]."²⁶ In a book published in 1921 by the British Museum, entitled *The Babylonian Legends of Creation: Fight between Bel and the Dragon,* the line describing Tiamat's endurance of the pain caused by the gods was not yet translated or available either. The account appears as follows:

> Tiamat was troubled and she … their guardian.
> Her belly was stirred up to its uttermost depths.
> ……
> Apsu (the watery abyss) could not diminish their
> brawl
> And Tiamat gathered herself together …²⁷

However, again Tiamat's anger at Apsu's infanticidal plan was clear: "Tiamat on hearing this / Was stirred up to wrath and shrieked to her husband. / … unto sickness. She raged all alone."²⁸ The editor has not overlooked this but reminds us that "Tiamat's wrath was roused by Apsu, who had proposed to slay the gods, her children. She took no part in the first struggle of Apsu and Mummu against the gods, and only engaged in active hostilities to avenge Apsu."²⁹

Now we turn to some more recent studies of *Enuma Elish.* By their date of publication, we would expect that fuller translations of the Babylonian tablets would have been available. The renowned Assyrian and Sumerian historian Thorkild Jacobsen published an essay entitled "*Enuma Elish* — 'The Babylonian

---

25 Leonard William King, *The Seven Tablets of Creation* (London: Luzac and Co., 1902), 7–8. All square brackets are in the original.
26 Ibid., 11.
27 Budge, *The Babylonian Legends of the Creation and the Fight between Bel and the Dragon,* 33. The omissions are original, showing untranslatable or heavily damaged parts of the tablets.
28 Ibid.
29 Murison, "The Serpent in the Old Testament," 33n1.

Genesis,'" included in *The Intellectual Adventure of Ancient Man* (1964),[30] in which he analyzes Mesopotamian cosmogony and the Babylonian Creation Epic. Envisaging the epic from the perspective of the creation of cosmic order, he summarizes the disturbance of the gods in Tiamat's belly, Apsu's plan to abolish them, Ea's killing of Apsu, and Marduk's battle with Tiamat, quoting extensively from the original myths.[31] Throughout the whole essay, however, we don't find a single line mentioning the moment when Tiamat endures the pain caused by the gods inside her belly and furiously refuses Apsu's plan of killing them. The endurance of Tiamat is translated as "and Tiamat is silent …" in the version of the epic the author quotes.[32] The lines that record Tiamat's motherly protection of the children from the father's anger have also been omitted. In his extensive citations of the epic, one fragment ends with: "[Apsu said to Tiamat] I will abolish, yea, I will destroy their ways, / that peace may reign (again) and we may sleep." The next quotation of the epic begins with the lines that appear in reality much later in the epic, "He [Ea] of supreme intelligence, skillful, ingenious, / Ea, who knows all things, saw through their scheme." In a flash, the lines that describe Tiamat's anger at Apsu are omitted.

Jacobson, however, seems to have noticed the motherliness of Tiamat in his later work, *The Treasures of Darkness.* There he briefly analyzes the "parricide theme" of *Enuma Elish,* and claims that "while the aspect of parricide is […] mitigated both by making the parents remote ancestors and putting them plainly in the wrong, part of this effect is countered […] by the stress on Tiamat's motherliness."[33] He believes that,

---

30 The version I have access to and quote from is included in Milton K. Munitz, ed., *Theories of the Universe: From Babylonian Myth to Modern Science* (New York: The Free Press, 1965), 8–20.

31 Ibid., 12–14.

32 No information is given in the essay as to which version of *Enuma Elish* the author uses. Considering that he is an eminent expert of the Akkadian language, it is possible that the English translation of the epic is his own.

33 Thorkild Jacobsen, *The Treasures of Darkness* (New Haven: Yale University Press, 1976), 187.

[s]o odd is this sympathetic treatment of the archenemy, Tiamat, that one can hardly escape feeling that the author is here in the grip of conflicting emotions: love, fear, and a sense of guilt that requires palliation.[34]

Albeit finding the sympathetic treatment of the so-called archenemy "odd," Jacobsen's observation of Tiamat's motherliness stands surprisingly alone in the epic's long history of reception. Perhaps due to its singularity, Jacobsen's influential work does not seem to have any bearing on other scholars after him when they decide to overlook precisely Tiamat's motherliness. For example, in the detailed examination of mythological traditions and the Bible by the so-called Danish School of biblical studies, *Myths in the Old Testament,*[35] *Enuma Elish* is summarized in a way that entirely ignores Tiamat's "motherly moments":

The poem tells us about the primordial gods Tiamat, representing the sea, and Apsu, the divinity of fresh water. Together they beget a number of gods, but when these later disturb the repose of the older gods, Apsu decides to annihilate them. Ea, one of the young gods, thereupon opposes Apsu and kills him. Tiamat creates an army of gruesome demoniac beings who with Kingu[36] (her new husband) as leader introduce a reign of terror. Chaos ruled among the gods, and *chaos is, above all in the figure of Tiamat, represented by the menacing and destructive waters.* Ea, however, *gives birth*[37] to

---

34 Ibid.

35 Benedikt Otzen, Hans Gottlieb, and Knud Jeppesen, *Myths in the Old Testament* (London: SCM Press Ltd, 1980).

36 In some translations, the transliteration "Kingu" is used instead of "Qingu."

37 Marduk is born to Ea the father and Damkina the mother. However, this short summary ignores Damkina, who for Harris represents the "good mother" (we will come to this study soon), smuggles the motherly "birthgiving" from Damkina, and creates quite literally a homosocial patrilineality (Rivkah Harris, "The Conflict of Generations in Ancient Mesopotamian Myths," *Comparative Studies in Society and History* 34, no. 4 [1992]: 621–35, at 631)

Marduk, *who dares to take up the battle against the goddess of chaos, Tiamat.*[38]

Two more recent examples will demonstrate what we can already call "the monstrification of Tiamat in scholarship," which systematically erases her endeavor to endure the childish disturbances and to protect them from paternal infanticide. We will show that the long reception history that essentializes Tiamat as *the* monster (or archenemy) even exerts influences on some studies that bear gender issues in mind.

In 1992, Rivkah Harris published a gender theory-informed study on the generational conflicts in the Mesopotamian myths. She reduces *Enuma Elish*'s pantheon to "images of the good father (Ea) and the bad father/progenitor (Apsu), of the good mother (Damkina) and the bad mother/progenitrix (Tiamat)."[39] Even though Harris is aware of Dalley's 1989 translation and has written extensively on gender in Mesopotamia from a feminist perspective, this does not seem to prevent her from repeating the same idea that "[t]he depiction of the old Tiamat as aggressive and powerful may reflect Mesopotamian views about gender differences in the personality of the elderly."[40] This argument is certainly not wrong. Tiamat *is* aggressive and powerful, but she/it is not only so. Her other aspect that is more gentle and indulgent is, however, again unfortunately overlooked even by a feminist scholar.

Victor A. Hurowitz, who scrutinizes the philological aspects of Akkadian, touches upon the issue of the representation of Tiamat. He follows Piotr Michalowski's suggestion about the possibility that *mummu* in "Mummu-Tiamat" means "noise," and translates the first lines of the epic as "Noisy Tiamat, birther of their noise."[41] Hurowitz continues to argue, rather stunningly:

---

38 Otzen, Gottlieb, and Jeppesen, *Myths in the Old Testament,* 13–14.

39 Harris, "The Conflict of Generations in Ancient Mesopotamian Myths," 631.

40 Ibid., 631n55.

41 Dalley's translation, as we have quoted earlier, has: "And maker Tiamat, who bore them all."

Unnoticed by Michalowski, this hidden meaning adds significant irony and even a bit of tragedy to the comic story given the decisive role of noise in the rest of the myth. Tiamat and Apsu are disturbed by their children's noisy frolicking and seek to destroy them. Giving Tiamat herself a name that means "noisy" would imply that by trying to rid herself of noise she is self-hating and bent on destroying herself. At the very least, calling her "birther of their noise" makes her, rather than her children, responsible for her own suffering.[42]

In a nutshell, Apsu's plan[43] becomes both his and Tiamat's. The whole scenario of Tiamat's emotion, indulgence, and protection is again erased. I am unable to locate in the epic the place where it is possible to read that Tiamat ever even tried to "rid herself of noise" and "seek to destroy them [the gods]." It is ironic to see how our 20th-century scholar has used the same allegation used by Marduk, by confusing Tiamat and Apsu and accusing Tiamat of rejecting motherly compassion when the sons are "disrespectful to their fathers" and of having planned infanticide. It is also difficult to understand how this epic, full of love, hatred, pain, violence, and death can ever be interpreted as a "comic story." What is more, Tiamat, the victim of unbearable disturbance and violent slaughter, is cruelly alleged to be "responsible for her own suffering."

Gregory Mobley, in his *The Return of the Chaos Monsters: And Other Backstories of the Bible* from 2012, the most recent example we have, also explicitly asks, "[w]ho are the bad guys in the *Enuma Elish*? There is Tiamat, a feminine personification of saltwater, and the gang of eleven monsters."[44] Marduk's spell

---

42 Hurowitz, "Alliterative Allusions, Rebus Writing, and Paronomastic Punishment," 78.

43 We might even add the vizier Mummu, who is complicit with Apsu in this plan of infanticide, and regard the plan as a murderous result of an eroticized homosociality.

44 Gregory Mobley, *The Return of the Chaos Monsters: And Other Backstories of the Bible* (Grand Rapids: Wm. B. Eerdmans Publishing Co., 2012), 18.

against Tiamat seems to have endured the *longue durée* of the *Enuma Elish*'s reception.

1.1.3 Monstrification/Feminization of Tiamat.

Through more than one hundred years of study, ranging from archaeologist, philologist, and biblical scholarly to feminist perspectives, only very few seem to have noticed the motherly aspect of Tiamat. Even those who are aware of gender issues, like Harris, tend to regard Tiamat at best as a figure of the demonized *femme fatale* easily found in "patriarchal mythologies." Certainly, some authors have not turned their eyes completely away from the possibility of *not* seeing Tiamat as the "bad guy," such as Budges and Jacobsen have claimed.[45] But almost all of them agree that Tiamat is feminine and represents chaos or a destructive force that opposes the order or creational force represented by the masculine Marduk.

After this short survey of the reception history of Tiamat in scholarship from the 19th and 20th centuries, I hope it has become clear that such scholarship is largely responsible for the monstrification and essentialization of Tiamat as the feminine chaos. In other words, Tiamat is not born, but *becomes* a female monster. This relationship between monstrosity and femininity is complex and worth further exploration. By the "monstrification of Tiamat," I do not suggest that Tiamat is essentially "good" and only became monstrified later, such as is argued by feminists adhering to New Age Spiritualism and the Goddess Movement, namely that the feminine Tiamat has been monstrified both within the course of *Enuma Elish* and through its reception history.

The problem of imagining a matriarchal past (represented by the primordial mother figure Tiamat) later replaced by patriarchy (represented by Marduk's victory over Tiamat), has been criticized by Carol Meyers from the perspective of biblical archeology and by Zainab Bahrani in the context of art histo-

---

45 Budge, *The Babylonian Legends of the Creation and the Fight between Bel and the Dragon,* 33n1; Jacobsen, *The Treasures of Darkness,* 187.

ry.[46] The weakness of an analysis that regards the monstrosity of Tiamat as largely a later construction or distortion through monstrification, either by the Babylonian cosmographers or by modern scholars, is that it fails to see the contingency of femininity, which is always a construction, i.e., feminization. Feminization and monstrification in this sense do not exist in an additive, but in a mutually constructive relationship. The question of feminization and monstrification becomes even more complex when "motherhood" or "motherliness" is introduced at the same time, which renders any facile dichotomy fully untenable. For the modern/colonial logic of "either/or" that establishes the divide between "good" and "evil," "light" and "darkness," "we" and "them," the term "motherliness" seems to be always associated with the former. This appears to be a main quandary in Tiamat's modern reception.

1.2 "Cutting Tiamat in Two": The Monstrification/Feminization of Tiamat or the "Bad Monster" versus the "Benevolent Mother"

He placed her head, heaped up [   ]
Opened up springs: water gushed out.
He opened the Euphrates and the Tigris from her eyes,
Closed her nostrils, [   ]
He piled up clear-cut mountains from her udder,
Bored waterholes to drain off the catchwater.
He laid her tail across, tied it fast as the cosmic bond,
And [   ] the Apsu beneath his feet.
He set her thigh to make fast the sky,
With half of her he made a roof; he fixed the earth.
He [   ] the work, made the insides of Tiamat surge,

46 Carol Meyers, "Contesting the Notion of Patriarchy: Anthropology and the Theorizing of Gender in Ancient Israel," in *A Question of Sex? Gender and Difference in the Hebrew Bible and Beyond,* ed. Deborah W. Rooke (Sheffield: Sheffield Phoenix Press, 2007), 84–105; Zainab Bahrani, *Women of Babylon: Gender and Representation in Mesopotamia* (London: Routledge, 2001).

Spread his net, made it extend completely.
He … [   ] heaven and earth.[47]

This fragment from the epic recounts the creation of heaven and earth by Marduk after defeating Tiamat. It is also one of the few instances in which we can imagine Tiamat as a snake/dragon-like creature through the depiction of "her" tail. We have a feminine designation of Tiamat, who is also said to have an "udder," a clearly feminine organ. This so-called heroic act of Marduk is extremely violent, though it is often read as "merely" metaphorical. The sheer violence is often masked as a "heroic" or "creational" act of Marduk, and therefore unquestionably good. In the epic as in scholarship, Marduk's violence against the highly feminized chaos seems to be justifiable, since it is allegedly exerted to enforce order. This again subsumes a logic that neatly separates good and evil, cosmos and chaos, younger generation and older generation, activity and passivity, masculinity and femininity, which can be ironically allegorized with Marduk's simple act of "cutting Tiamat in two."

At least in the early stage of *Enuma Elish,* Tiamat can be regarded without any ambiguity as a caring and loving mother who indulges her children and protects them from the anger of Apsu, the "father." This moment is largely, if not completely or successfully, erased in scholarly works that so eagerly represent Tiamat as "a huge dragon of chaotic water that resists order"[48] or one of "the bad guys in *Enuma Elish.*"[49] The story shows her motherly moments three times. Let us first revisit these moments, strikingly distorted in scholarship, without the need of sophisticated hermeneutics, and by following the "textual evidence" as it is revealed in the epic.

---

47 The square brackets are in the original.
48 Paul S. Evans, "Creation, Progress and Calling: Genesis 1–11 as Social Commentary," *McMaster Journal of Theology and Ministry* 13 (2011): 67–100, at 72.
49 Mobley, *The Return of the Chaos Monsters,* 18.

Before it runs into the irrevocable conflict almost at the end of Tablet I,[50] the epic never portrays Tiamat as monstrous or frightening. This is true for the young gods both inside the text and inside Tiamat's body, who are fearlessly naughty and make restless noise. Indeed, the gods disturb Tiamat and stir up her belly, but she silently accepts it: "However grievous their behavior to her, / However bad their ways, she would indulge them." We are presented here with an indulgent and compassionate mother figure rather than a "bad mother/progenitrix."[51] However, she is not a passively suffering, giant metaphoric womb, either.[52] When Apsu, the impatient father, goes to Tiamat and tells her about his infanticide plan, she turns furious, actively protecting her children from the paternal violence. Why would he need to ask Tiamat's permission at all, if the Babylonian poets were really simply just promoting patriarchy through myth making? This is a separate issue, though it is not an exaggeration if Apsu complains to Tiamat, "Their ways have become very grievous to me, / By day I cannot rest, by night I cannot sleep," and reveals his plan of killing: "I shall abolish their ways and disperse them!" Apsu then suggests a mutual benefit for Tiamat, "Let peace prevail, so that we can sleep." As could be expected from a mother, Tiamat, after hearing this plan,

> was furious and shouted at her lover;
> She shouted dreadfully and was beside herself with rage,
> [...]
>> "How could we allow what we ourselves created to perish?
>> Even though their ways are grievous, we
>> should bear it patiently."

---

50 The version I am using contains seven tablets.
51 Harris, "The Conflict of Generations in Ancient Mesopotamian Myths," 631.
52 Julia M. O'Brien, ed., *The Oxford Encyclopedia of the Bible and Gender Studies* (Oxford: Oxford University Press, 2014), 70.

This could be the first time in the epic when we might, despite the benevolent intention, sense a certain degree of "monstrosity" due to her dreadful rage, which has even "suppressed the evil in her belly." This is also the second moment when we see the enactment of Tiamat's motherliness. The third time comes after the death of Apsu and before the dawn of the final combat with Marduk. The epic states that after overhearing the plan of Apsu and Mummu, the god Ea, "[s]uperior in understanding, wise and capable," casts a spell to kill Apsu and capture Mummu. This time, we do not have any information about Tiamat. She seems mercilessly indifferent to the death of her lover Apsu, who in the beginning of the epic has already mingled with her, that is, has become part of Tiamat. The birth of Marduk follows: "And inside Apsu, Marduk was created; / Inside pure Apsu, Marduk was born." At this time, Apsu has already been de-personified and has once again become the fresh-water ocean, which somehow also feminizes Apsu and makes him/it a womb-like space. The epic spends several lines telling us how superior this newly born god is. "Four were his eyes, four were his ears; [...] / Highest among the gods, his form was outstanding." The masculine cult of exalting power with concrete manifestations is at its worst in this representation. Like any macho lad, especially being encouraged by his indulgent grandfather who gives him the weaponized winds to play with, Marduk is bound to do something naughty: "He made the flood-wave and stirred up Tiamat. / Tiamat was stirred up, and heaved restlessly day and night." Again Tiamat indulges the wrongdoings of the younger grandson. This time, it is some of the children gods who cannot bear this younger brother or nephew's restlessness:

> They plotted evil in their hearts, and
> They addressed Tiamat their mother, saying,
>> "Because they slew Apsu your lover and
>> You did not go to his side but sat mute,
>> He has created the four, fearful winds
>> To stir up your belly on purpose, and we simply cannot sleep!

Was your lover Apsu not in your heart?
And (vizier) Mummu who was captured? No wonder you
    sit alone!
Are you not a mother? You heave restlessly
But what about us, who cannot rest? Don't you love us?"
[...]
Tiamat listened, and the speech pleased her.
    "Let us act now, (?) as you were advising!"

Tiamat is pleased by this appeal, which is similar to the one
Apsu made to them before and which, in that instance, had en-
raged them. She is so pleased, in fact, that she decides to fight
against the Marduk band for the same reason that Apsu had giv-
en her, "I cannot rest." While she had rejected the plan of Apsu,
the father, earlier, now she is "pleased" to act for her children,
despite the insults and mockery of the younger gods. If indeed,
we might initially have had only a vague sense of monstrosity in
Tiamat's rage at Apsu, it is only now that we can indeed associate monstrosity with Tiamat's deed for "she bore giant / snakes, /
Sharp of tooth and unsparing of fang (?) / She filled their bodies
with venom instead of blood"; "Whoever looks upon them shall
collapse in utter / terror!" However, should we thus simply accept the conclusion that Tiamat *is* a monster? Should we ignore
the fact that this "utter terror" is meant to protect her innocent
children from the bullying of the disturbing gangs led by the
four-big-ear-and-eye Marduk? Should we then consent to the
sheer monstrosity of Marduk just because the epic intends to
elevate him as the hero, representative of order, even to the extent of glorifying his battle with Tiamat as "the template for all
subsequent epic showdowns between monster and hero?"[53]

What is even more unfortunate, is that if the first motherly
indulgence was ignored, the second insurgence prompted by a
motherly desire to protect Tiamat's bullied children has been
consistently misrepresented as her personal revenge for the
murder of her lover Apsu. For example, Black and Green sum-

---

53 Mobley, *The Return of the Chaos Monsters,* 18.

marize Tiamat's "revolt" as: "When Ea slew Apsu, Tiamat determined to be avenged and created eleven monsters."[54] Tiamat's threat to order is only banished through Marduk's "heroic contest." Jacobsen, even though he has rightly argued that "when she [Tiamat] is finally roused to fatal action, it is by appealing to her motherly instincts of protection — not from lack of patience or forbearance on her part,"[55] represents the conflict as follows:

> [T]heir [the young gods'] fathers were in their eyes acting unjustly toward them when Apsu sought to destroy them; and now she, their mother, hates them and is bent on attacking them, as is abundantly clear from her standing here in the midst of an army fully armed by her.[56]

This binary opposition takes the form of a generational conflict. The young gods, those who oppose both Marduk and the Marduk gang, are grouped together in opposition to the "older gods," who are Apsu, the one who indeed seeks to annihilate the young gods, and Tiamat, the one who only acts against Marduk, not an undifferentiated "them." The internal discrepancies of both the younger and older generations are reduced for the sake of neatly dichotomizing "order/young versus chaos/old." The plot is most misleadingly summarized in Takayoshi Oshima's introduction to *Enuma Elish*:

> However, Ea, of the fourth generation from Apsu and Tiamat, learns *their* plan [to exterminate them] and kills Apsu by means of an incantation [...]. After having been accused for coolly allowing the death of Apsu, Tiamat decides to wage war against her children.[57]

---

54 Jeremy Black and Anthony Green, *Gods, Demons and Symbols of Ancient Mesopotamia: An Illustrated Dictionary* (London: British Museum Press, 1992), 177.

55 Jacobsen, *The Treasures of Darkness*, 187.

56 Ibid., 178.

57 Oshima, "The Babylonian God Marduk," 352.

These short summaries univocally read the Tiamat–Marduk battle as one between two antagonistic groups, Tiamat versus her
grandsons and allegorically woman against man, chaos against
order. However, some feminist works, notably those from the
"Goddess Movement" or New Age Spiritualism, do not seem to
follow this dichotomous reasoning. They believe in a primordial
mother goddess and find their sound supporter in the Ancient
Near East, which is believed to be the home of a matriarchal past
suppressed by patriarchy. In this conception, Tiamat is without
any doubt regarded as one of the most eminent matriarchal
mother goddesses, and *Enuma Elish* is consequently read as a
story of patriarchy defeating matriarchy or goddess worship,[58]
indeed a document of culture, "which is […] simultaneously
one of barbarism."[59] In light of this argument, Tiamat is often
represented essentially as a loving mother, while her more malign aspect is believed to be a result of the patriarchal distortion
(monstrification).

This kind of reading is equally problematic. The goddess-
worship interpretation of Tiamat arbitrarily divides (or may
we say, violently cuts) her/it into two supposedly incompatible

58 Such view can be found in blogs of "goddess worship," such as: "Goddess
Tiamat," *Journey into the Goddess*, July 30, 2012, https://journeyingtothe-
goddess.wordpress.com/2012/07/30/goddess-tiamat/; "Tiamat: Lady of
Primeval Chaos, the Great Mother of the Gods of Babylon," *Gateways to
Babylon*, http://www.gatewaystobabylon.com/gods/ladies/ladytiamat.html;
and Warlock Asylum, "The Worship of Tiamat in Ancient History," *Warlock
Asylum International News*, September 17, 2010, https://warlockasylumin-
ternationalnews.com/2010/09/17/the-worship-of-tiamat-in-ancient-histo-
ry/. For scholarly works in similar vein, see, for example: Bettina Liebowitz
Knapp, *Women in Myth* (New York: State University of New York, 1997);
Ruby Rohrlich, "State Formation in Sumer and the Subjugation of Women,"
Feminist Studies 6, no. 1 (1980): 76–102; and Marti Kheel, "From Heroic
to Holistic Ethics: The Ecofeminist Challenge," in *Ecofeminism: Women,
Animals, Nature*, ed. Greta Gaard (Philadelphia: Temple University Press,
1993), 243–71. For a general introduction to the closely related "ecofemi-
nism," see the foundational work of Susan Griffin, *Woman and Nature: The
Roaring inside Her* (New York: Harper & Row, 1978).
59 Walter Benjamin, "Theses on the Philosophy of History," in *Illuminations:
Essays and Reflections*, trans. Harry Zohn, ed. Hannah Arendt (New York:
Schocken Books, 1969), 253–64, at 256.

characteristics: on the one hand a benevolent mother and on the other a bad monster. Just like Marduk created the world by butchering Tiamat's body to form heaven and earth, it transforms the genuine "good mother" from the outset of the myth "into a negative and destructive personality type during the course of the myth [which] signals a sharp cultural and psychological shift from a [*sic*] quasi-matriarchal to patriarchal tendencies in Babylonia."[60] This anti-patriarchal argument unintentionally reinscribes the very dichotomous logic of phallogocentrism[61] through a careless acceptance of an original "ideal mother" type, which only indulges and endures sufferings. Anything contrary to this expectation is doomed to be read either as monstrous femininity representing chaos, or as a monstrified victim of patriarchal conspiracy.

What has been sacrificed in this account is the complexity of Tiamat's motherhood, which involves both love and monstrosity.[62] What is even more dangerous, is that the profound hegemonic phallogocentric logic underwriting the hierarchical

---

60 Knapp, *Women in Myth,* 21.
61 For a discussion of "phallogocentrism," a combination of logocentrism and phallocentrism, see Part O and Part II in this volume.
62 As this work intends to get closely "within" the ancient text, it intentionally has not engaged with the exciting works in "monster studies" per se. However, this volume shares with the critical vision of this exciting field, especially those with critical energies from feminism, queer theory, and critical race studies. Readers interested in monster and monstrosity, see Jeffrey Jerome Cohen (ed.), *Monster Theory: Reading Culture* (Minneapolis: University of Minnesota Press, 1996), and, more recently, Asa Simon Mittman and Peter J. Dandle (eds.), *The Ashgate Research Companion to Monsters and the Monstrous* (London: Routledge, 2012); monster and the monstrous have been, at least in the West, intricately linked with what the dominant white male culture deems "other": women, queers, people of color, and the working class, see Julia Kristeva, *Pouvoirs de l'horreur: Essai sur l'abjection* (Paris: Seuil, 1980); Jack (then Judith) Halberstam, *Skin Shows: Gothic Horror and the Technology of Monsters* (Durham: Duke University Press, 1995); and Christina Sharp, *Monstrous Intimacies: Making Post-Slavery Subjects* (Durham: Duke University Press, 2010). On the closely related issue of monstrosity and motherhood, viewed through the lens of psychoanalysis, see Sabrina Spielrein, "Destruction as the Cause of Coming into Being," *Journal of Analytical Psychology* 39, no. 2 (1994): 155–86, among others.

dichotomy of gender is left unquestioned. If Braidotti is correct in pointing out that "the misogyny of discourse is not an
irrational exception but rather a tightly constructed system that
requires difference as pejoration in order to erect the positivity of the norm,"[63] the misogynist representation of Tiamat as
pure monstrosity results from a necessity, in the very logic of
difference, to erect the positivity of Marduk, who is constructed
in this process as the norm/order opposing the stigmatized difference as monstrosity/chaos. Feminization thus runs together
with monstrification. In the same analysis, which intentionally
conflates "Mothers, Monsters, and Machines," Braidotti points
out succinctly that

> hatred for the feminine constitutes the phallogocentric econ-
> omy inducing in both sexes the desire to achieve order, by
> means of a one way pattern for both. As long as the law of the
> One is operative, so will be the denigration of the feminine,
> and of women with it.[64]

Without making the inner mechanism of phallogocentrism or
"patriarchy" clear, simply reversing its polarities will continue
to fall prey to this detrimental logic. Going back to our earlier
metaphor, the inverse strategy of goddess-worship's critique of
the "patriarchal monstrification" of Tiamat has equally cut them
into two incompatible parts, the Tiamat as the "original" or "authentic" loving mother-goddess and the Tiamat who becomes
the lethal monster because of a "misogynist distortion." Regarding this matter, the ancient text leaves an immense ambiguity
that cannot be easily categorized as "phallogocentric" or "patriarchal," even though Marduk seems to fight with his penis-
cum-weapon.[65] Tiamat's ambiguity or "queerness," which will be

---

63 Rosi Braidotti, *Nomadic Subjects: Embodiment and Sexual Difference in
    Contemporary Feminist Theory* (New York: Columbia University Press,
    1994), 80.
64 Ibid., 81.
65 See Ilona Zsolnay, ed., *Being a Man: Negotiating Ancient Constructs of Mas-
    culinity* (London; New York: Routledge, 2017).

discussed in the next chapter, is achieved precisely through the blending between motherliness and monstrosity, watery space and personified embodiment. If we take the "text" as an organic, unstable, and "chaotic" wholeness rather than a separable (or "orderly") quasi-matriarchal outset and patriarchal ending, we might then read the epic against its phallogocentric design without reinforcing the erection of the positivity of Marduk (in the name of order from chaos), or of Mother Tiamat (in the name of matriarchy before patriarchy). The unsettled text can be further read as resembling Tiamat's watery body, which is *already* always mingled with Apsu, inside which Marduk is born and erected as the supreme power.[66] After all, how can one separate the fresh-water "father" and the salt-water "mother," if they form a whole from the very beginning?

Before going to discuss what I call the queer Tiamat-Apsu (substituting the "/" for "-") in the next chapter, it is necessary to devote one last section to a discussion of the complex issue of motherhood and monstrosity. Are monstrosity and motherliness incompatible? Or can allegedly incompatible characteristics exist within one subject? Do we really need to make a decision between the "good mother" and the "bad monster," or find out a reason when the two run together in one entity?

1.3 Motherhood and Monstrosity: The Irreducible Complexity

Enuma Elish has served the highly sexist ideology of the Babylonian state, an argument supported by the epic, for example in overtly misogynous statements like: "However strong a woman's strength, it is not equal to a man's," or "My son, (don't you realize that) it is Tiamat, of / womankind, who will advance against you with / arms?" Ruby Rohrlich argues that Mesopotamian state

---

66 And in Chapter 2 I will discuss further the "unstable" and "chaotic" Babylonian text as a pretext for the Biblical Genesis and the postbiblical theological efforts of cleansing it from monotheism's chaotic beginning and religious, "pagan" origins, as opposed to the doctrine of *creatio ex nihilo* underlying not only orthodox Christian theology but also the colonial logic.

formation, first in Sumer and later in Babylon, "was a complex interaction among the processes of class stratification, militarism, patriarchy, and political consolidation."[67] Following this argument, the colonial undertone of *Enuma Elish* is revealed especially when Marduk, patron god of the Babylonian state, asks for the recognition of his legitimacy and supremacy over all *other* gods and is confirmed in his claims:

> And let me [Marduk], my own utterance, fix fate instead of you.
> Whatever I create shall never be altered"
> [...]
> "May your utterance be law, your word never be falsified.
> None of the gods shall transgress your limits.
> May endowment, required for the gods' shrines
> Wherever they have temples, be established for your place."

Oshima argues that "as political power of Babylon grew, so did the position of its national god, Marduk, who was also gradually elevated within the polytheistic religious system of Babylonia."[68] The political meaning of Marduk's petition for supremacy in compliance with a patriarchal logic, which literally suppresses what is taken to be at once feminine and chaotic, cannot be clearer. But could or should we therefore assume that such phallogocentric politics is successfully completed in the epic? Should we conflate the volitive pronouncement of Marduk's supremacy, which actually had to be renewed every year during the New Year Festival by reiteration and repetition, with the indicative narrative of the epic as to how things really were?

Even if — despite its necessity of renewal, which implies potential failure or constant threat — we were to accept the misogyny of *Enuma Elish,* the theory that sees the monstrosity of Tiamat as merely patriarchal monstrification/distortion is still bought at a price, namely that of depriving Tiamat of her own

---

67 Rohrlich, "State Formation in Sumer and the Subjugation of Women," 98.
68 Oshima, "The Babylonian God Marduk," 348.

agency and her own decision to be malign. Cutting Tiamat into either the "bad monster" who kills or the "good mother" who protects, two supposedly incompatible entities, is a result of modern and colonial categorical logics, unable to fathom the coexistence of two supposedly oppositional characteristics.

In a different context, Richard Rorty asserts that "one cannot find anybody who says that two incompatible opinions on an important topic are equally good."[69] The alleged incompatibility of "motherliness" and "monstrosity" does not permit them to be "equally good" in one figure, Tiamat. She/it has to be *either* a lethal monster *or* a loving mother. The misogynists choose to accept the former, while the "Tiamat-worshippers" stick to the latter. This "either/or" logic requires the researchers to either univocally ignore the benevolent Tiamat and reiterate her monstrosity, or look for the reason why the essentially good mother is later monstrified. If the former readings are explicitly sexist, the latter counterarguments, once examined closely, also appear to reproduce the same dichotomous logic, typical of the patriarchy that they seek nominally to oppose.

We have seen the continuous efforts to interpret the battle between Tiamat and Marduk as the battle between chaos and order and Marduk's victory as the defeat of chaos, an interpretation that can be traced back to the first modern studies of the epic. The early feminist effort to read the epic as a textual reflection of the historical shift between (quasi-)matriarchy to patriarchy is designed to counteract the naturalization of patriarchy which presents itself as inevitable. This "colonizing epistemological strategy that would subordinate different configurations of domination under the rubric of a transcultural notion of patriarchy"[70] is contested in archaeology. Studying artistic representations in ancient Babylonia, Bahrani argues in her *Women of Babylon* that "prehistoric matriarchy is a mythic construction

69 Richard Rorty, *Consequences of Pragmatism* (Minneapolis: University of Minnesota Press, 1982), 166.
70 Judith Butler, *Gender Trouble: Feminism and the Subversion of Identity* (London: Routledge, 1999), 48.

which is part and parcel of the same narrative of patriarchy it wishes to overthrow."[71]

What is more unfortunate is that the readings in favor of or in opposition to Marduk have unfortunately subscribed to the same dichotomous logic, and assisted a phallogocentrism that is *far from* being successfully installed in the epic. The repetition of the epic's creation story both in Babylonia and through scholarly works that confuse volition with actuality, has performatively "attributed and installed" the "patriarchy" that the former wishful pronouncement anticipates and later feminist critiques seek to oppose.

However, the "split" of Tiamat in *Enuma Elish* and in reception history is never and can never be completed. The "monster" always returns.[72] For this very reason, the Babylonian kings deemed it necessary to reiterate and renew Marduk-*qua*-Babylonia's supremacy every year. For even the Bible, which is often seen as claiming an absolute supremacy of Yahweh in its linearity from creation to revelation, would have to face a recurrent "threat" of the sea-dragon, either in the name of Leviathan or Satan, a form of *l'éternel retour*:

He laid hold of the dragon, that serpent of old, who is the Devil and Satan, and bound him for a thousand years; and he cast him into the bottomless pit,[73] and shut him up, and set a seal on him, so that he should deceive the nations no more till the thousand years were finished. But after these things he must be released for a little while. (Revelation 20:1–3)

---

71 Bahrani, *Women of Babylon,* 17.

72 See Jon D. Levenson, *Creation and the Persistence of Evil* (San Francisco: Harper & Row Publishers, 1988); Jeffrey J. Cohen, "Monster Culture (Seven Theses)," in *Monster Theory: Reading Culture,* ed. Jeffrey J. Cohen (Minneapolis: University of Minnesota Press, 1996), 3–25; Mobley, *The Return of the Chaos Monsters.*

73 The "bottomless pit" here both etymologically and semantically remains us of the primordial *tehom* before God's creation in Genesis 1.

Beyond the allegedly patriarchal distortion of Tiamat, let us read closely this particular moment after which she/it goes into battle against Marduk, and reexamine the seemingly incompatible characteristics of Tiamat. Perhaps, at this stage, I should emphasize that this reading attempts to go *below* rather than beyond the previous readings that I see as being caught in the logic of "either/or." "Below" circumvents the transcendental and supersessionist undertone of "beyond," and, more importantly, it suggests an adherence to the "queer" space (and Apsu) that are there. We read: "Inside pure Apsu, Marduk was born." He begins to make noise inside Tiamat's belly just like the other gods have done before. That is to say, while he is "born inside Apsu," he also remains within Tiamat's watery body, which should not be surprising, because, as we have repeatedly stated, Apsu's and Tiamat's waters have been mingled into one since the beginning. If we stick to these primordially mingling waters as they are eternally present, the efforts to separate them and destroy their unity, either by Marduk's mighty winds or by modern/colonial categorization, are doomed to fail.

But now let us leave this question for a moment and continue our story. Marduk's turbulence inside Tiamat annoys the other gods. This leaves us wondering *where* those gods actually were, but, strangely, Jacobsen wonders about *the reason* of their annoyance, suggesting that "[t]hese objecting gods [those against Marduk] were a group of deities who for some reason or other were siding with Tiamat."[74] Who else could a child turn to, if not the mother, especially if the father is dead?

The disturbed children selfishly accuse their mother of betraying her "lover" and coldly mock her, "no wonder you sit alone." Yet, "Tiamat listened, and the speech pleased her." Is this a reaction one could expect from a "female dragon, queen of a hideous host, who are hostile to the gods"?[75] The young gods clearly know that they are not facing an evil monster, but an indulgent mother who would not get angry as she did with a

---

74 Jacobsen, *The Treasures of Darkness,* 173.
75 Barton, "Tiamat," 12.

similar complaint from Apsu. She is even so pleased to hear their childish petulance and agrees to their petition to punish the bullying Marduk. If we keep in mind the inseparability of Apsu and Tiamat, Tiamat's anger towards Apsu would get an unexpected twist. We could ask whether this anger is directed towards what Julia Kristeva calls the *étranger à nous-mêmes*.[76] Even for Marduk and his father Ea, it is a surprise that mother Tiamat should prepare war against them:

> Ea listened to that report,
> And was dumbfounded and sat in silence.
> When he had pondered and his fury subsided,
> He made his way to Anshar his father;
> [...]
> And began to repeat to him everything that Tiamat had planned.
>> "Father, Tiamat who bore us is rejecting us!
>> She has convened an assembly and is raging out of control.
>> The gods have turned to her, all of them,
>> Even those whom you begot have gone over to her side,
>> [...]"

In the French version, "Tiamat who bore us" is even translated explicitly as "Tiamat, our mother."[77] Finally, the battle is reported to Ea's great-great-grandparents: "Lahmu and Lahamu listened and cried out aloud. / All the Igigi then groaned dreadfully."[78] They ask: "What have we done so wrong that she should have

---

76 Julia Kristeva. *Etrangers à nous-mêmes* (Paris: Librairie Arthème Fayard, 1988).

77 Talon, *The Standard Babylonian Creation Myth Enūma Eliš*, 83: "Tiamat, notre mère."

78 "Lahmu and Lahamu" are the very first ones born to Apsu and Tiamat, that is to say, the great-grandparents of Ea, father of Marduk. "Igigi" are the gods in general.

made such a decision towards us?"[79] For the same reason, Ea is confused and remains silent. The Marduk troop also considers Tiamat as their mother and for that very reason they are shocked and sad with tears when they know that the mother who once indulged their noise and saved them from Apsu's anger now "collected battle-units against the gods his / offspring [and] did even more evil for posterity than Apsu." Even Marduk himself states: "Just because the sons were noisy (and) / disrespectful to their fathers, / Should you, who gave them birth, reject / compassion," or as the French version has it, again more explicitly: "The children have made noises (that is true), they have bullied their fathers / but you, *their mother,* you have abandoned all compassion!"[80]

Inside Tiamat's body, inside the epic, both groups assume the motherliness of Tiamat. They all remind Tiamat, "are you not a mother?" and "should you, who gave them birth [*leur mère à tous*], reject compassion?" The young gods, both those who side with her and those who finally fight against her, in no sense see her as a threatening primordial chaos/monster. The pun "(m)other," that is, mother as other, which only works in the English language, is thus at best only partially true in *Enuma Elish.*

After all, Tiamat does not set out to "kill" all her children but tries to eliminate the disturbing part in order to save the innocent ones. The studies that identify Tiamat as essentially monstrous have assumed the (m)other economy so that the benevolent "motherly moments" before the final battle between Tiamat and Marduk would be accepted as internal contradictions to be overlooked. If the essential nature of femininity is seen as monstrous (and the monstrous as feminine), seeking to oppose the order allegedly represented and restored by Marduk, then the benevolent moments at the outset of the epic could only be seen

---

79 Talon, *The Standard Babylonian Creation Myth Enūma Eliš,* 90: "Qu'avons-nous fait de mal pour qu'elle ait pris à notre égard une telle décision?" All translations to English from non-English sources, unless stated otherwise, are mine.

80 Ibid., 93, emphasis mine. "Les enfants ont crié (c'est vrai), ils ont malmené leurs pères / mais toi, leur mère à tous, tu as rejeté toute pitié!"

as a temporary deception. Alternatively, these benevolent moments are read as her "real" identity, only later distorted in the epic. In Bettina Knapp's analysis, "Tiamat […] is not depicted as a monstrous force at the outset in the myth, she is maligned by mythologists, philosophers, critics and literati after she assumes a confrontational position."[81]

Marduk seems to have already set the rules of the game for the mythologists (and to some extent, also some feminist interpreters). Listen to what he has to say to Tiamat, about this "discrepancy" in Tiamat, "before" and "now": "While you showed good will before / now your heart is plotting to mount an attack."[82] The problem of those misogynist interpretations is perhaps not the fact that they have intentionally monstrified Tiamat in a kind of patriarchal conspiracy. A theory of the essentially monstrous femininity that menaces the masculine order does not need *Enuma Elish* to support its claim. In this scenario, any evidence contrary to the monstrous rendering of Tiamat would have been either erased as irrelevant or simply overlooked. Motherliness and monstrosity do not in nature oppose each other (as the feminist critiques would like it) nor do they run together with each other (as the misogynist accounts would like it).

In this chapter, we have revisited the complex narrative of *Enuma Elish,* especially its ambiguity regarding the "mother" figure Tiamat and her relationship with Apsu her lover, and the younger gods, her children. As I have shown, the modern reception of the epic has largely simplified and essentialized Tiamat. In fact, it appears that the complex figure that is at once

---

81 Knapp, *Women in Myth,* 21.
82 Talon, *The Standard Babylonian Creation Myth Enūma Eliš,* 93: "alors qu'avant tu manifestais de bons sentiments, / maintenant ton coeur complote-t-il de lancer l'assaut?"

the primordial salt water already mingled with the fresh water and the personified primordial mother "who bore them all" has been consolidated in scholarship as the monster. The benevolent "motherly" moments of Tiamat have been either ignored by those who eagerly associate her with chaos, or oversimplified as her "true identity," notably by the goddess feminists who hold that the malign representation of Tiamat is a result of misogynist distortions. Neither interpretation has turned out to be satisfactory. By assuming the separability of the allegedly incompatible characteristics of Tiamat, both antifeminist and feminist critiques have continued Marduk's violence of cutting Tiamat in two. However, the split of Tiamat *inside* the epic is hardly successful, if we follow closely the narrative that *all* happens within Tiamat(-Apsu), and if we situate the epic in its renewal ritual of the New Year Festival. The other kind of split of Tiamat, in her/its scholarly reception is not complete either; the "good/motherly"–"bad/monstrous" dichotomy imposed on Tiamat is primarily sustained by the categorical logic of modernity/coloniality, rather than by the epic itself.

Last but not least, if I have nevertheless "cut" the mingled water Tiamat-Apsu in two, so that they are separated with a slash instead of being linked with a hyphen, I did so consciously. The mingling water(s) of Tiamat and Apsu is/are at once separated and united, yet profusely inundating the whole epic, *below* the logic of either/or. This is not to be confused with the undifferentiated mixture of the two distinct waters. Studies that conflate Tiamat with Apsu often do so at the price of charging her with the same infanticidal cruelty as Apsu. The challenge that Tiamat-Apsu poses to us is how to move below not only the "either/or" logic of exclusivity that previous critiques seek to either overthrow or reverse, but also below the quick solution of the swampy "both…and." *Enuma Elish,* distinct from the modern/colonial logic of insurmountable differences, offers us rich insights into rethinking beyond both "either/or" and "both…and" and *below* the transcendental "beyond."

Adhering to the luxuriant withinness of the mingling Tiamat-Apsu, the fusing primordial waters of *Enuma Elish,* we will move

one step further in the next chapter and dwell in the inseparability of Tiamat-Apsu, to inquire what this mingling entails and
discuss the "queer" divine waters of Apsu-Tiamat(-Mummu).

2

Queer Divine Waters

有物混成先天地生。寂兮寥兮独立不改，
周行而不殆，可以为天地母。
—道德经—第二十五章　老子[1]

Our gods are Queer, because they are what we want them to be.
— Marcella Althaus-Reid, *Indecent Theology*[2]

The Chinese novel 西遊記 (*Journey to the West*) by Wu Chen'en from the Ming Dynasty (14th–17th century CE) begins with a heavenly disorder created by a naughty yet mighty monkey, the "Great Sage" Monkey King, who revolts against the gods. The Buddha Tathāgata (如來) captures him, but bets with him that if he can fly out of the right hand of the Buddha with a single somersault, he will not be punished for the revolt. The Monkey King can cover thirty-six thousand miles with a single somersault and thinks to himself that the Buddha must be an idiot, for his hand is less than a foot large! He makes the jump, thinks that he is already at the end of the sky, and thus leaves an inscription as proof. He writes, "齊天大聖到此一游" ("The Great Sage who

---

1   "Something is chaotically and confusingly formed before heaven and earth, so tranquil and so fragile yet independent and unchanging. It circulates and never ends. It can be regarded as the mother of all." *Daodejing*, ch. 25.

2   Marcella Althaus-Reid, *Indecent Theology: Theological Perversions in Sex, Gender and Politics* (London: Routledge, 2000), 67.

equals heaven was here") on one of the five giant pillars in front of which he also urinates. He returns and the Buddha tells him, "You never left the palm of my hand!" The Great Sage refuses to believe him, looks at the Buddha's right hand, and sees his inscription on the Buddha's middle finger, where one also gets a whiff of smelly monkey pee. The name Tathāgata (如來), which means the "one who has attained full realization of thatness (Tathā-ta) [… and who] neither comes from any where […] nor goes to any where,"³ should have already warned the Monkey King of the omnipresence of the Buddha. S/he is beyond time and space, and certainly beyond gender.

If the body of the Buddha metaphorically represents the cosmos beyond the limits of conceivable space and time, the story about the Monkey King's revolt and subsequent failure to escape the Buddha's palm is an allegory of the omnipresent natural order. This ultimate harmony or orderedness is only temporarily disrupted by the smelly chaos that tries in vain to conquer it. *Journey to the West* offers an understanding that is seemingly the opposite of the Babylonian *Enuma Elish.* The Monkey King is the one who tries to induce chaos through "culture," including writing, onto the harmonious and orderly nature, whereas Marduk, also representing "culture," is the one who brings order by subjugating Tiamat/nature, who, as a result of this imposed order, becomes known as the chaos that ought to be tamed. The Chinese text regards nature as represented by the Buddha as an "order as such." 自然, the Chinese word for "nature," coincides philosophically with the idea of the Sanskrit name of the Buddha Tathāgata. The Babylonian text *seems* to suggest the contrary; that "nature" as represented by Tiamat (and Apsu) is chaotic and therefore should be organized by a "righteous" order represented by Marduk, who, allying himself with "culture," conquers not only through a spell but also with weaponry.

This quick comparison of the two texts installs a dichotomy between chaos and order, culture and nature, as if they were

---

3   K. Krishna Murthy, *A Dictionary of Buddhist Terms and Terminologies* (New Delhi: Sundeep Prakashan, 1999), 41.

ahistorical, separable, and self-sufficient entities. Putting the two culturally diverse stories together, we can see, at least, how different cultures understand these allegedly dualistic pairs in different and even contradictory ways. However, neither the Chinese story nor the Babylonian *Enuma Elish,* it seems, has assumed a dualistic separation, whose sustaining binary oppositional logic can be extended to nature/culture, passivity/activity, and femininity/masculinity in modernity. The Monkey King, the male-gendered "Great Sage," and also the male-gendered Marduk all represent the temporary injection (seen as chaos or order) into "nature-as-it-is" or 自然 (seen as order or chaos). Expressed in the language of complexity theory, as Edgar Morin puts it, "disorder […] is the generalized dispersion and order […] is an arbitrary constrain imposed onto this diversity."[4] In both the Chinese and Babylonian texts, however, the so-called disorder and order are interchangeable concepts. What is at stake is how the dominant voice promotes the "generalized dispersion" and/or the "imposed arbitrariness."

While the Buddha Tathāgata is gendered male, given the historical figure of the founder of Buddhism, Siddhartha Gautama, but ultimately transcendental in terms of gender, Tiamat is gendered female, given the motherly personification of the primordial sea in the Babylonian Epic of Creation, but is ultimately unstable and uncategorizable. Scholars of the ancient Near East remind us that "the sex of a god is not assigned based on his or her genitalia, nor is the gender of a god assigned based on the god's sex."[5] This chapter will survey several moments in this vast and complex array of cultures and histories of the very diverse, unstable, and often confusing gendering (and ungendering) of primordial divine figures associated with water, from the Sumerian oceanic mother goddess Nammu and the Babylonian Tiamat-Apsu, to the biblical "deep" *tehom.*

---

4   Edgar Morin, *Introduction à la pensée complexe* (Paris: ESF Editeur, 1990), 126: "le désordre […] est la dispersion généralisée et l'ordre […] est une contrainte arbitraire imposée à cette diversité."

5   Julia M. O'Brien, ed., *The Oxford Encyclopedia of the Bible and Gender Studies* (Oxford: Oxford University Press, 2014), 70.

While the Sumerians personify their primordial ocean "(the) Apsu" with a mother goddess figure Nammu, Tiamat of *Enuma Elish* assumes the male gender in Tablet II when she prepares for war with Marduk: "Tiamat assembled his creatures / And collected battle-units against the gods his / offspring." In the post-Babylonian biblical Genesis, the primordial deep, *tehom,* even though morphologically resembling "Tiamat," is semantically related to "Apsu."[6] Instead of trying to work out the confusions of the fluctuating mythological sources, we will wander back and forth with Tiamat-Apsu of *Enuma Elish* and inquire into the "queerness" of this commingling, resistant, and gender-blurred watery spaces. Like the inescapable palm of Tathāgata, the "chaotic" and "queer" Tiamat seems to have been constantly haunting Marduk's self-appointed supremacy and righteousness. We will see how these "queer" divine waters might leak into our time and nurture our imagination for different, if not "new," ways of thinking, embodying, and practicing queerness.

2.1 Primordial Waters

Before the "beginning" there are always other worlds, deep down. *Enuma Elish,* in any case, has not claimed to be an absolute beginning. Before *Enuma Elish,* the Sumerians had their mythology regarding the primordial waters. Author of *Sumerian Mythology,* Samuel Kramer asserts that "the Sumerian origin of the *Enuma Elish* is obvious and certain."[7] Nammu, "written with the ideogram for 'sea,' is described as 'the mother, who gave birth to heaven and earth.'"[8] In the myth *Enki and Ninmah,* Enki,

---

6 David Toshio Tsumura, *The Earth and the Waters in Genesis 1 and 2: A Linguistic Investigation* (Sheffield: Sheffield Academic Press, 1989), 62.

7 Samuel Noah Kramer, "The Babylonian Genesis: The Story of Creation by Alexander Heidel," *Journal of American Oriental Society* 63, no. 1 (1943): 69–73, at 70n3. In a review of one of the most classical translations and studies of *Enuma Elish* by Alexander Heidel, Kramer points out that the only problem with Heidel's study is that he has not adequately studied Sumerian mythology.

8 Samuel Noah Kramer, *Sumerian Mythology: A Study of Spiritual and Literary Achievement in the Third Millennium B.C.* (Philadelphia: University of

the supreme god, is born to Nammu in the *abzu,* the primordial sea and Nammu herself. Slightly changing his name, Enki later becomes Ea in *Enuma Elish,* overhears the infanticidal plan of Apsu and Mummu, and manages to kill them. Ea then builds his "dwelling" upon "the *apsu*" after he kills Apsu, the personification of the *apsu/abzu.*[9] Similar to the Sumerian Enki, Ea's son Marduk, the so-called hero god, is born and remains in the *apsu.* In the *Codex Hammurabi,* which marks Babylon's supreme power in the region, we have a sort of synchronization of the Mesopotamian pantheon with the elevation of Marduk to the position of their patron god:

When the august god Anu, king of the Anunnaku deities, and the god Enlil, lord of heaven and earth who determines the destinies of the land, allotted supreme power over all peoples to the god Marduk, the firstborn son of the god Ea, exalted him among the Igigu deities, named the city of Babylon with its august name and made it supreme within the regions of the world, and established for him within it eternal kingship whose foundations are fixed as heaven and earth.[10]

In *Enuma Elish,* Tiamat occupies a role similar to that of Nammu, namely the primordial creatrix of all. This role is quickly balanced with a male-gendered creator Apsu at the outset of

Pennsylvania Press, 1972), 39.

9   *Abzu* is the Sumerian pronunciation, while *apsu* is the Akkadian one.

10 Martha T. Roth, *Law Collections from Mesopotamia and Asia Minor* (Atlanta: Scholars Press, 1995), 76. "Anunnaku" (Kramer transliterates it as "Annunaki") means the "attendant of gods": see Kramer, *Sumerian Mythology.* "Igigu," also transliterated as "Igigi," means "gods" in Stephanie Dalley, *Myths from Mesopotamia: Creation, The Flood, Gilgamesh, and Others* (Oxford: Oxford University Press, 2008) and Talon's English and French versions of *Enuma Elish* (Philippe Talon, *The Standard Babylonian Creation Myth Enūma Eliš* [Helsinki: Neo-Assyrian Text Corpus Project, 2005]). Other deities in this quote, "Anu," "Enlil," and "Ea," all appear in various Sumerian myths. For more discussion on this, see Takayoshi Oshima, "The Babylonian God Marduk," in *The Babylonian World,* ed. Gwendolyn Leick (New York: Routledge, 2007), 348–60.

the epic, and Tiamat is violently slaughtered by the "hero" Marduk, after which the epic proceeds to credit Marduk as "creator of heaven and earth." In her feminist study on the relationship between the subjugation of women and state formation
in Sumer, Rudy Rohrlich explains these changes as follows:
"[W]ith the institutionalization of the patriarchal family, economic stratification, militarism, and the consolidation of the
state in the hands of a male elite, male supremacy pervaded every social stratum."[11] Similarly, Tikva Frymer-Kensky points out
in *In the Wake of Goddess* that "among the changes in religion,
one trend that becomes very clear is the ongoing eclipse and the
marginalization of the goddesses" in Sumerian society and the
whole Mesopotamian region.[12]

As one piece of evidence, Rohrlich invokes the goddess
Nammu, whose supreme creation of heaven, earth, and human
beings was transformed into "the combined efforts of Nammu;
of the goddess Ninmah [...]; and of the water-god Enki."[13] Similarly, the deity An, now known as the first son born to Nammu,
was initially "seen as female and referred to the overcast sky,"[14]
while being in some traditions "both male and female [... dis-
tinguishing] the god An (Akkadian: Anum) from the goddess
An (Akkadian: Antum) to whom he was married."[15] Rohrlich
further points out that at a later point in history Nammu, whose
epithet *ama-tu-an-ki* actually means "the mother who gave birth
to heaven and earth,"[16] is described as merely An's consort.[17]
Most alerting is Frymer-Kensky's slippage in defining Nammu,

---

11 Ruby Rohrlich, "State Formation in Sumer and the Subjugation of Women,"
    Feminist Studies 6, no. 1 (1980): 76–102, at 84.
12 Tikva Frymer-Kensky, *In the Wake of the Goddesses: Women, Culture and
    the Biblical Transformation of Pagan Myth* (New York: The Free Press, 1992),
    70.
13 Ibid., 85.
14 Jacobsen, *The Treasures of Darkness*, 137.
15 Ibid., 95.
16 Kramer, *Sumerian Mythology*, 114n41.
17 Rohrlich, "State Formation in Sumer and the Subjugation of Women," 86.

Enki's mother, "the Sumerian prototype" of the later Tiamat of the *Enuma Elish,* as "the mistress of the watery deeps."[18]

The feminist political usefulness of works like Rohrlich's and Frymer-Kensky's notwithstanding, what is left severely unquestioned is the seemingly *straight*-forward "naturalness" of the deities' gender. Although "visual presentation or textual description of a god occurs after the sex has been agreed on by a culture, if any sex has been decided at all," we are told, "how these designations are assigned is obscure and eludes any simple rationale."[19] If we dwell on this obscurity for a second and insist upon the fact that all the deities concerned are related to primordial waters, which were literally liquid and fluid, we might want to entertain the idea of an unstable gender system at play in these interrelated mythologies and deities.

The Sumerians personified the primordial (fresh water) ocean the Apsu/*abzu* as a goddess, Nammu "the mother, the ancestress who gave birth to all the gods."[20] In his much earlier review of Heidel's book from 1943 mentioned above, Kramer briefly summarizes this difference of gender in Sumerian and Babylonian myths:

[B]oth the Sumerians and Babylonians conceived the primeval sea, itself probably eternal and uncreated, as the prime originator of the universe. In *Enuma Elish,* however, the primeval sea is conceived as consisting of two principles, the male Apsû (Apsû is a Sumerian loan word) and the female Tiâmat (Tiâmat is a word of Semitic origin). No such dichotomy is recognizable in the extant Sumerian mythological material and it is not unreasonable to conclude, therefore, that the introduction of Tiamat is a Semitic innovation.[21]

18 Frymer-Kensky, *In the Wake of the Goddesses,* 71.
19 O'Brien, *The Oxford Encyclopedia of the Bible and Gender Studies,* 70.
20 Kramer, *Sumerian Mythology,* 114n41.
21 Kramer, "The Babylonian Genesis," 72.

Thorkild Jacobsen contests Kramer's association of Nammu-Apsu with the sea, arguing that "the sign with which her name is written does not [...] mean 'sea' [... but] denotes — if read *engur* — primarily the body of sweet water [...] below the earth." Hence, he proposes to interpret Nammu-Apsu-engur as "the 'watery deep' of the Mesopotamian marshes."²² He further supports this judgment by pointing out that even occasional usage of *engur* or *abzu* (*apsu*) to connote sea was very unlikely; since the sea was "an almost negligible factor" in the Mesopotamian life, it would be very strange if they chose it to worship it as a divine manifestation.²³ However, the distinction between a sweet-water deep and salt-water sea "was not always as precise as modern people expect," Tsumura contends, and "there is no evidence for distinguishing the sweet and the bitter sea [... and] in Sumerian the sea [...] was conceived as a single body of water."²⁴

This Sumerian "single body of water" might not be recognizable at the outset of *Enuma Elish,* where Apsu is said to personify the sweet-water "deep," and Tiamat the salt-water "ocean." What is more, the *Atra-Hasis* epic written in Akkadian, "known from several fragments from the Old and Neo-Babylonian period, as well as from Neo-Assyrian tablets,"²⁵ depicts Enki/Ea as possessing "'the bolt, the bar of the sea' [... which] may have kept Tiam(a)t(um) out, i.e. to stop its waters from mixing with the waters of Apsu."²⁶ This hypothesis, however, cannot stand. As we have seen in the first chapter, Tiamat and Apsu have been mingled from the beginning and all the gods have been dwelling in their shared watery space, which is occasionally referred to as "the Apsu," and occasionally only as "Tiamat." Marduk is said to have let out the great rivers Tigris and Euphrates from the eyes of Tiamat after he defeated her, suggesting that the "salt water

22 Thorkild Jacobsen, "Sumerian Mythology: A Review Article," *Journal of Near Eastern Studies* 5, no. 2 (1946): 128–52, at 139.
23 Ibid., 140n21.
24 Tsumura, *The Earth and the Waters in Genesis 1 and 2,* 61.
25 Leick, *A Dictionary of Ancient Near Eastern Mythology,* 64.
26 Ibid., 60. According to Tsumura, *The Earth and the Waters in Genesis 1 and 2,* 61, *tiāmtum* or *tâmtum* "could refer to both salt- and sweet-waters."

sea" Tiamat is at this point also the "subterranean sweet water" formerly associated with Apsu. This comes without surprise, given that Apsu and Tiamat have become one.

If we stick to the Tiamat-Apsu mingling, it would be equally problematic to think of the two (in *Enuma Elish* at least) as a "dichotomy," as Kramer has suggested in his summary of the differences between the Sumerian and Babylonian gendering of the primordial sea(s).[27] Dichotomy, translated into an essentialized hierarchy of sexual differences, is very much a modern/colonial invention. As we have seen in the previous chapter, the reception history's continuous monstrification of Tiamat is simultaneously constructive with the feminization of Tiamat, a result of the misogynist imaginary imbued in a phallocentric economy that renders the feminine side negative in the modern/colonial reception history. A firmly feminized and monstrified identification of the fluctuant and fluid *Tiam(a)t(um)* (Tiamat, the personified all-mother, and *tiamtum,* the Akkadian word for the sea) is not present in the original text, which occasionally refers to "her" as "him." How much of a "her" is Tiamat after having mixed with the he-water-Apsu from the beginning, we better stop calculating.

What is more, as Jacobsen reminds us, "Sumerian does not differentiate semen and water: one word stands for both."[28] It is very thought-provoking, to say the least, that the semen-*qua*-water body should have been personified primarily as a goddess. Not only that, but Enki, the god who produces powerful semen, could also get himself pregnant.[29] Outside the fantastic world of myths, we also have Nammu, the name of a goddess, used as the name of the most important Sumerian King Ur-Nammu, who apparently did not seem to be afraid of being "emasculated" by adopting a goddess's name. The big ocean of semen personified as a goddess certainly moves Nammu's creation story beyond

27 Kramer, "The Babylonian Genesis," 72.
28 Thorkild Jacobsen, *The Treasures of Darkness* (New Haven: Yale University Press, 1976), 111.
29 Frymer-Kensky, *In the Wake of the Goddesses,* 49.

the impoverished cliché of the so-called fertility myth, which is often no more than just a facile heteronormative self-consolation when faced with something as queer as a semen-goddess.

It is time for us to abandon or unlearn the very heteronormative and gender-essentialist logic that equates *straight*-forwardly a goddess with female or woman, or sees in the "sexual transformation" of An and Apsu an ontological metamorphosis between allegedly fixed identities: from female to female and male, and then to male. If we take seriously what feminists and queer theorists have reminded us of for decades, namely that gender (and sex, for that matter) is socially constructed, we need also to actually believe that it is also historically contingent, culturally variant, and textually ambiguous. It is, after all, absurd to think of mythical divinities, especially watery ones, with the vocabulary of "sexes," a seemingly objective vocabulary contested from historical and biological perspectives.[30]

The Nammu-Tiamat-Apsu conjunction into/as the primordial waters has not, however, entailed their blurring into one undifferentiated and ungendered mesh. Deities of these creation myths are no exemplars for gender-ambiguity or genderqueerness. Highly identifiable individual deities "Tiamat," "Apsu," or "Nammu" exist in their own right and for their own sake. The Mesopotamian wor(l)d of seas and semen does not surrender to either identity politics or political nihilism, and precisely because of this, it seems to entail a queerness able

both to occupy such sites [subject positions] and to subject them to a democratizing contestation in which the exclusionary conditions of their production are perpetually reworked (even though they can never be fully overcome) in the direction of a more complex coalitional frame.[31]

---

30 See Thomas Laqueur, *Making Sex: Body and Gender from the Greeks to Freud* (Cambridge: Harvard University Press, 1990) and Anne Fausto-Sterling, "The Five Sexes: Why Male and Female Are Not Enough," *The Sciences* (March/April 1993): 20–25.

31 Judith Butler, *Bodies That Matter: On the Discursive Limits of "Sex"* (London: Routledge, 1993), 115.

This forecast of "queerness" — I remind those who associate what is queer with poststructuralist US academia or a certain type of "lifestyle" in the "post-Stonewall" era that David Eng succinctly calls "queer liberalism"[32] — is made to us from the deep waters of ancient myths and history.

While the primordial waters of Mesopotamia may be recognizably gendered, often through anthropomorphic renderings, their confluences in the deep, *tehom*, of the biblical Genesis appear to be ungendered, or even unseen, as a result of the combined efforts of theologians and philosophers who attempt to reduce it to an uncreated nothingness.

2.2 The Deep

Genesis 1 is said to give testimony to the Christian orthodoxy of *creatio ex nihilo*:

> In principio creavit Deus caelum et terram, terra autem erat inanis et vacua et tenebrae super faciem abyssi et spiritus Dei ferebatur super aquas. (Gen 1:1–2)

Despite the generations of theological and philosophical efforts that have transformed it into the most representative text on *creatio ex nihilo*, the text of Genesis itself continuously resists the *ex nihilo* doctrine. The text leaves many traces "before" and "within" God's creation that resist this orthodoxy. The deep "abyss" (*tehom* in Hebrew), vibrating and dissident, has never surrendered to this purging doctrine. "Her" roaring existence *before/within* the creation insists. The giant watery space of the deep abyss leaks out and constantly haunts the theological efforts to ignore, erase, and murder her/it.

The text of Genesis does place an article before *tehom*, which potentially makes it a proper name. However, in Hebrew *tehom* is a feminine noun, which might suggest her/its connection to

---

32 David L. Eng, *The Feeling of Kinship: Queer Liberalism and the Racialization of Intimacy* (Durham: Duke University Press, 2010).

some earlier feminine deity in the region.[33] Catherine Keller traces the biblical *tehom* to *Enuma Elish*: "[T]he face of the deep was first — as far as we can remember — a woman's. Tiamat, 'salt water, primal chaos,' lay in primordial bliss with Apsu."[34] The primordial deep, in fact, goes even further, wider, and deeper than *Enuma Elish*. The philologist David T. Tsumura, working on Ancient Near East languages, contends that "Akkadian *tiāmtum* or *tâmtum*, Arabic *tihāmat* […] together with the […] Ugaritic [*thm(t)*] and Hebrew indicate that all these forms are the reflections of a common Semitic term **tihām-*."[35]

"The primeval sea […] conceived by the Sumerian as eternal and uncreated"[36] travels back and forth, from Sumer and Babylon and to the Bible. Nammu was the life-generating primordial all-mother, personification of the *abzu/apsu,* the fresh water that lies in the deeper memory of the "water deep." Many discussions have been devoted to whether it was the Babylonians or the Canaanites who influenced the writing of Genesis. In his *God's Conflict with the Dragon and the Sea,* John Day claims that "so far as tehom's mythological background is concerned this is not Babylonian at all, but rather Canaanite," although he does not deny the fact that "both tehom and Tiamat are derived from a common Semitic root."[37] He only contests a theory of "direct borrowing" from the Akkadian Tiamat into Hebrew *tehom*.

The influences on the Bible from myths in the region problematically called the Ancient Near East cannot be overstated.[38]

---

33   John Day, *God's Conflict with the Dragon and the Sea* (Cambridge: University of Cambridge Oriental Publications, 1985), 50 and Catherine Keller, *Face of the Deep: A Theology of Becoming* (London: Routledge, 2003), 239n4.

34   Catherine Keller, *Face of the Deep: A Theology of Becoming* (London: Routledge, 2003), 28.

35   Tsumura, *The Earth and the Waters in Genesis 1 and 2*, 51–53. Here Tsumura points out that -*t* is the feminine ending for the Ugaritic word *thm* (ocean).

36   Kramer, *Sumerian Mythology,* 73.

37   Day, *God's Conflict with the Dragon and the Sea,* 50–51.

38   By "problematic," I mean that the concept of "(Ancient) Near East," like "the Americas" or "the Orient," is not a value-free and constative geographical denomination. The near-ness of "Near East" or far-ness of "Far East" marks Europe as the zero point of observation.

Just like the ineffaceable *tehom* vis-à-vis the so-called *ex nihilo* God, it cannot be erased. Given the frequent interchanges between culturally and linguistically diverse yet connected groups in this region, and especially the Israelites' exile during the "Babylonian Capture" when part of Genesis was written,[39] any clear distinction between a "direct" or "indirect" borrowing is not very relevant to our discussion. The rejection of a direct, or, shall we say, straightforward borrowing is an unnecessary but certainly not naïve effort to try to neatly compartmentalize one fluctuant ocean of merged wor(l)ds.

The Hebrew *tehom* and Ugaritic *thm(t)* are "semantically corresponding closer to *apsu* than to *tiamtum* though morphologically corresponding to the latter."[40] That is to say, *tehom* becomes a "male" semanteme (i.e., gender) with a "female" morphology (i.e., body). The watery bodies, like trans bodies, are therefore not simply a surgical or sartorial mutation or "transgression" from one self-enclosed gender/sex to the supposedly oppositional other.[41]

The clear waters of biblical misogyny, in accord with the phallic *creatio ex nihilo,* become blurred through their own lexicality. In the same way that modern reception history has monstrified Tiamat by joining the Babylonian rulers in reiterating the masculine mono-power of Marduk in the name of order, Christian orthodoxy propagates the doctrine of *creatio ex nihilo* and condemns any interpretation of Genesis that is not accordingly heteronormative as heresy. However, "the habit of producing heretics as outer boundary markers for orthodox identity also exposes a repressive evasion of evident Christian complexity."[42]

---

39 Barry L. Bandstra, *Reading the Old Testament: An Introduction to the Hebrew Bible* (Belmont: Wadsworth Publishing Company, 1995).

40 The Akkadian *tiamtum,* which Tiamat derives from, "has a much wider semantic field than its West Semitic cognate terms" (Kramer, *Sumerian Mythology,* 73).

41 Susan Stryker and Stephen Whittle, eds., *The Transgender Studies Reader* (London: Routledge, 2006).

42 Catherine Keller and Laurel C. Schneider, eds., *Polydoxy: Theology of Multiplicity and Relation* (New York: Routledge, 2011), 2.

Self-appointed, authoritarian orthodoxy tries in vain to impose monochromatic and lifeless doctrine onto the rainbow-hued and vibrant act of creation. Hardly successful, the use of the Genesis account to condemn any *other* interpretations as either "paganism" outside Christian monotheism or blasphemy within is protested by the text of Genesis itself. A text made of a multiplicity of *sources*[43] (a watery concept already) can be reread *other-wise*. I continue to learn to learn from non-modern texts to understand how they have resisted the modern categorical and hierarchical logic of segregation, long before "queer theory" was coined in the 1980s. It is also in this sense, as commitment to the ethics of queering, that I reject the *ex nihilo* narrative of the single "origin of queer theory" and consequently its unsolicited canonization.

"Bereshit, bara elohim" (Gen 1:1), the most commented on line of the Old Testament, engenders numerous interpretations. The multiplicity of possible meanings from the "beginning of beginnings" is already at odds with any attempt to coerce them into *one* well-closeted doctrine (or the doctrine of oneness). What does the Hebrew text tell us? Sticking to the original text, by the way, only contradicts the decolonial and queer promise of pluralism, if either one pretends that the original text has or can only have one meaning, one reading and one truth; or more dangerously, if one believes that one can do just anything despite the original (by chanting the orthodoxy of the death of God, author, and so on, even though these were *originally* liberating).

This first sentence of Genesis has two drastically different interpretations reflected in the wording and syntax of the trans-

---

43 The two Genesis accounts that we are dealing with, Genesis 1 and Genesis 2, are made from several sources, namely the "Elohist Source," "Yahwist Source," and "Priestly Source" that "came into existence out of this context […] in the period of the Babylonian exile (587–538 B.C.E)" (Barry L. Bandstra, *Reading the Old Testament: An Introduction to the Hebrew Bible* [Belmont: Wadsworth Publishing Company, 1995], 31).

lated versions.[44] Different versions have translated Genesis 1:1–2 as follows:

When God began to create heaven and earth, and the earth then was welter and waste and darkness over the deep and God's breath hovering over the waters. (Robert Alter's translation[45])

In the beginning God created the heaven and the earth. And the earth was without form, and void; and darkness was upon the face of the deep. And the Spirit of God moved upon the face of the waters. (King James Version)

在起初天主創造了天地。大地還是混沌空虛，深淵上還是一團黑暗，天主的神在水面上運行。(思高本，*Studium Biblicum*[46])

Au commencement, Dieu créa le ciel et la terre. La terre était informe et vide: il y avait des ténèbres à la surface de l'abîme,

---

44 I have chosen two English versions: the King James Version and Robert Alter's translation; one Chinese version: the Studium Biblicum Version (高斯本); one French version: la Bible de Jérusalem; and one Spanish version: la Biblia Latinoamericana. They are all translated directly from the original languages (Old Testament — Hebrew; New Testament — Greek) and represent large speaking populations.

45 For the English translation I use the version accompanied by many useful commentaries by Robert Alter, *Genesis: Translation and Commentary* (London: W.W. Norton & Company Inc., 1996). This work focuses exclusively on Genesis and is also a translation that is meant to correct "something seriously wrong with [...] the familiar English translations [...] of the Hebrew Bible" and to provide a new version "in a language that conveys with some precision the semantic nuances and the lively orchestration of literary effects of the Hebrew" (ix).

46 This version is used by Chinese Catholics, translated from various primal sources in Hebrew, Greek, and Latin versions and manuscripts. Another influential version in Chinese is the *Chinese Union Version* (和合本), used mainly by Protestants, translated from English instead of from Hebrew and Greek.

et l'esprit de Dieu se mouvait au-dessus des eaux. (*La Bible de Jérusalem*[47])

En el principio, cuando Dios creó los cielos y la tierra, todo era confusión y no había nada en la tierra. Las tinieblas cubrían los abismos mientras el espíritu de Dios aleteaba sobre la superficie de las aguas. (*La Biblia Latinoamericana*[48])

These various versions of the Bible in different modern languages are all translated from the original texts in Hebrew with reference to versions in Latin and Greek. Despite the linguistic specificity of these modern languages, I roughly divide these translations into two major groups concerning Genesis 1:1. The first group is, following the first words of the Latin Vulgate Bible, called "in principio." The King James Version, the Chinese *Statium Biblicum,* and the French *La Bible de Jérusalem* belong to this group. The syntactic rendering of these translated versions resembles the Latin Vulgate: "in principio creavit Deus caelum et terram." The reader is told that "in the beginning," "在太初," "au commencement" (*in principio*) it was God who created (*creavit Deus*) the heaven and the earth. This group, opening the Bible with a full sentence describing God's creation in line with the doctrine of *creatio ex nihilo,* renders the Hebrew "bereshit bara elohim" as "some comprehensive creative act on the first day."[49] However, it contradicts the following Genesis account of creation, in which "the heaven was created on the second day to restrain the celestial water (1:7–8), and the earth on the third day (1:9–10)."[50]

The second group is what I would call "enuma elish," the Akkadian phrase that marks the beginning of the Babylonian Epic of Creation, meaning "when on high," a temporal clause in

---

47 The French translation from Hebrew by biblical scholars.

48 The Spanish version translated by biblical scholars and widely used in Spanish-speaking countries.

49 Jon D. Levenson, *Creation and the Persistence of Evil* (San Francisco: Harper & Row Publishers, 1988), 5.

50 Ibid.

grammatical terms closer to the Hebrew *bereshit* (also the Hebrew title of the book of Genesis). "Bereshit bara elohim" is here understood as a temporal clause, which highlights the connection between *Enuma Elish* and Genesis, and thus the "chaotic beginnings of Christianity."[51] More importantly, it suggests a totally different theological take on the creation act compared to the "in principio" group. In Robert Alter's version and *la Biblia Latinoamericana,* the first sentence is translated as a temporal clause: "En el principio, *cuando* Dios creó los cielos y la tierra." In the Rabbinic commentary by the medieval rabbi Rashi, the phrase is translated as "in the beginning of God's creation,"[52] echoing the same theological interpretation. How is this rendering different from the "in principio" group in terms of theological understanding of the creation act and how is it relevant to our discussion?

In his classic study of the Homeric and biblical narratives, Eric Auerbach argues that "the Biblical narrator was obliged to write exactly what his belief in the truth of the tradition [...] demanded of him. [...] What he produced [...] was oriented toward truth."[53] In other words, the authors of Genesis do not nor ought to prove that God created the world. That God has created the world (*in principio* or not, from nothingness or not) needs no specification, narration, or, perhaps more unlikely, explanation in the text. Rather, one has to accept the action of creation as a given fact once informed by the authoritarian voice of the biblical narrator who speaks for God. The task of the narrator is to claim this truth through a narrative strategy that erases any suggestion of the need to prove the fact. That is to say, this claim to absolute truth should not rely on a narrated "reality," but can

---

51 Bauman, *Theology, Creation, and Environmental Ethics,* 30.
52 For a complete commentary, see "The Complete Jewish Bible with Rashi Commentary," *Chabad,* http://www.chabad.org/library/bible_cdo/aid/8165/ jewish/Chapter-1.htm.
53 Eric Auerbach, *Mimesis: The Representation of Reality in Western Literature* (Princeton: Princeton University Press, 2003), 14.

only be achieved through what Auerbach recognizes as a tyran-nical gesture: "Woe to the man who did not believe it!"[54]

In this sense, we are neither sure, nor do we need to care, about whether God has created everything out of absolute noth-ingness. The subject of this creation, announced to the world through a tyrannical gesture, is naturally expected to be a tyrant himself who would control man made-in-his-likeness. Don Cu-pitt points out:

> The classical God-centered vision and the modern Man-cen-tered visions both sought to unify the world by focusing it around a Centre, conceived in each case as a centre of under-standing, power, control and self-affirmation. But precisely that wish to see the world fully understood and controlled by a self-affirming Ego is what we ought to give up. It is a sexist dream of mastery: nature as a fantasy-woman, com-pletely subservient, responsive to one's slightest desire […]. I am saying that our life-practice needs to be freed from the old sexist-political ideal of a strong Ego, omnipotent power, fixed boundaries and total control.[55]

Yet, if we move closer to the original text, to the crisp and com-plex Hebrew words, and listen to what *bara elohim* has to say, we might be surprised to find out that *elohim,* the plural form of *eloh* (god), is followed by *bara,* a verb in third person singu-lar. The grammatically erroneous and unlawful phrase *bara elo-him* occupies the very first sentence of the proclaimed absolute beginning of all beginnings, ruthlessly irritating those efforts, generation after generation, to suppress him/her/them into one enclosed, finite, and dead doctrine of the phallus. The grammat-ical rule of subject–predicate agreement exerts so trivial an in-fluence on the vibrant creational force. Already in archaic times, and always inside the tyrannical narrative, we find a campy jux-

---

54 Ibid.
55 Don Cupitt, *Creation Out of Nothing* (London: SCM Press Ltd, 1990), 200–201.

taposition that would be echoed by the young queer firebrand Arthur Rimbaud in the 19th century: "je est un autre." As Catherine Keller has noted, "Centuries before the deconstruction of 'the subject,' the western hypersubject, the subject of subjects, quietly drops out."[56]

Elohim's plurality remains ineffaceable and makes the biblical God, at least in its Elohist account, the "One" that is not one. "God 'himself' is unsure whether he is plural or singular."[57] Many suggest that this apparent discrepancy in the sacred text of monotheism should be understood as an expression that suggests the "plural of majesty" or "plenitude of might."[58] Those strictest monotheists who insist on *elohim*'s singularity, despite the original text's dissident indecisiveness, however, find it acceptable that the multiple should come from the one, so much so that they feel obliged to multiply the majesty of the One God into a plural Trinity.

Keller reconciles the discrepancy between *elohim* and monotheism, subject and predicate, by coining a concept that preserves the playfulness of the original text: the pluri-singularity of creation.[59] "Elohim," as the "singular-plural being,"[60] move(s) to create *'adam,* the human. And *elohim* said, "let us make a human in our image, by our likeness" (Gen 1:26); "male and female He created them" (1:27). The original text is unsettled again: with *elohim vaiyomer* the pluri-singular *elohim* enunciate(s) through a singular voice (*vaiyomer* ["said"] is third personal singular) a collective invitation: *na'aseh* (let *us* make). The plural verb *na'aseh* is not an expression of royalty, for "the 'royal we' was not part of the vocabulary of kings or individual gods in the ancient Near East."[61]

---

56 Keller, *Face of the Deep,* 178.

57 Danna Nolan Fewell and David M. Gunn, *Gender, Power & Promise: The Subject of the Bible's First Story* (Nashville: Abingdon, 1993), 23.

58 J.H. Hertz, ed., *The Pentateuch and Haftorahs: Hebrew Text with English Translation and Commentary* (London: Soncino Press, 1988), 2.

59 Keller, *Face of the Deep,* 172.

60 Jean-Luc Nancy, *Être singulier pluriel* (Paris: Galilée, 1996).

61 Levenson, *Creation and the Persistence of Evil,* 158n14.

The biblical text seems confusing only to a mind that is trained to strictly compartmentalize everything, even divine beings, and to dogmatically follow grammatical propriety. *Elohim* is/are pluri-singular. "God's own blurred and slipping self-definition suggests that things [...] might in fact be as inherently indeterminable as the identity that creates [them]."[62] *Elohim* might even seem "feminine," though the grammatical gender of *-im* here is masculine plural. The "femininity" I am suggesting is not in the essentialist sense of a "primordial all Mother," but in the playfulness and creativity of Luce Irigaray's "this sex that isn't one."[63] Only a male-female "He" could have created *them* in "His" likeness (Gen 1:27).[64]

When the pluri-singular *elohim* began the creation of heaven and earth, his breath (*ruah*) hovered over the waters of deep *tehom,* which was covered by darkness. The "verb attached to God's breath-wind-spirit (*ruah*) [*merachefet* ...] might have a connotation of parturition or nurture as well as rapid back-and-forth movement."[65] Hornsby and Stone ponder queerness and chaos in the context of Genesis, link it with *Enuma Elish,* and suggest that the deep is "the undefined, the chaos" like Tiamat, "the symbol of the deep and of disarray, [...] from [whose] eviscerated, divided body come the earth and sky."[66] Reading against the grain of the binary opposition in which heterosexuality is aligned with order and queerness with chaos, the authors of *Bible Trouble* are ready to conclude, "it is from *queerness* that

62 Fewell and Gunn, *Gender, Power & Promise,* 23.

63 Luce Irigaray, "Ce sexe qui n'en est pas un," *Les Cahiers du GRIF* 5, no. 1 (1974): 54–58, at 55–58.

64 Elsewhere I have written about the queerness of the creation of *'adam.* See: "'*adam* Is Not Man': Queer Body before Genesis 2:22 (and After)," in *Unsettling Science and Religion: Contributions and Questions from Queer Studies,* eds. Whitney Bauman and Lisa Stenmark (Lanham: Lexington Books, 2018), 183–97.

65 Alter, *Genesis,* 3n2.

66 Teresa J. Hornsby and Ken Stone, *Bible Trouble: Queer Reading at the Boundaries of Biblical Scholarship* (Atlanta: Society of Biblical Literature, 2011), xi.

all creation comes."[67] The pre-*fiat lux* scene in Genesis 1:1–2 are either read as an unstable, chaotic, useless state of "uncreatedness" or erased as negligible nothingness, ironically prepared for *creatio ex nihilo*. Yet, this moment of poetic juxtaposition, transgressive grammar, and roaring vibrancy echoes the indeterminate, multiple, and inclusive ethic of queerness. Let us suspend the *lux* for a second and venture (back) into the cosmic darkroom.

Temporal (*bereshit*), plural (*elohim*), watery (*tehom*), airy (*ruah*), and rhythmically moving back and forth (*merachefet,* as Alter explains it; *tohu vabohu,* as Keller explains it), the opening words of Genesis sound reparative: non-discriminating, relational, erotic, and full of life. Darkness (*choshek*), perhaps immediately falling prey to all thinkable negative connotations in and beyond Christian heteronormativity, was with *elohim* from the beginning and in many other instances[68]: "He [*elohim*] made darkness his secret place" (Ps 18:11). Darkness (*choshek* or not) is particularly dear to queers. Through a reading of Samuel R. Delany's memoir *The Motion of Light in Water,*[69] José Muñoz ties his theorization of queer futurity, that is hope, to the fraternal and fleshy night of cruising at the end of Christopher Street near the Hudson River in New York City "under the cover of a protective darkness."[70] Darkness was over the deep and God's breath hovering over the waters (Gen 1:2).

Dark nights compress linear time (past–present–future) into queer temporality. The point of queer (time) "may be to trail behind actually existing social possibilities [... and] to be bathed in the fading light of whatever has been declared useless."[71] Queer

---

67 Ibid.
68 Gen 15:12–13, Ex 14:20–21.
69 Samuel R. Delany, *The Motion of Light in Water: Sex and Science Fiction Writing in the East Village* (Minneapolis: University of Minneapolis Press, 2004).
70 José Esteban Muñoz, *Cruising Utopia: The Then and There of Queer Futurity* (New York: New York University Press, 2009), 52.
71 Elizabeth Freeman, *Time Binds: Queer Temporality, Queer Histories* (Durham: Duke University Press, 2010), xiii.

futurity finds accommodation in the past. The earth, "welter and waste" (*tohu vabuhu*), declared useless and negative in the usual defense of *creatio ex nihilo,* resides with the deep waters (*tehom*) and is protected by the gentle darkness (*choshek*). *Tohu vabuhu* regains dignity in this moment of queer inclusivity, however trivial and problematic, as the *prima materia.*[72] For the queer Delany, the "numberless silent sexual acts" declared welter and waste, even satanic and menacing to the public good, are "'reassuring' and 'very human,'" since "the men in this space took care of one another not only by offering flesh but by performing a care for the self that encompassed a vast care for others — a delicate and loving 'being for others.'"[73]

The same intensity of entanglement is found in Pedro Almodóvar's film *Entre tinieblas* (*Dark Habits*) from 1988 (*tinieblas* the Spanish word used to translate *choshek*). There, the impossible love of a drug-addicted Catholic nun for a female singer is declared through her dubbing of the song "Encadenado" ("Chained") by Lucho Gatica: "Beloved, since our [love] is a punishment / that is in the soul until death /My luck needs your luck / and you need me more."[74] In between (*entre*) the obscurity (*tinieblas*) of the convent, the eccentric queer nuns throw a continuous carnival in which "individual identities dissolve and social oppositions break down" in an open text that is able to capture this "infinite interrelationship of interpretation."[75]

What is menacingly felt in every step of theo-political efforts to erase the *prima materia-qua*-chaos from the creation so as to secure a colonialist *creatio ex nihilo,* is the deep, *tehom,* a deep fear that is beyond the fears of darkness and *tohu vabuhu* altogether. I will now return to the intermingled primordial wor(l)ds: *tehom,* the *abzu,* Apsu, Tiamat, and Nammu. Their stories might reveal drastically different and visionary meanings

---

72 Keller, *Face of the Deep,* 184.

73 Muñoz, *Cruising Utopia,* 51.

74 "Cariño como el nuestro es un castigo / Que se lleva en el alma hasta la muerte / Mi suerte necesita de tu suerte / Y tu me necesitas mucho mas."

75 Mark C. Taylor, *Erring: A Postmodern A/Theology* (Chicago: University of Chicago Press, 1984), 15–16.

once the clichés of creation myths' "archetypical" order winning over chaos, allegedly represented in the Bible, have been swept away with the help of the original Hebrew lexicon.

2.3 Queer Primordial Waters

Kafka's short story "Beim Bau der Chinesischen Mauer" ("The Great Wall of China") may be read as a "commentary on the topic of differentiation."[76] This "building of the Great Wall of China" as the "whole ideological process of creating the notion of 'you and me' by searching and producing alterity"[77] dissolves for queers who participate in cruising, protected by nightly darkness, *entre tinieblas*. Kafka might not know that in one of the "four greatest folk tales" of China, a disfranchised woman, Meng Jiangnü, brings down the wall. After learning that her newly married husband, who was forced to build the Great Wall, lies dead at the construction site, Meng weeps so plaintively that one section of the wall collapses. The mourning woman does not care about the empire's reasons for building the wall, allegedly to separate good and bad at the expense of common life in the name of protecting their home(land) from the nomads. She stands together with the monstrified "barbarians" as the order-threatening *tohu vabuhu*. The "production of alterity," of you and me, she and he, we and they needs to be rethought from her perspective, that of the disenfranchised, the "illegal," and the queer, who have no choice but to be (with) the so-called "chaos," to weep the so-called "order" into collapse.

In the very beginning of *Enuma Elish,* Apsu and Tiamat "[h]ad mixed their waters together." We know that they become one because "gods were born within them." But we also know that Apsu is the "father" and Tiamat the "mother." The epic reveals these parental identities through Mummu, the "vizier." After Tiamat's rage against Apsu's plan of infanticide, Mummu

---

76 Dorothee Kimmich, "'Interzones': Spaces of a Fuzzy Cultural Logic," in *Charting the Interzone,* 42–49 (EMJD Interzones Official Website, 2010), 48.
77 Ibid., 47.

"did not agree with the counsel of his / earth [sic] mother. / [and spoke to Apsu], 'O father, put an end to (their) troublesome ways." The mingled watery "one" between Tiamat and Apsu is likely forgotten, as we proceed to read more conflicts based on individual characters that talk to, kiss, or kill each other. If the previous discussion intends to multiply the oneness of the biblical God and the Genesis account in order to contaminate the monolithic, monotheist orthodoxy, this section takes an opposite direction by reuniting the seemingly separated divine beings into a queer one-ness. This one-ness, however, will be discussed in this section as "the open mesh of possibilities, gaps, overlaps, dissonances and resonances, lapses and excesses of meaning when the constituent elements of anyone's gender, or anyone's sexuality aren't made (or *can't* be made) to signify monolithically."[78]

The conflict between the primordial couple after Tiamat's angry rejection of Apsu's infanticide plan is followed in the epic by an interesting encounter between Mummu and Apsu, both gendered male:

(Vizier) Mummu replied and counseled Apsu;
[…]
Apsu was pleased with him [Mummu], his face lit up
[…]
(Vizier) Mummu hugged him,
Sat on his lap and kissed him rapturously.

Talon's French version has the above-quoted verses as: "Then Apsu clung to Mummu's neck,"[79] and Mummu kisses back. This rather homoerotic moment has rarely been commented on. Mummu promptly comes out in the epic and as a troublesome figure. Before the Apsu–Mummu encounter, in the epic's first stanza, *mummu* is already there, written together with Tiamat,

---

78 Eve Kosofsky Sedgwick, *Tendencies* (London: Routledge, 1994), 8.

79 Talon, *The Standard Babylonian Creation Myth Enūma Eliš*, 80: "Apsu lança alors le cou de Mummu."

transliterated as *mu-um-mu tia-amat mu-al-li-da-at gim-ri-šú-un*.[80] In "The Seven Tablets of Creation," Wallis Budge translates this as "'Mummu' Tiâmat, who bare each and all of / them,"[81] rendering *mummu* an epithet of Tiamat. Leonard W. King, however, translates *mummu* as independent from Tiamat as both the "son" of Tiamat-Apsu and as the "chaos." He also states that *mummu* is also a name of Marduk. To move out of this confusion, he argues, much like his followers who firmly hold onto the rivalry between chaos and order, that

> it is possible that the application of the title to Tiamat and her son was suggested by its ambiguity of meaning; while Marduk (and also Ea) might have born the name as the 'form" or "idea" of order and system, Tiamat and her son might have been conceived as representing the opposing "form" or "idea" of chaos and confusion.[82]

Heidel dedicates an article to the discussion of different opinions regarding the meaning of *mummu,* understanding it as the remnant of a Sumerian goddess or as another title for Tiamat.[83] Reviewing these interpretations together, it almost seems that *mummu* also intends to confuse rigid modern (gender) boundaries. *Mummu,* a word borrowed from Sumerian, should be a feminine noun to the extent that some suggest it was the name for a Sumerian goddess,[84] although in *Enuma Elish* they[85] undergo a masculinization and becomes the "son" of Apsu and Tiamat and also occasionally goes by the name of Marduk, "the

---

80 Ibid., 33.

81 Budge, *The Babylonian Legends of the Creation and the Fight between Bel and the Dragon,* 32.

82 Leonard William King, *The Seven Tablets of Creation* (London: Luzac and Co., 1902), xxxviiin1.

83 Alexander Heidel, "The Meaning of Mummu in Akkadian Literature," *Journal of Near Eastern Studies* 7, no. 2 (1948): 98–105.

84 Ibid., 100.

85 I am borrowing the singular usage of the plural pronoun "they" used by the transgender community to evade the over-determination of gendered pronouns when referring to most of the deities.

creator of heaven and earth."[86] Mummu has joined Tiamat and Apsu to have "mixed their waters together." Heidel argues that "Mummu was the personified fog or mist rising from the waters of Apsû and Tiâmat," their "son" in mythological language.[87] As a conclusion, he suggests that this understanding of Mummu is "in full accord with the statement in *Enûma eliš* that the three deities Apsû, Mummu and Tiâmat 'mingled their waters together,' or 'mingled their waters as one.'"[88] The heterosexual nuclear family rendering of the trio is hardly convincing, not because it is anachronistic, but because the text of *Enuma Elish* actively discredits this facile modern imposition. Mummu–Apsu's erotic encounter is one of those "dissident" instances.

To console the angry "father," Mummu sits on Apsu's lap and kisses him rapturously. The "lap" in the original text is *birku*.[89] *The Assyrian Dictionary of the Oriental Institute of the University of Chicago* lists several meanings for the entry *birku*. The editors exemplify one of the many connotations of *birku*, "lap — physically, referring to human beings," with the line from *Enuma Elish*, "*ušbamma bir-ka-ašú unnaššaq šâšu* — he (Mummu) sat on his lap and began to fondle him."[90] We are told that *birku* is also "a euphemism for male and female sexual parts."[91] When Mummu and Apsu engage in the act of hugging, kissing, and fondling, it is difficult not to see such a euphemistic definition at play here. It might as well be a loving expression between father and son, or even between "bros." The intensive eroticism between two "men" is explicitly described in the epic but silently ignored in reception history, whereas the intermingling of Tiamat and Apsu is immediately read as heterosexual intercourse that foregrounds fertility. One might argue that Mummu–Ap-

---

86 Heidel, "The Meaning of Mummu in Akkadian Literature," 102.

87 Ibid., 104.

88 Ibid., 105.

89 Talon, *The Standard Babylonian Creation Myth Enūma Eliš*, 35.

90 Ignace J. Gelb et al., eds., *The Assyrian Dictionary of the Oriental Institute of the University of Chicago (Volume 2: B)* (Chicago: The Oriental Institute and J.J. Augustin Verlagsbuchhandlung, 1965), 256.

91 Ibid., 257.

su's encounter is an unimportant moment, which is at most overlooked but not deliberately silenced. The point is not to claim victimhood for some kind of primordial gay fathers, but to reveal the arbitrariness of rendering Tiamat-Apsu-Mummu in terms of a nuclear-family-like papa-Apsu + mama-Tiamat + son-Mummu; and to highlight the queer complexities of the Mummu–Apsu eroticism, Mummu–Tiamat connection, Mummu ambiguity — in another words, to perform a "perverse reading." The work of Eve Sedgwick provides guidance here:

[B]ecoming a perverse reader was never a matter of my condescension to texts, rather of the surplus charge of my trust in them to remain powerful, refractory, and exemplary. And this doesn't seem an unusual way for ardent reading to function in relation to queer experience.[92]

Mummu shakes up the certainty of the heterosexuality of the primordial couple. Right after this homoerotic moment, Ea overhears Mummu and Apsu's plan and decides to kill them. The Apsu-Mummu pair might be easily read as a certain kind of proto-patriarchal *hom(m)osexualité*.[93] Their effacement in reception history, however, has locked them in the closet of heteronormativity as the queer-chaos that should be controlled, rather than the hom(m)osexual patrilineality exalted by the Anshar-Ea-Marduk family (and the epic at large). Further on in *Enuma Elish,* Ea puts Apsu and Mummu to sleep and kills them: "He held Apsu down and slew him; / Tied up Mummu and laid him across him. / He set up his dwelling on top of Apsu."[94] Hav-

---

92 Sedgwick, *Tendencies,* 4.

93 *Hom(m)osexualité* is a term coined by Luce Irigaray that combines the French word *homme* (man) and *homosexualité* (homosexuality) through her reading of Sigmund Freud. *Hom(m)osexualité* points to the "homosexuality" — the desire for the (male) same — of patriarchy. See Luce Irigaray, *Speculum de l'autre femme* (Paris: Éditions de Minuit, 1974), 120–29.

94 Talon translates it as "Il enchaîna Apsû et le mit à mort / après avoir enfermé Mummu et tiré sur lui le verrou" (*The Standard Babylonian Creation Myth Enûma Eliš,* 80).

ing killed Apsu and chained Mummu, Ea rests in his dwelling with his lover Damkina. Marduk is also born.

> Then he [Ea] rested very quietly inside his private quarters
> And named them Apsu and assigned chapels,
> Founded his own residence there,
> And Ea and Damkina his lover dwelt in splendor.
> […]
> Bel,[95] cleverest of the clever, sage of the gods, was begotten.
> And inside Apsu, Marduk was created;
> Inside pure Apsu, Marduk was born.

Even if "Apsu" at this moment already becomes the de-personified primordial fresh waters, it is still intriguing to notice that Marduk is born inside Apsu, in a way similar to how his elders were born inside Tiamat.[96] Apsu thus becomes a womb-like place that generates life. Meanwhile, it is not difficult to notice that Marduk is also inside Tiamat, for at least two reasons. First, after the initial disturbances by the gods born inside Tiamat and the killing of Apsu by one of them, Ea, the epic has never indicated to us that the gods have moved outside of Tiamat's belly. Second, the fact that Marduk can continue to make noise inside Tiamat in the manner of the elder gods, which at the same time annoys some of these gods, seems to suggest that they are *all* still inside Tiamat. That is to say, Marduk is at the same time inside Apsu and Tiamat. In fact, from the very beginning Apsu and Tiamat have mingled together. The verb *ihîqû* (to be intermixed), used in the epic's first stanza, Tsumura contends, "does not even indirectly suggest the initial state of the primordial ocean as 'chaotic' [but] this 'intermingling' of these two waters was orderly in itself, i.e. 'as one.'"[97] Yet, as should be added at this point, this is a "one" that is not one.

---

95 *Bel* means "king," and in some versions Marduk is called Bel-Marduk. That is to say, Bel is another name of Marduk.
96 "Then Gods were born within them."
97 Tsumura, *The Earth and the Waters in Genesis 1 and 2,* 60n70.

The one-that-is-not-one defies the facile solution of seeing Apsu as "bisexual." Bi-/homo-/hetero-sexuality ceases to hold much meaning when Apsu's genders are regarded as malleably changeable with regard to the flux of their textual and historical resurgences. This changeability however, is not anything-goes. The skillful subterranean liquids of Tiamat and Apsu leak out from the closet of both queerphobia and essentialized identities, resonating with contemporary theorizations of queerness. Attending to their "queerness" is "to make invisible possibilities and desires visible […] to smuggle queer representation in where it must be smuggled and […] to challenge queer-eradicating impulses frontally where they are to be so challenged."[98] It is important to highlight the possibilities excluded (by epistemological and physical means) in order to demarcate the boundaries of intelligibility and of normativity.

Through the reception history of *Enuma Elish,* the queer moment of homoeroticism between Apsu and Mummu is overlooked and the unstable *mummu* adjacent to "Tiamat" has been either erased in translation or fixed as the "son." Also a primordial chaos (let us accept this simplistic rendering for just a moment), Apsu has been largely forgotten. The oblivion or erasure of the masculinized aspect of the primordially *one* ocean made of mingling salt, sweet, and steamy waters secures "the chaotic" as thoroughly feminine by ways of Tiamat, the essentialized "mother goddess." Whenever the "deep" is evoked, whether in studies of *Enuma Elish* or the Bible, the immediate image that comes up is a feminized Tiamat, a sea/she monster, "queen of a hideous host,"[99] or the "bad mother/progenitrix."[100] Even if the primordial waters could be seen as chaos battling against order/creation, why is Apsu in his order-menacing function very seldom remembered, not to mention that he indeed plans

---

98 Sedgwick, *Tendencies,* 3.

99 George A. Barton, "Tiamat," *Journal of American Oriental Society* 15 (1893): 1–27, at 12.

100 Rivkah Harris, "The Conflict of Generations in Ancient Mesopotamian Myths," *Comparative Studies in Society and History* 34, no. 4 (1992): 621–35, at 631.

to kill the newly born gods for their lively noisiness? And why is Tiamat not only remembered, but also repeatedly monstrified as the proto-enemy of order/creation who "opposed creation, *at every step resisted God, tempted* and *seduced* man?"[101] The masculinized aspect of the primordial "chaos" (Apsu) has to be completely erased together with his suspicious "homoeroticism," so that the allegory of order winning over chaos can justify itself through a series of phallocentric binaries: man controlling woman, activity overcoming passivity, and culture dominating nature.

"Tehomophobia," Keller argues, is a manifestation of misogyny that complies with the doctrine of the masculine *creatio ex nihilo* through a "sexual economy of colonized wombs, ruled by a disembodied Word."[102] She alludes on several occasions to the centrality of homophobia in thinking about tehomophobia. Weaved into the imaginary of the threatening "deep," tehomophobia is directly linked to homophobia, the masculine hatred/fear of femininity in general, including one's own passivity embodied by the anus/rectum.[103] In *Policing Desire,* Simon Watney analyses homophobia as a "displaced misogyny [… that is] a hatred of what is projected as 'passive' and therefore female, sanctioned by the subject's dominant heterosexual drives."[104] This is a dear observation to the feminist queer Asian man that I am, constantly threatened by the fascist extirpation "no asians!," which has become almost a slogan of a white supremacist gay "community" that coerces Asian men "to occupy the most unsexy, undesirable position […] seen as soft, effeminate, and poorly endowed"[105] — in other words, to occupy tehomic bottomhood.

---

101 Barton, "Tiamat," 27.
102 Keller, *Face of the Deep,* 223.
103 Gregory W. Bredbeck, *Sodomy and Interpretation* (Ithaca: Cornell University Press, 1991), 31.
104 Simon Watney, *Policing Desire: Pornography, AIDS and the Media* (London: Comedia, 1987), 50.
105 Hoang Tan Nguyen, *A View from the Bottom: Asian American Masculinity and Sexual Representation* (Durham: Duke University Press, 2014), 2.

Racialized tehomophobia goes further and deeper than the hatred and fear of the womb or "bottom." After lingering so long on a lexical excavation aimed at resisting the modern, heteronormative dichotomization of etymological "beginnings," I propose a critical survey of the correlation between these two forms of tehomophobia, misogyny and homophobia, to understand how they come together in the stigmatization of the anus, a womb-like open "scar" on the human body that makes sex/gender/sexuality irrelevant.

What holds together misogyny and homophobia is the fear of femininity reiterated through all kinds of social and cultural practices. Deeply buried below or *behind* this hatred and anxiety, in its modern/colonial context (that is to say, in a context in which the male/female dichotomy accompanied by heterosexuality is naturalized and normalized), is a wounded anus, an innocent organ demonized into the equivalence of immorality, transgression, "sin," or simply being stupid, and not to mention, if penetrated, annihilation. Beatriz (now Paul) Preciado argues that the privilege of the heteronormative masculine subject is won at the price of "anal castration":

The boys-of-castrated-anus established a community of what they called City, State, Fatherland, whose power and administrative authority excluded all those bodies whose anus remained open: women are doubly perforated as a result of their anuses and vaginas [with] their entire body transformable into a uterine cavity capable of housing future citizens; however also the bodies of faggots, which the power was not able to castrate; bodies that repudiated what others would consider anatomic evidence and that create an aesthetic of life from this mutation.[106]

---

106 Beatriz Preciado, "Terror anal," in *El deseo homosexual de Guy Hocquenghem,* 133–72 (Santa Cruz de Tenerife: Editorial Melusina, 2009), 137: "Los chicos-de-los-anos-castrados erigieron una comunidad de la que llamaron Ciudad, Estado, Patria, de cuyos órganos de poder y administrativos excluyeron a todos aquellos cuerpos cuyos anos permanecían abiertos: mujeres doblemente perforadas por sus anos y sus vaginas, su cuerpo entero trans-

In a nutshell, the Spanish queer theorist has subverted the phallocentric obsession with the penis in the Freudian fantasy of male "castration anxiety" and female "penis envy," with the almost inconceivable idea of "anal castration." After all, how can the anus be castrated if it does not even "exist?" The phallocentric psychoanalysis coerces all men to have "castration anxiety" and all women to envy the penis. Because of their "dispossession" of the penis, women were, as if by *nature,* already castrated. All these alleged fears or envies could only make sense in an androcentric culture so obsessed with the penis.[107]

This obsession is explicitly shown in dictionary entries. After having surveyed the Spanish definitions of *ano, pene,* and *vagina,* offered by the Real Academia de Español, Preciado finds that only the penis enjoys the biopolitical privilege of being considered a sexual organ. The *Oxford English Dictionary* offers almost the same, far from simply objective definitions in English of "anus" as the "posterior opening of the alimentary canal in animals, through which the excrements are ejected"; "penis" as the "male genital organ used (usually) for copulation and for the emission or dispersal of sperm [...] and serving also for the elimination of urine"; and "vagina" as the "the membranous canal leading from the vulva to the uterus in women and female mammals."[108] It is no coincidence that "penis envy" is adjacent to the entry of "penis" and "vagina dentata" to "vagina." These ad-

---

formable en cavidad uterina capaz de albergar futuros ciudadanos, pero también cuerpos maricas a los que el poder no pudo castrar, cuerpos que reniegan de lo que otros consideran evidencia anatómica y que hacen de la mutación una estética de vida."

107 I am aware of the differences between the biological penis (Freud's focus) and symbolic phallus (Lacan's focus); however, I follow Jane Gallop's suggestion that although the "penis is what men have and women do not; the phallus is the attribute of power which neither men nor women have [...] As long as the attribute of power is a phallus which refers to and can be confused with a 'penis,' this confusion will support a structure in which it seems reasonable that men have power and women do not" (Jane Gallop, *The Daughter's Seduction: Feminism and Psychoanalysis* [Ithaca: Cornell University Press, 1982], 97).

108 All of these definitions are from the *Online Oxford English Dictionary.*

jacent entries seem to confirm the widespread (and theorized) belief that the penis is appealing and should be envied; whereas the vagina is abhorrent and should be feared.[109] However, this penis–vagina dichotomy doesn't really apply in the text of *Enuma Elish*. Apsu, as shown above, is in a suspicious relation with the enviable phallus/penis, for "he" is, after all, a watery cavity. Apsu's existence quite literally marks the lack. "He" is the hom(m)osexual father forgotten in the closet of modern receptions. In order to secure this oblivion, the feminized/monstrified "primordial monster" Tiamat has to be deflated, first by Marduk in *Enuma Elish* and then repeatedly by the reception history that continues this cry:

> Let him defeat Tiamat, constrict her breath and shorten her life
> So that for future people, till time grows old,
> She shall be far removed, not kept here, distant forever.

The social scientific endeavor of deciphering the past is not just an innocent act of interpretation. In the critical light of queerness, Marduk's creation act of slaughtering Tiamat is hardly righteous. Paul Ricoeur is perhaps the first to read *Enuma Elish* in this social context, especially that of "justified violence." Despite the overt pessimism that sees violence as inscribed at the origin of things, he aptly observes:

---

109 "Penis Envy" is defined as "(supposed) envy by the female of the male's possession of a penis, postulated by Freud to account for some aspects of female behaviour," suggesting possible fraud in this theory with the bracketed "supposed." However, "Vagina Dentata" is defined as "the motif or theme of a vagina equipped with teeth which occurs in myth, folklore, and fantasy, and is said to symbolize fear of castration, the dangers of sexual intercourse, of birth or rebirth, etc." in which the male subject who fantasizes the fear of being castrated is rendered transparent. Additionally, the alleged "fear of castration" cannot accommodate Preciado's "anal castration," and "sexual intercourse" is assumed to be a heterosexual penetrative one without the question of how a vagina equipped with teeth would be fearful for, say, non-vaginal sexual intercourse, whether homosexual, heterosexual, or anysexual.

In the battle between Marduk and Tiamat, Marduk appears as the brutal power, as unethical as Tiamat's anger. Marduk represents the creation and the destruction; by Marduk's enthronement by the gods, human violence is then justified by the original one. The creation is a victory over an Enemy older than the creator.[110]

Chanting the victory of Marduk, justifying his murderous violence with a rhetoric of order winning over chaos, sounds utterly familiar to the colonial discourse that propagates colonization as a process of bringing "light and sweetness" to the unenlightened "barbarians," which will be looked at more closely in the two Parts to come. Here, let us take a temporal leap to look at its continuation in the "murderous representations of homosexuals unleashed and 'legitimatized' by AIDS" in the US media during the AIDS epidemic in the 1980s.[111]

Leo Bersani, in his essay "Is the Rectum a Grave?" written at the peak of the AIDS epidemic, denounces the crimes of the Reagan government's non-response, and the increased policing of those "unacceptable ones in the AIDS crisis [who] are, of course, male homosexuals and IV drug users (many of the latter, [...] poor blacks and Hispanics)."[112] Despite his argument's ethnocentric assumption that "all people of color are straight, all gay men

---

110 Paul Ricoeur, *Philosophie de la volonté: Finitude et culpabilité 2, 2: La symbolique du mal* (Paris: Aubier, 1960), 173: "Au cours de la lutte qui oppose Mardouk à Tiamat, Mardouk apparaît comme puissance brute, aussi peu éthique que la colère de Tiamat. Mardouk figure l'identité de la création et de la destruction ; lors de l'intronisation de Mardouk par les dieux [... la] violence humaine est ainsi justifiée par la violence originelle ; la création est une victoire sur un Ennemi plus vieux que le créateur."

111 Leo Bersani, "Is the Rectum a Grave?" in *Is the Rectum a Grave? And Other Essays* (Chicago: University of Chicago Press, 2010), 3–30, at 28.

112 Including "criminal delays in funding research and treatment, obsession with testing instead of curing." Besides, the US Justice Department issued a "legal opinion stating that employers could fire employees with AIDS if they had so much as the suspicion that the virus could be spread to other workers, regardless of the medical evidence." The American Secretary of Health and Human Services "argued against the need for a deferral law guaranteeing the confidentiality of HIV antibody test results" (ibid., 4–6).

are white," as criticized by José Muñoz,[113] Bersani's righteously angry criticism is particularly relevant to my analysis of the discursive mechanism of tehomophobia when he argues, "*power* is in the hands of those who give every sign of being able to sympathize more with the murderous 'moral' fury of the good vicar than with the agony of a KS patient."[114]

The justified violence (homophobia in this case) is cunningly fed by the strategy of accusing and monstrifying the victim, much like the unethical treatment of Tiamat in *Enuma Elish* reproduced by modern scholarship, as I have shown throughout these two chapters. Simon Watney explains the overt public homophobia during the AIDS epidemic to the representation of female prostitutes in the 19th century that condemned them "as contaminated vessels, conveyancing 'female' venereal diseases to 'innocent' men."[115] Through Watney, Bersani further points out that homosexuals, "those belonging to the group hit most heavily by AIDS [...or] those being killed are [demonized as the] killers" and the intentional vectors of AIDS.[116]

Thus, far from an *ana*chronistic "application" of queer theory to a remote antiquity, almost in an absurd gesture to coerce a reading that would interpret the primordial watery deities as the densely symbolized modern/colonial heteronormative asses, what I want to show is the great political potential of an "unclean," non-identitarian, undifferentiated deep. This is at odds with the tehomophobic interpretations that are no less absurd in forcing the mingling ancient waters into the modern/colonial hetero-monogamous nuclear family composed of papa, mama, and son,[117] however metaphorical these personifications might

---

113 Muñoz, *Cruising Utopia*, 33–35.
114 This alludes to the headline of London newspaper *Sun*: "I'd Shoot My Son If He Had AIDS, Says Vicar!" that the author mentions earlier in his analysis (Bersani, "Is the Rectum a Grave?" 5–6).
115 Watney, *Policing Desire*, 33–34.
116 Bersani, "Is the Rectum a Grave?" 17.
117 Preciado ironically points out in a parody of Freudian family drama/trauma of the penis, "Los miembros de la familia no tienen ano. Papá no tiene ano. Mamá no tiene ano. El niño no tiene ano. La niña, ni siquiera importa si tiene ano o no lo tiene" ("The members of the family have no anus. Papa has

claim to be. Opposing these monolithic and seemingly *straight-forward* interpretations and appropriations is to oppose the murderous logic that translates violence on the symbolic level of mythology into a physical violence in everyday politics.

The miraculous survival of queer subjects under the life-threatening impulses to eradicate them from epistemic intelligibility and material livability in the name of "order" — be it Marduk in his "creation of heaven and earth" or the general public's murderous moral fury against any sexual dissident — has fortunately revealed the limits and inadequacies of the dominant system. While Apsu is locked in the heteronormative closet of tehomophobia, his sexual partner Mummu leaks out, by adhering to Tiamat, "mu-um-mu tia-amat mu-al-li-da-at gim-ri-šú-un."[118] As monstrified chaos, Tiamat-Apsu (and Mummu) keep(s) their body open, penetrable, and malleable. The imageries of the sometimes separated, yet always mixed, Tiamat-Apsu-Mummu-Nammu-Tehom, of penetrable "male" bodies and of long-silenced but ineradicable homoeroticism, haunt not only Marduk and the Babylonian Kings, but also the Bible and the whole tehomophobic and phallogocentric tradition of their receptions.

The survival strategies of these antique queer beings urge us to suspend our facile gender identifications and respect their embodiments as complex entanglements. Our ordinary experiences of the rectum — "the terminal, usually relatively *straight,* section of the large intestine in humans and other mammals, ending in the anus" (OED) — can help us to understand these queer divine beings, who convey a kind of gender parody that "reveals that the original identity after which gender fashions itself is an imitation without an origin."[119]

These perpetually displaced primordial fluids lying at the *origins* of human imagination that oscillate between unclassifi-

no anus. Mama has no anus. The son has no anus. The girl, it does not even matter if she has it or not") (Preciado, "Terror anal," 139).

118 Talon, *The Standard Babylonian Creation Myth Enūma Eliš,* 33.

119 Judith Butler, *Gender Trouble: Feminism and the Subversion of Identity* (London: Routledge, 1999), 175.

able indifference, *undifferentiation,* and killable differences, *are* forms of chaos that can never be conquered.

PART 0

—

NULLA

Creatio ex Nihilo Contested

Yo no cruzé la frontera, la frontera me cruzó.
— Los Tigres del Norte[1]

Situated between the Mesopotamian "Waters" and the Meso-american "Earth" of the book comes this long part deliberately named *O/nulla* (zero), as a gesture of critiquing the theo-political concept of *creatio ex nihilo* (creation out of nothingness). We will see how *creatio ex nihilo* has had a decisive influence on colonialism and coloniality, an influence that persists in the scholarly reception of mythologies and critical theories. As Catherine Keller argues in her book *Face of the Deep: A Theology of Becoming,* the initial theological topic of creation out of nothingness became common sense and "took modern and then secular form, generating every kind of western originality, every logos creating the new as if from nothing, cutting violently, ecstatically free of the abysms of the past."[2] *Creatio ex nihilo* is what enabled Catholic Spain and Europe to claim their "discovery" of a pre-inhabited land later renamed as "America." In *La invención de América,* Edmundo O'Gorman asserts: "the

---

1   "I did not cross the border. The border crossed me." From the song "Somos más Americanos" (1993) by the Mexican *norteño* band Los Tigres del Norte.
2   Catherine Keller, *Face of the Deep: A Theology of Becoming* (London: Routledge, 2003), xvi.

fundamental concept for well understanding the image they had of the world at the time of Columbus is that the world was created *ex nihilo* by God."[3] This sense of originality that creates as if from nothingness is still largely operative.

If nothing can be made out of nothing, there is always something in the so-called "nothingness." This something might even be a lot of things, more than can be addressed in a single chapter. These somethings are what colonialism has tried, most of the time violently yet in vain, to erase and to reduce to "nothingness." In this chapter, we will see how *creatio ex nihilo* operates discursively in the many facets of modern colonialism, such as the "(re)invention of printing by Gutenberg" and the aforementioned "discovery" or "invention of America," as well as in the persistence of coloniality in knowledge production, especially in the areas of postcolonialism and gender/queer studies. More concretely, we will look at the gender of *creatio ex nihilo* in relation to the reception of Sojourner Truth's famous speech "Ain't I a Woman?" and the broader issue of the coloniality of gender(ing).

0.1 How to Create out of Nothingness?

French sinologist René Étiemble's work *L'Europe chinoise* (1988) opens Chapter 1 with a case regarding the invention of printing by asserting, "the masterpiece of the Eurocentric imposture: that Gutenberg should be the inventor of printing."[4] Étiemble reviewed numerous scholarly works, encyclopedias, and museum introduction texts, and found that they univocally affirmed

---

3   Edmundo O'Gorman, *La invención de América: El universalismo de la cultura occidental* (México D.F.: Universidad Nacional Autónoma de México, 1958), 72: "el concepto fundamental para entender a fondo la imagen que se tenía del universo en tiempos de Colón es el de haber sido creado ex nihilo por dios."

4   René Étiemble, *L'Europe chinoise I: De l'empire romain à Leibniz* (Paris: Gallimard, 1988), ch. 1: "le chef-d'oeuvre de l'imposture européocentriste: Gutenberg serait l'inventeur de l'imprimerie." All translations to English from non-English sources, unless stated otherwise, are mine.

the invention of printing in the 1450s by the German craftsman Johann Gutenberg. Many works acknowledge the existence of similar technology (movable type) already invented by the Chinese craftsman Bi Shen around 1040 and 1050, that is, some thousand years after the first books were printed, though with other methods, during the Han Dynasty (around 250 BCE). The sources reviewed by Étiemble either ignore this historical fact or assert that it was Gutenberg who invented movable type printing, or they articulate this "invention" in a peculiar way. Étiemble observes that

> they would like us to admit that Gutenberg, a German, certainly, but also a European, is one of the greatest geniuses of humanity because, being so ignorant of what people then could not *not* know, and of which [sc. printing] many others had shown the path from China to Germany, he alone would have invented printing himself.[5]

One of the most curious cases Étiemble cites is from a book published in 1961, *L'univers des livres: Étude historique des origines à la fin du XVIIIe siècle* by Albert Flocon, who argues that

> all the techniques and essential materials for the multiplication of writing have been developed in the Far-East. Nothing can prove that the only [way of] manufacturing paper has followed the silk road; why wouldn't books and printed images, like any other goods, have reached the western frontiers of the Asiatic continent, or at the very least quite precise in-

---

5 Ibid., 39: "ils voudraient nous faire admettre que Gutenberg, un Allemand, certes, mais oui bien un Européen, est l'un des plus grands génies de l'humanité parce que tout seul, comme un grand ignorant de tout ce que tant de gens alors ne pouvaient pas ne pas savoir, et dont plusieurs du reste avaient démontré le cheminement de la Chine vers l'Allemagne, il avait inventé l'imprimerie."

formation about their mode of production which would have allowed, in due course, for a Western *reinvention*?[6]

The peculiar word *reinvention* drew Étiemble's attention. Despite Flocon's prudent tone — he uses interrogative phrasing and the conditional tense which can be construed as leaving space for uncertainty — it was baffling to Étiemble that after a work such as *The Invention of Printing in China and its Spread Westward* by Thomas Francis Carter (1925) had already been "enthusiastically received" and "immediately became the standard work on the Chinese origins of printing,"[7] Flocon could still credit Gutenberg with inventing (or more precisely *reinventing*) printing.

Suspicious of the outdatedness of Étiemble's work, I have reviewed some more recent scholarly studies, encyclopedias, and museum introduction texts. Changes remain to be seen. For example, the website of the Gutenberg Museum in Mainz, Germany briefly mentions Bi Sheng in the section "Beweglich Lettern vor Gutenberg" under the introduction of printing in East Asia. The text nuanced and prudent yet problematic, states, "Records tell us that in c. 1040 a man called Bi Sheng began experimenting with moveable ceramic printing stamps, using them to compose and print texts."[8] In this version, Bi Sheng is said to (*so ist überliefert*) have experimented (*experimentierte*) with printing, but not necessarily to have succeeded, ones assumes, in engen-

---

6 Quoted in ibid., 30: "toutes les techniques et les matériaux essentiels pour la multiplication des écrits ont été mis au point en Extrême-Orient. Rien ne prouve que la seule fabrication du papier a suivi la route de la soie; pourquoi, comme d'autres marchandises, les livres et les images imprimés ne seraient-ils pas parvenus aux confins ouest du continent asiatique, ou tout au moins des renseignements assez précis sur leur mode de fabrication qui pouvait permettre une réinvention occidentale le moment venu?" Emphasis mine.

7 Quoted in ibid.

8 "Ostasien," *Gutenberg-Museum Mainz,* http://www.gutenberg-museum.de/122.0.html: "Um das Jahr 1040 experimentierte ein Mann namens Bi Sheng, so ist überliefert, mit beweglichen Druckstempeln aus Keramik, aus denen er Texte zusammensetzte und abdruckte."

dering a "print revolution in China comparable to that usually associated with Gutenberg in the Western world."[9]

The entry for "Johannes Gutenberg" in the online version of the *Encyclopedia Britannica* credits him with having "originated a method of printing from movable type."[10] The same online encyclopedia has no entry for Bi Sheng. The *New York Times,* on January 27, 2001, published an article entitled "Has History Been Too Generous to Gutenberg?" A physicist and a rare books scholar using new technology to examine early printings credited to Gutenberg, questioned the "one, heroic discovery" of printing by Gutenberg, though the article is quite confident in noting that "the new research [...] does not dislodge Gutenberg from his historic position as the inventor of the printing press."[11] At the end of the article, surprisingly, the author adds that

> the Koreans had been *using sand casting to make metal letters* [...] for at least 30 years, but the scholars found no direct evidence that Gutenberg had contact with them. It has also long been known that the Chinese were *making movable type* out of clay and mass-producing books in the 11th century A.D., *although that process was unknown in Europe.*[12]

While the Koreans were "using sand casting letters to make metal letters" and the Chinese were "making movable type," it was Gutenberg, or "someone else about 20 years after Gutenberg [who] printed his bible" and "invented" movable type printing.[13] This is an example of "the kinds of colonial representation that, at least superficially, do not stigmatize or overtly distance the

---

9   Andrea Janku, "'Gutenberg in Shanghai. Chinese Print Capitalism, 1876–1937' by Christopher A. Reed. [Book Review]," *The China Quarterly* 182 (2005): 443–45, at 445.

10 "Johannes Gutenberg," *Encyclopedia Brittanica,* https://www.britannica.com/biography/Johannes-Gutenberg.

11 Dinitia Smith, "Has History Been Too Generous to Gutenberg?" *New York Times,* January 27, 2001, http://www.nytimes.com/2001/01/27/arts/27PRIN.html.

12 Ibid., emphasis mine.

13 Ibid.

other as a type, as a primitive or Asiatic savage."[14] East Asia, and especially China, were seldom considered "barbarian" or "primitive" by the Europeans, as was the fate of the Amerindian cultures. Nevertheless, the modern/colonial mind, locked in the logic of *creatio ex nihilo,* finds it difficult to grapple with the idea that Gutenberg might not have invented movable type printing out of nothingness. It thus invented the "reinvention."

The troublesome suffix *re-* is not a singular case. Naming is renaming and populating is repopulating. In his *Historia de las Indias,* Bartolomé de Las Casas explains that Cristóbal Colón[15] means *poblar de nuevo* (to repopulate).[16] The Spanish expression *de nuevo* means doing something again, as does the *re-* prefix of repopulate or rename, but it contains the curious word *nuevo,* "new" as in Vespucci's nomination *mundus novus.* This implies an "unconscious arrogance and deep belief that what for him was not known had to be, of necessity, new; that whatever was not known to him, naturally did not exist."[17] But when it comes to re-populating the land with new inhabitants, *de nuevo,* like *ex nihilo,* begs the question of the old inhabitants of whose existence the colonizer is consciously aware. O'Gorman asks us to make a distinction between "invention" and "creation," connecting the latter term with *ex nihilo* in a religious context.[18] He suggests that the task is to reconstruct not a history of "discovery," but of how the idea that America was discovered came into

---

14 Nicholas Thomas, *Colonialism's Culture: Anthropology, Travel and Government* (Princeton: Princeton University Press, 1994), 37.

15 The Italian-born navigator's name is written as Christopher Columbus in English and Cristoforo Colombo in Italian. However, during his life, he insisted on using the Spanish Cristóbal Colón, which has interesting theological connotations closely related to the "discovery of America," as argued in Tzvetan Todorov, *La conquête de l'Amérique: La question de l'autre* (Paris: Éditions du Seuil, 1982). I thus maintain the Spanish Cristóbal Colón throughout the text.

16 Bartolomé de Las Casas, *Historia de las Indias, Tomo I* (Madrid: Imprenta de Miguel Ginesta, 1875), 43.

17 Walter Mignolo, *The Darker Side of the Renaissance: Literacy, Territoriality and Colonization* (Ann Arbor: University of Michigan Press, 1995), 264.

18 O'Gorman, *La invención de América,* 14.

being.[19] McClintock suggests that these "implosive anxieties [...] were just as often warded off by fantastical rites of imperial violence,"[20] by imagining the unknown-become-known as the "new," demonizing the old-now-known through "cannibalization," then erasing the old-made-new/barbarian people and their culture, religion, memory, and history through the rhetoric of "civilization conquers/converts barbarism."

0.1.1 Renaming: Modern Colonialism and the Invention of America

The "(re)invention" of printing by Gutenberg and the "(re)naming" of America by the Europeans are sustained by the same logic of *creatio ex nihilo*. One of the most significant functions of the West's "sense of originality" is reflected in the act of "naming," which is always a renaming of non-Western others. The invention of "America" is filled with this desire for and anxiety of naming-appropriating. The inhabited lands of Cemanahuac (for the Nahuas) and Tawantisuyana (for the Inca), with their highly sophisticated civilizations, are reduced to a *terra nullius* to be "discovered," then "named," and eventually appropriated by Christian Europeans.

Not only was the *terra nullius* perfectly inhabited, it was also no stranger to colonialism. Non-modern[21] types of colonialism abound. Colonization or colonialism has existed throughout human history and across the world. The Babylonian state and the Aztec empires were great colonial powers in their respective regions at certain historical moments. The Greeks, the Romans, the Chinese and the Mongols, to name but a few, were also re-

---

19 Ibid., 24
20 Anne McClintock, *Imperial Leather: Race, Gender and Sexuality in the Colonial Contest* (New York: Routledge, 1995), 27.
21 I follow María Lugones to designate societies that are not considered "modern" as "non-modern" rather than "pre-modern." She argues that the "modern apparatus reduces [non-modern societies] to premodern ways [while] non-modern knowledges, relations, and values, and ecological, economic, and spiritual practices are logically constituted to be at odds with a dichotomous, hierarchical, 'categorical' logic" (María Lugones, "Toward a Decolonial Feminism," *Hypatia* 25, no. 4 [2010]: 742–59, at 743).

gional colonizers who exerted colonial control over the lands of others. Modern colonialism started from the 16th century through the European conquest of "America," while "[t]he colonial relations of previous periods […] were not the corner stone of any global power."[22] The uniqueness of modern colonialism lies precisely in its intimate connection with a global capitalism that "originates and globalizes from America."[23] "America," or, more precisely, the invention of "America," is the threshold of our discussion of modern colonialism and coloniality, "one of the constituent and specific elements of the global matrix of capitalist power."[24]

0.1.1.1 From Colonialism to the Invention of America and Modern Colonialism
The two ancient cultures we are studying can be regarded as colonial ones. The Babylonians colonized their neighbors and rose to a dominant power in the Mesopotamian region before they were brought down by the Persian Empire. The Aztecs were a nomadic group in the northern Mesoamerican region which gradually migrated to central Mexico, subjugating the indigenous inhabitants of the Mexican Valley and building up their empire with its center at the emerging metropolis Mexico-Tenochtitlan.[25]

The Babylonian creation myth *Enuma Elish* became important and was repeatedly recited at the "New Year's Festival" only after the rise of the Babylonian state. Marduk consequently became the patron god not only of the Babylonians, but of the entire Mesopotamian region. Similarly, the foundation of the

---

22 Aníbal Quijano, "Coloniality and Modernity/Rationality," *Cultural Studies* 21, nos. 2–3 (2007): 168–78, at 170.

23 Aníbal Quijano, "Colonialidad del poder y clasificación social," *Journal of World-Systems Research* 6, no. 2 (2000): 342–86, at 342: "se origina y mundializa a partir de América."

24 Ibid.: "uno de los elementos constitutivos y específicos del patrón mundial de poder capitalista."

25 The name "Aztec" refers to the myth of "Aztlan," which the Nahuatl-speaking nomadic group believe to be their place of origin. "Mexica" (the Nahua rule) refers to the people of Mexico-Tenochtitlan.

city Mexico-Tenochtitlan by the Aztecs on the island in Texcoco Lake was justified as the "divine will" of their patron god Huitzilopochtli, who is said to have guided them to the promised land where they had seen an eagle devouring a snake on top of a cactus. The expansion of the Aztec empire made Tenochtitlan its spiritual and political center. In the center of the center, at the Templo Mayor, the myth in which Huitzilopochtli defeated Coyolxauhqui (the moon goddess) and the Centzonhuitznahuac (the four hundred southern stars), was often performed. The sun god Huitzilopochtli, patron god of the Aztec tribe, thus became the patron god of the Mexican Valley. Upon a superficial reading, the myth propagates victory of the masculine power over the feminine ones, and the colonizer (Huitzilopochtli representing the Aztecs) over the colonized (Coyolxauhqui and Centzon Huiznahuac representing the conquered and feminized tribes).

Both cultures have used creation myths heavily charged with justifications for their colonial power over previous inhabitants of the conquered land. *Enuma Elish* was performed on multiple occasions every year, as a reiteration of Marduk's — and thus the Babylonian's — superiority; sacrificial rituals at the Templo Mayor served similar ends. Despite the differences between non-modern and modern forms of colonialism, *creatio ex nihilo* persists as a justificatory discourse. It appears in the Spanish conquest of the Aztec Empire and the genocide of the indigenous American population, as well as in the Israeli occupation of Palestinian land.[26]

What makes modern European or Western colonialism unique in global history is its relationship to capitalism. In this sense, "America" — which was not known as such either by the inhabitants of the land, who knew it as, for example, *cemanahuac* (Nahuatl: "earth entirely surrounded by water") or by its "discoverer," who thought he had arrived in India — encapsulates both the historical event and the ideological specificity of modern Eu-

---

26 See Ilan Pappe, *The Ethnic Cleansing of Palestine* (London: Oneworld Publications, 2006).

ropean colonialism. Starting in the 16th century with the Spanish and Portuguese, moving on to global dominance through direct political control in the 19th century, predominantly by the British and French, and in the 20th century by the United States, the legacy of modern European colonialism has been arguably passed on to neoliberal multinational corporations.[27]

"America" is a concept enunciated from a European, Christian perspective through the myth of the "great discovery" of a pre-habited continent with diverse populations, civilizations, empires, and even non-modern colonial powers, in order to appropriate and dominate these conquered cultures on the continent as a whole, and keep Europe as the only locus of enunciation. "America" is then used as the name appropriated by the United States to refer to the country, symbolically suggesting its neocolonial and capitalist domination over the whole American continent, which makes "'Latin' America [...] a dependent subcontinent that is subaltern to the continental totality, America."[28]

Once again, the question of naming is crucial here. In the Judeo-Christian imaginary, God speaks the world into existence and subsequently asks the human 'adam[29] to call and name the creatures so that "whatever the human called a living creature,

---

27 For an early exploration of this issue in the context of Africa, see O.E. Udofia, "Imperialism in Africa: A Case of Multinational Corporations," *Journal of Black Studies* 14, no. 3 (1984), 353–68. For a recent study in the context of Latin America, see Macarena Gómez-Barris, *The Extractive Zone: Social Ecologies and Decolonial Perspectives* (Durham: Duke University Press, 2017).

28 Walter Mignolo, *The Idea of Latin America* (Oxford: Blackwell, 2005), 153.

29 Rather than the proper name Adam, according to Robert Alter, the Hebrew 'adam should be translated as *human,* as in the Hebrew text the term "afterward consistently with a definite article, which is used both here [in the first account of the creation of the human being in Genesis I] and in the second account of the origins of humankind." Robert Alter, *Genesis: Translation and Commentary* (London: W.W. Norton & Company Inc., 1996), 5. For a discussion on the queerness of 'adam, see my essay "'adam Is Not Man': Queer Body before Genesis 2:22 (and After)," in *Unsettling Science and Religion: Contributions and Questions from Queer Studies,* eds. Whitney Bauman and Lisa Stenmark, 183–97 (Lanham: Lexington Books, 2018).

that was its name" (Gen 2:19).[30] A similar act of (re)naming, thus (re)creating, was repeated by Colón when he arrived on the continent, which he himself did not know as "America" either. Tzvetan Todorov, in his study of the "Great Discovery," *La conquête de l'Amérique* (1982), tells us, "like Adam in the garden of Eden, Columbus is passionate about picking names for the *virgin* world before his eyes."[31] Cristóbal Colón is often credited as the first to "discover" America. The honor of being the "first one" was said to be already implicit in his name: Cristóbal, *Christum ferens,* the bearer of Jesus Christ: "[I]n fact, [he] was indeed the first one to open the doors of the Ocean from where he entered and took to those lands so remote and those kingdoms unknown until then, our Savior Jesus Christ."[32] It was the Spanish version of his family name that he insisted on using: Colón, that made him the "legitimate" colonizer. As de Las Casas points out, Colón means *poblador de nuevo,* the one who re-populates.

The sustaining logic of colonialism, that of *creatio ex nihilo,* often works discursively to eliminate the *re-* or *de nuevo* part of the renaming, reinvention, and repopulating process — i.e., to erase physically and/or discursively the preexistence of people, cultures, and languages to a zero-degree *nihil* or nothingness (although most of the time in vain). "America," today a part of the "natural" division of the world, was not known to the "natural inhabitants" (a term used by de Las Casas) of those *tierras remotas,* nor even to Colón himself. None of them lived in "America." Tracing the history of the renaming of the continent now known as "America," Mignolo contends that

---

30 For all biblical references to Genesis, unless otherwise noted, I will be quoting from Robert Alter's detailed research translation *Genesis: Translation and Commentary* (London: W.W. Norton & Company Inc., 1996).

31 Ibid., 39, emphasis mine: "comme Adam au milieu de l'Éden, Colon se passionne pour le choix des noms du monde vierge qu'il a sous les yeux."

32 De Las Casas, *Historia,* 43: "en la verdad haya sido el primero que abrió las puertas deste mar Océano, por donde entró y él metió á estas tierras tan remotas y reinos, hasta entonces tan incógnitos, á nuestro Salvador Jesucristo."

since Vespucci [the Italian navigator] conceptually "discovered" (in the sense of "discovering for oneself" or "realizing") that Europeans were confronting a New World, the continent was renamed "America" after Amerigo Vespucci himself, with a slight change to the ending to make it fit with the already existing non-European continents Africa and Asia.[33]

0.1.1.2 *Critiques of Modern/Colonial/Categorical Logic*

This brief account of different cultural groups and their colonial legacies, as well as the quintessential moment of modern European colonialism that is the "discovery" or invention of America, also intends to problematize the dichotomous division between the "colonizer" and the "colonized." Homi Bhabha has criticized the fallacious self/other dichotomy through the concept of hybridity, the mixed-ness of cultures, especially in his work on colonial India. Through close reading of colonial literature, he detects an "intrinsic anxiety" of the British colonizers about the colonial project. Drawing insights from psychoanalysis, Bhabha argues that "the tension between the illusion of difference and the reality of sameness leads to anxiety." For him, the "colonial power is anxious, and never gets what it wants — a stable, final distinction between the colonizers and the colonized."[34] We should be careful not to maintain such divisions that reproduce and reinforce the (wishful) colonial logic of hierarchical categorization and anti-miscegenation.

The caution against the absolute division between colonizer and colonized is an important development in postcolonial theory. It radically moves beyond the logic of insurmountable difference that underpins modern colonialism. As Bauman argues, this logic of difference, the "claim of purity, transcendence, and objectivity is exactly what the logic of domination promises, but to the detriment of the relational, contextual world in and from

---

33 Mignolo, *The Idea of Latin America*, 3.
34 David Huddart, *Homi K. Bhabha* (London: Routledge, 2006), 4.

which all epistemological claims are made."[35] Using Bhabha's concept of the interstice, that is, "the overlap and displacement of domains of difference,"[36] Bauman further relates this logic to foundationalism or essentialism. He shows that the "binary ordering of the world destroys the creative 'third space' or 'interstitial' space in which self-other are mutually formed."[37] Bauman frames this discussion through an analysis of the decisive role that *ex nihilo* theology plays in Christian orthodoxy, one that denies the "chaotic beginnings of Christianity from disparate traditions, and the borrowing from other traditions in the biblical texts."[38] Put another way, the doctrine of *creatio ex nihilo* erases the context from which Christianity emerges and pretends that "Christianity need begin nowhere but with the story of Genesis and the reading of Genesis from the perspective of *ex nihilo* creation."[39]

Here however, we need to situate Bhabha's analysis of "colonial anxiety" in the modern history of Western colonialism operating hand in hand with Christianity. A good example is seemingly homogenous 19th-century Victorian Britain, which is traditionally credited with highly stringent Christian morals, but was in fact undergoing great social and religious crises and changes. The development of science, especially the theory of evolution, shook the Christian attribution of the world's origin to God; Robert L. Stevenson's *Strange Case of Doctor Jeckyll and Mr Hyde* (1886) showed signs of suppressed homosexuality rising to the surface;[40] Bram Stoker's *Dracula* (1897) exemplified the fear of a reverse colonization;[41] the changing role of women, "guardians" of Victorian values, culminated in a masculinist cri-

---

35 Whitney Bauman, *Theology, Creation, and Environmental Ethics: From Creatio Ex Nihilo to Terra Nullius* (London: Routledge, 2009), 13.

36 Homi K. Bhabha, *The Location of Culture* (London: Routledge, 1994), 2.

37 Bauman, *Theology, Creation, and Environmental Ethics,* 32.

38 Ibid., 30.

39 Ibid.

40 See Elaine Showalter, *Sexual Anarchy: Gender and Culture at the Fin de Siècle* (London: Bloomsbury, 1991).

41 See Arata Stephen, "The Occidental Tourist: *Dracula* and the Anxiety of Reverse Colonization," *Victorian Studies* 33, no. 4 (1990): 621–46.

sis evident in such texts as the extremely popular *King Solomon's Mines* (1885) and *She: A History of Adventure* (1887), both written by Henry Rider Haggard after his service in British colonial administration in South Africa.[42] All these texts can also be read in the light of the colonial anxiety around racial degeneration through contact with other "inferior races" in the British colonies or at home.

This colonial anxiety of influence should be thought within modernity as a "categorical, dichotomous, hierarchical logic," and as one that is "central to modern, colonial capitalist thinking about race, gender and sexuality."[43] If we change the context of 19th-century Britain to that of the pre-conquest colonial Aztecs — i.e., a non-modern culture operating differently from the same modern categorical hierarchy — it is not clear how the Aztec colonial authorities would experience the same "colonial anxiety."

In his book about the urban complexity of Mexico City from the Aztec period to the post-Independence era, Louis Panabière suggests that cultural shock was frequent in Mexico, but asks, "has it provoked crises or enabled fertile enrichment?"[44] He reviews different historical periods under different cosmologies and political rules in order to answer this question. Tenochtitlan, under the rule of the Aztecs, is the center of the empire. He contends, "the Aztec empire is not a center that imposes itself to the periphery by destroying the values, but it is a[n] [imperial] body that is nourished by contacts and relations with the peoples and cultures it has encountered."[45] According to Panabière, therefore, non-Aztec cultures were able to survive and integrated into the new empire.

---

42 See *McClintock, Imperial Leather*.

43 Lugones, "Toward a Decolonial Feminism," 742.

44 Louis Panabière, *Cité aigle, ville serpent* (Perpignan: Presses Universitaires de Perpignan, 1993), 12: "est-ce qu'il a provoqué des crises ou est-ce qu'il a donné lieu à de féconds enrichissements?"

45 Ibid., 17: "l'empire aztèque [...] n'est pas un centre qui s'impose à la périphérie en en détruisant les valeurs, mais c'est un corps qui se nourrit des contacts et des relations avec les populations et les cultures rencontrées."

For example, despite the privileged position of Huitzilo-pochtli in Aztec politics, pre-Aztec deities such as Quetzalcoatl and Tlaloc were incorporated and remained in prestigious positions to continue their worship.[46] This is shown in the structure of Templo Mayor, the twin pyramid that is believed to be in the center of the universe and is dedicated to Huitzilopochtli, patron god and also god of sun and fire, as well as to the older, pre-Aztec deity Tlaloc, god of rain. In front of the twin pyramid of Templo Mayor, we find a separate altar dedicated to Quetzalcoatl, the plumed serpent, an ancient god present throughout the Mesoamerican region.[47]

Panabière explains that, as opposed to Spanish monotheism, which "tends to reduce the individual to the unique essence,"[48] the Aztec religion proposes plurality, participation, and coherence, for which "the internal contradictions do not take away the coherence and the unity."[49] In Part II, I will analyze in detail the strange case of Tlaltecuhtli, the Aztec earth deity, and argue that the combination of Aztec religious thought, the particularity of its writing system, and its philosophical plurality gave greater freedom to representations of Tlaltechuhtli, who appeared in feminine, masculine, and zoomorphic guises, as well as in the guise of other deities who shared a similar physiognomy to Tlaloc. While Panabière might be right to point out the contradiction-in-coherence, his observation might be too generous to the Aztec colonizers, who were actually also haunted by a certain anxiety towards their colonial project and the encountered "others."

---

46 See Eduardo Matos Moctezuma, *Vida y muerte en el Templo Mayor* (México D.F.: Editorial Océano, 1986).

47 Among the Mayans, Quetzalcoatl appears under the guise of Kukulcan, depicted on the famous pyramid of Chichen Itza; in Teotihuacan, one of the three major pyramids is dedicated to him; finally, he was worshipped in Tula, the capital of the Toltecs.

48 Panabière, *Cité aigle,* 18: "tend à ramener l'individu à une essence unique."

49 Ibid., 20: "les contradictions internes n'enlevaient rien à la cohésion et à l'unité."

The Mexican Nobel laureate Octavio Paz, for example, believes that "the incessant theological speculation that combined, systematized and unified scattered beliefs, of themselves or of the others,"[50] performed not by the proletarians at a popular level but by certain castes and theocrats at the top of the social hierarchy, was superficial. He asserts that "the religious unification only affected the consciousness superficially while the primitive beliefs were left intact."[51] As opposed to Panabière, Paz regards the religious and cultural incorporation of the non-Aztec ones as a superficial unification or even imposition, which he believes laid the ground for the introduction of Catholicism: "[I]t is also a religion superimposed onto an original and always living religious background [... and therefore] laid the ground for the Spanish domination whose arrival seems like a liberation for the people submitted to the Aztecs."[52]

The analogy Paz draws between the Aztec religion and Catholicism ignores that monotheism marks the fundamental difference between the two. The superimposition of Catholicism works from within its orthodox theological dictum, where there is no space for negotiation. The conquered people of the Americas had two options regarding their "demonic beliefs": conversion to Christianity or death.[53] In his fanatical *Requerimiento* (1513), Juan López de Palacios speaks to the indigenous

---

50 Octavio Paz, *El laberinto de la soledad* (Madrid: Fondo de Cultura Económica, 2007), 102: "la incesante especulación teológica que refundía, sistematizaba y unificaba creencias dispersas, propias y ajenas."
51 Ibid.: "la unificación religiosa solamente afectaba a la superficie de la conciencia, dejando intactas las creencias primitivas."
52 Ibid.: "también es una religión superpuesta a un fondo religioso original y siempre viviente [... entonces] preparaba la dominación española [y su] llegada [...] parece una liberación a los pueblos sometidos por los aztecas."
53 Laiou traces this religious impulse underpinning the conquest of the Americas to a previous period of European expansion, the Crusades, and argues that the "Second Crusade, preached against the Slavs as much as against the Muslims in the Holy Land, produced an unequivocal and powerful ideological conceptualization, precisely that of conversion or annihilation" (Angeliki E. Laiou, "Many Faces of Medieval Colonization," in *Native Traditions in the Postconquest World,* eds. Elizabeth Hill Boone and Tom Cummins [Washington, DC: Dumbarton Oaks, 1998], 13–30, at 21).

people of the Americas in the name of the Spanish Crown, whom he defines as the *domadores de pueblos bárbaros* (tamers of barbarians):

And if you would not do this or viciously make delay in it [conversion to Christianity and subjection to the Castilian Monarchs], I assure you that, with the help of our God, we shall powerfully enter (your land) to oppose you and wage war everywhere in all ways we can; and we will subject you to the yoke and obedience to the Church and Their Majesties; we will take you, your wives and children and make them slaves, who we will sell and dispose them as Their Majesties would command; and we will possess your goods and do all the bad things and damages that we can, as to the vassals who do not obey, refuse to receive their lord, resist and contradict him; and we protest that the deaths and damages caused by this are your fault but nor that of Their Majesties, nor ours, nor these gentlemen who come with us.[54]

The attitude as shown in the above quote is fundamentally different from that of the Aztec theocrats. Theo-political monotheism intersects with the categorical logic of modernity/coloniality. A critique of the modern form of colonialism should be very careful not to fall into the same categorical and linear logic, for instance, believing that the colonial project has successfully

---

54 Juan López de Palacios, *Requerimiento* (1513): "Y si así no lo hicieseis o en ello [conversión al Cristianismo y sometimiento a los Reyes de Castillas] maliciosamente pusieseis dilación, os certifico que con la ayuda de Dios nosotros entraremos poderosamente contra vosotros, y os haremos guerra por todas las partes y maneras que pudiéramos, y os sujetaremos al yugo y obediencia de la Iglesia y de Sus Majestades, y tomaremos vuestras personas y de vuestras mujeres e hijos y los haremos esclavos, y como tales los venderemos y dispondremos de ellos como Sus Majestades mandaren, y os tomaremos vuestros bienes, y os haremos todos los males y daños que pudiéramos, como a vasallos que no obedecen ni quieren recibir a su señor y le resisten y contradicen; y protestamos que las muertes y daños que de ello se siguiesen sea a vuestra culpa y no de Sus Majestades, ni nuestra, ni de estos caballeros que con nosotros vienen."

eliminated the indigenous knowledges, cosmologies, and beings to the level of *nihil*. Or even worse, assuming that colonialism only started (as if *ex nihilo*) in the 19th century.

This global, capitalist, colonial system that seeks to pave its way through the conquered worlds is "continually resisted and being resisted today."[55] In the case of the Christianization and colonization of the Nahuas, research shows that "the dualistic categories of 'Christian' and 'pagan' […] were highly meaningful to Europeans but foreign to indigenous self-conceptions."[56] It was the Nahuas who "manipulated their friars into presiding over a church founded not upon abstract Christian theological or moral tenets but upon an exuberant pageantry; [a phenomenon which] tended to mask a slower and more subtle process by which world view and philosophy were renegotiated by the Nahuas without there being any abrupt rupture with the past."[57]

In Ang Lee's film *Life of Pi* (2012), the young protagonist Piscine Patel from the former French colony Pondicherry in India went home one day after a symbolic encounter with a Christian priest, who gave him a cup of water and brought him the gospel of Jesus Christ. Before sleep that night, he touched his Vishnu statuette and prayed, "Thank you Vishnu, for introducing me to Christ." We learn later that the young boy had no problem believing and practicing piously and simultaneously in Hinduism, Christianity, and Islam. Put differently:

[C]olonial authority thus produces ironic, split identifications; these threatening expressions of hybridity disrupt and subvert colonial hegemony, in the sense that they exclude the possibility of total epistemic mastery, and because they constitute "a variously positioned native who by (mis)appro-

---

55 Lugones, "Toward a Decolonial Feminism," 748.

56 Louise M. Burkhart, "Pious Performances: Christian Pageantry and Native Identity in Early Colonial Mexico," in *Native Tradition in the Postconquest World,* eds. Elizabeth Hill Boone and Tom Cummins (Washington, DC: Dumbarton Oaks, 1998), 361–81, at 362.

57 Ibid., 363.

priating the terms of the dominant ideology" is able to resist colonial typification.[58]

The epigraph at the beginning of this chapter is an excerpt from a song called "Somos más Americanos" ("We are more Americans") by the Mexican *norteño* band Los Tigres del Norte. "I did not cross the border. The border crossed me" acutely summarizes the violent imposition of categorization (the drawing of borders) through colonialism, which cuts across the organic living experience, memories, and intersubjective relationships, and causes enduring problems at borders of all kinds. Needless to say, one of the most prominent, artificially constructed borders that violently cut across both epistemological (symbolical) and material (physical) bodies is that of sex and gender, the central focus of this book. Most noticeable in that context is the practice of coercive "sex assignment" for pathologized intersex people.[59]

0.1.2 Colonialism ex Nihilo: *The Problem of Postcolonialism*
After heated debates on colonialism and postcolonialism by preeminent scholars such as Edward Said, whose *Orientalism* (1979) is a foundational text of postcolonial studies, and Gayatri Spivak, whose article "Can the Subaltern Speak?" (1988) has been widely cited and criticized, the *Columbia Encyclopedia* presents to its reader a definition of "colonization" in 1993. This publication comes from the same university where Said and Spivak produced their influential works, works that are credited as foundational of what later came to be known as postcolonial studies:

Colonization: Extension of political and economic control over an area by a state whose nationals have occupied the area and usually possess organizational or technological *su-*

---

58 Thomas, *Colonialism's Culture*, 40.
59 See Thomas Laqueur, *Making Sex: Body and Gender from the Greeks to Freud* (Cambridge: Harvard University Press, 1990); Anne Fausto-Sterling, "The Five Sexes: Why Male and Female Are Not Enough," *The Sciences* (March/April 1993): 20–25; María Lugones, "Heterosexualism and the Colonial/Modern Gender System," *Hypatia* 22, no. 1 (2007): 186–209.

periority over the native population. […] IMPERIALISM, *more or less aggressive humanitarianism,* and a desire for adventure or individual improvement are also causes. […] Modern colonization, frequently preceded by an era in which missionaries and traders were active, has been largely exploitative. Moreover, it has not in the long run proved directly lucrative to the colonial power […] Colonization in its classical form is rarely practiced today and is widely considered to be immoral.[60]

The entry perpetuates the colonial myth of "superiority" of the colonizer over the "native" population, a distinction that already carries the colonial linear logic that is reflected by the very concepts of modern ("state") and traditional ("native"), with the latter locked "in the lower scale of a chronological order driving towards 'civilization.'"[61] Positing the "superiority" of the colonizer comes close to suggesting that colonization is inevitable or at least in most cases ("usually") justifiable. It quickly explains colonization as caused by "more or less aggressive humanitarianism" and a desire "for adventure or individual improvement," which is usually regarded as positive, especially in Western and Westernized societies (the potential readers of the *Encyclopedia*). A long recapitulation of examples of colonization throughout ancient and modern history follows. All examples are European, except for the Phoenicians, who are loosely related to Europe, and the Japanese, whose colonial history in Asia followed its Westernization during the Meiji Restoration in the late 19th century.[62]

According to this definition, therefore, colonization is usually undertaken by Western "states" at the expense of organization-

---

60 Barbara A. Chernow and George A. Vallasi, eds., *The Columbia Encyclopedia,* 5th edn. (New York: Columbia University Press, 1993), 600–601, emphasis mine.
61 Walter Mignolo, *The Darker Side of Western Modernity: Global Futures, Decolonial Options* (Durham: Duke University Press, 2011), 153.
62 See, for example, Yan Lu, *Re-Understanding Japan: Chinese Perspectives, 1895–1945* (Honolulu: University of Hawai'i Press, 2004), 228–29.

ally and technologically inferior populations (whose inferiority is already woven into the text through the opposition between the modern/advanced "state" and traditional/backward "native"). It is caused, at least sometimes, by individualism manifesting as the desire for personal adventure and improvement, or by some form of "humanitarianism" that can be "more or less aggressive." One wonders if the enslavement and genocide of indigenous Amerindian and African human beings, or the environmental disaster that continues and intensifies today through globalized capitalist expansion, would qualify as the more aggressive forms of such "humanitarianism." But the degree of aggression is probably irrelevant after all, since colonialism, we are told, is not entirely profitable for the colonial power. The entry ends with an observation on the immorality of colonization, not as a matter of fact, but of reception ("considered to be").

Certainly, one encyclopedia entry published about twenty-five years ago might not have so decisive an influence to be considered too seriously. This entry serves, however, as an example of how colonial discourse can survive political and scholarly efforts to disavow it and make its way into a prestigious university-published encyclopedia, under the guise of a scientific, truth-claiming, carefully fabricated language that at brief glance does not appear overtly colonialist. Colonial discourse, in its modern logic, posits the colonizer as the white man and his culture as the superior center, the "measure of all things," while the other — men, women,[63] cultures — are considered inferior and thus colonizable. From "inferiority" to "colonizability," the modern linear logic of progression provides persistent theories. This linearity, for example, might take the form of biblical salvation from sin, or as a transition from the old world toward the new "America." In short, it is believed that "Europe and the Europe-

---

63 Western women play an ambiguous role in colonialism. The question of women and colonialism is a good example of the problem of assuming that race and gender can be treated as issues independent from each other. As I have repeated throughout this text, they are already intersected. See also Indira Ghose, *Women Travellers in Colonial India: The Power of the Female Gaze* (Delhi: Oxford University Press, 1998).

ans were (at) the most advanced moment and level in the lineal, unidirectional and continuing path of the species."[64]

The ongoing global dominance of European colonial expansion is maintained through coloniality and the control of knowledge. Critique of the "colonizing epistemological strategy" of subordinating differences to transcultural notions should be consistent and kept alive.[65] This is equally true to the field of postcolonial studies. I have emphasized that Bhabha's theorization of colonial anxiety should be contextualized in 19th-century British colonialism, by using a counterexample from non-modern forms of colonialism. Scholars of postcolonialism, whose main historical focus is on the 19th century, consciously or inadvertently ascribe a uniqueness to these imperial powers to the extent that the British and French invasion of the world becomes presented as, precisely, *creatio ex nihilo* in the 19th century. Fernando Coronil, for example, enumerates the systematic exclusion of Latin America from several anthologies of postcolonial studies, including classics such as *The Post-Colonial Studies Reader* edited by Ashcroft, Griffiths, and Tiffin from 2006.[66] The brutal genocide of Amerindians and the continuous colonial policy toward indigenous populations in the form of so-called internal colonialism, still pervasive in Latin American countries, have been largely disregarded.

The exclusion or ignorance of Latin American anti-colonialist endeavors on the global map of decolonization is tellingly present in a dialogue between John Comaroff and Homi Bhabha, who divide postcoloniality into two periods: "the decolonization of the Third World marked by India's independence in

---

64 Quijano, "Colonialidad del poder y clasificación social," 344: "Europa y los europeos eran el momento y el nivel más avanzados en el camino lineal, unidireccional y continuo de la especie."

65 Judith Butler, *Gender Trouble: Feminism and the Subversion of Identity* (London: Routledge, 1999), 46.

66 Fernando Coronil, "Elephants in the Americas? Latin American Postcolonial Studies and Global Decolonization," in *Coloniality at Large: Latin America and the Postcolonial Debate,* eds. Mabel Moraña, Enrique Dussel, and Carlos A. Jáuregui (Durham: Duke University Press, 2008), 396–416.

1947; and the hegemony of neoliberal capitalism signaled by the end of the Cold War in 1989."[67] No wonder Spivak has claimed that "Latin America has *not* participated in decolonization!"[68] In this sense, as I will discuss further in a moment, not only did 19th-century colonialism posit itself as *creatio ex nihilo,* but so did its astute critic, "postcolonialism."

More than a disciplinary "attack" on postcolonialism *per se,* what we understand from this critique is the tendency of post-colonialism to claim universality by neglecting other political and intellectual endeavors that aim at decolonization parallel to or even much earlier than postcolonial studies. There is also the danger that postcolonial studies "would become an imperial design as any other [… that it] would compete with Marxism for global dominance."[69] "Global dominance" almost always goes hand in hand with universal claims. Nicholas Thomas for example, says of Bhabha that

[although] most of his [Homi Bhabha's] other references are to 19th century texts […] the limits and conditions of possibility of colonial discourse remain unspecified; it is as though the brute fact of the significance of imperialism in modern history exempts the critic from the need to locate its enunciations and reiterations.[70]

Joseba Gabilondo points out that, being blind to his own locality, Bhabha turns his discussion about postcoloniality "not into

---

67 Quoted in ibid., 402.
68 Gayatri Chakravorty Spivak, *Outside in the Teaching Machine* (New York: Routledge, 1993), 63.
69 Ibid.
70 Thomas, *Colonialism's Culture,* 43. Nicolas Thomas's critique of Bhabha's failure to take into consideration other forms of colonialism, however, differs from decolonial critics' insistence that "modernity" started in the Americas. He argues that Bhabha's focus on the 19th century "suggests either that colonial discourse is understood to be peculiarly modern — and hence did not exist, for example, in the period of the conquest of America — or that it is assumed that the logic identified is equally applicable in that case, and in others."

a particular position, but a negative and thus universal position defined by modernity," which for Bhabha is "no longer particularly Western, but rather hegemonically universal."[71]

Sara Castro-Kláren investigates the polemic reception in Latin America of Edward Said's influential book *Orientalism,* often credited with having generated the school of "postcolonial studies." She recounts that students in Latin American studies have experienced "the shock of recognition" when reading *Orientalism* precisely because the previously mentioned Mexican writer Edmundo O'Gorman has already analyzed, in a line of argument similar to that in Said's book, the "invention of America."[72] Rather than trying to undermine the importance and influence of Said's work, that "sweeping inquiry [that] was a brilliant investigation of Europe's invention of the Orient as its 19th century other,"[73] Castro-Kláren opens up a question that Mignolo later picks up: how come O'Gorman's thesis was only popularized through Said's work twenty years after he first proposed it? He argues that the reason lies in the "geopolitical ranking of knowledge, [in which] both the history and the scholarship of core imperial languages (English, French, and German) are more visible."[74]

"Visibility," when it comes to decolonial thoughts and struggle however, is a tricky issue. On the back cover of the English translation of the Mexican philosopher Enrique Dussel's *Politics of Liberation: A Critical World History,* Ivan Petrella contends: "[I]f Enrique Dussel had been born in the United States, France or Germany he would be an intellectual celebrity. Author of dozens of books in Spanish, few have been translated into

---

71 Joseba Gabilondo, "Introduction to 'The Hispanic Atlantic,'" *Arizona Journal of Hispanic Cultural Studies* 5 (2001): 91–113, at 97.

72 O'Gorman, *La invención de América.*

73 Sara Castro-Kláren, "Posting Letters: Writing in the Andes and the Paradoxes of the Postcolonial Debate," in *Coloniality at Large: Latin America and the Postcolonial Debate,* eds. Mabel Moraña, Enrique Dussel, and Carlos A. Jáuregui (Durham: Duke University Press, 2008), 130–57, at 131.

74 Mignolo, *The Darker Side of Western Modernity,* 56.

English. This book seeks to begin to remedy this injustice."[75] Let us not forget first that Enrique Dussel writes in Spanish, one of the major *colonial* languages most spoken in the world as a consequence of the *Conquista,* but not in Nahuatl, Tagalog, or Slovene. Petrella's comment falls into the trap of a strange logic that if one is not considered a "celebrity" (of any kind) by the English-speaking audience, one suffers from "injustice." Injustice for whom and by whom? Enrique Dussel is widely read in the Spanish-speaking world and native Spanish speakers make up the second largest linguistic group after Chinese and before English. Is their readership countable to render some "justice" for Dussel's works?

Here we come to two important points. First, the "locus of enunciation" of globally validated knowledge is still largely rooted in the West, that is, in the United States and Europe, written in English (of which this book plays a part), French, or German. From the self-avowed epistemic "zero point" of the West, knowledges from the "rest" of the world are not fully legitimate ones. Second, 18th-century "orientalism" did not happen *ex nihilo.* Indeed it would have been impossible without 16th-century colonial competition over the Americas, through which Occidentalism, the self-fashioning of the West as the embodiment of modernity, was shaped.[76] The foundational theo-political ideology of *creatio ex nihilo* is to be found, and criticized, not only in colonialism, but also in metropolitan postcolonialism.

Thus the critique of the blindness of postcolonial studies to America and the focus on anti-colonial thought theorized from the Americas should not be understood as promoting a "new" theoretical field (as if created *ex nihilo*) to claim dominance over the previous ones. Thus, "decoloniality" is not a new field, let alone a new "turn," but points to all theoretical and political en-

---

75 Enrique Dussel, *Politics of Liberation: A Critical World History,* trans. Thia Cooper (London: SCM Press Ltd, 2011), back cover.

76 Fernando Coronil, "Beyond Occidentalism towards Post-Imperial Geohistorical Categories," *Transformations: Comparative Studies of Social Transformations,* Working Paper 72 (May 1992): 1–29, at 14.

deavors throughout the history of colonization in order to make sense of the colonial experience and to resist colonialism.

In recent years, the research on decolonization across the "non-West" and the call for further decolonization (within and beyond the academia) by a handful of contemporary thinkers have been gradually received and turned into another "school of thought," alternatively named "decolonial option" or "decolonial theory." It seems sufficient to just quote Mignolo (or Quijano, for that matter) in order to "decolonize something." The local variants of political resistance, anti-colonial and anti-capitalist struggles, and non-heterosexualist cultural practices that "decolonial theorists" urge us to learn from, remain overshadowed by this allegedly new theoretical trend. This is a rather worrisome phenomenon for decolonization, because decolonial struggles *have always existed,* since day one of colonization in different localities, languages, and ways. If, as the now widely cited (including in this book) decolonial thinker Mignolo points out: "The colonial experience in South America and the Caribbean did not have to wait until the word *postcolonialism* entered the U.S. academy in the early 1980s, after the word *postmodernism* was introduced in France,"[77] decolonial endeavors have preceded and will surpass the conveniently named "decolonial theory."

Supersessionism, a temporal cousin of *creatio ex nihilo,* produced by the incessant theoretical "turns," manifests itself in the above quotation in which Mignolo reproduces the myth of postmodernism's French origin. The strong advocate of studying decoloniality from Latin America has, in his repudiation of postcolonialism, overlooked that both modernism and postmodernism "were born in a distant periphery rather than at the center of the cultural system of the time: they come not from Europe or the United States, but from Hispanic America."[78]

The "decolonial turn," as it has been more and more frequently used, should not be taken as an overarching proper name for a supposedly newly emergent school of thought. It is, however, an

---

77 Mignolo, *The Darker Side of Western Modernity,* 57.

78 Perry Anderson, *The Origins of Postmodernity* (New York: Verso, 1998), 3.

invitation to learn to learn from decolonial struggles, theories, and practices that abound in the colonized world.

0.1.3 The Gender of Creatio ex Nihilo
Nothingness, produced through the reduction and erasure of preexisting realities in colonial history and imaginaries, is directly linked with the image of the feminine body as a void, an empty place, a womb waiting for masculine inscription or insemination. This is an issue I touched upon in Part I and will be the central focus of the next section and Part II.

The feminization of the colonized is an old story. In her book *Imperial Leather: Race, Gender and Sexuality in the Colonial Contest* from 1995, Ann McClintock captures the "doubling in male imperial discourse" represented in Jan van der Straet's painting *America* (c. 1575). The painting represents "America" as a naked woman in a position of lust, luring the European discoverer Vespucci as a fully clothed, technologically equipped "man of letters," who, with his "godlike arrival, is destined to inseminate her with the male seeds of civilization, fructify the wilderness and quell the riotous scene of cannibalism in the background."[79] The dichotomous coupling is easily discernible as "earth–sky; sea–land; male–female; clothed–unclothed; active–passive; vertical–horizontal; raw–cooked," yet McClintock sharply points out the colonial/masculine anxiety present in the representation of the cannibalistic scene between Amerigo and America on the background amidst the natural landscape, with the dismembered body, a (phallic) leg, being grilled by a group of female cannibals. She concludes that the scene "is a document both of paranoia and of megalomania." What is more, the supposedly "passive" feminine figure in the foreground is "riotously violent and cannibalistic" in the background, ready to engulf the lonely erected "civilization."[80] The passivity and cannibalism contradicting each other, yet projected onto the "feminized" land, trouble the impulse of dichotomization and hierarchiza-

---

79 McClintock, *Imperial Leather,* 26.
80 Ibid., 26–27.

tion: It becomes uncertain whether the correlation femininity/
passivity/colonized, or masculinity/activity/colonizer, for that
matter, is clearly maintained.[81]

Naming, and therefore controlling, the unknown is vividly
shown in the Amerigo–America connection. The inscription of
the painting reads in Latin, "Americen Americus retexit & Se-
mel vocauit inde Semper excitam."[82] McClintock interprets the
"rediscovery" as a way for Amerigo Vespucci to assert himself
as being the first man to "discover" the "New World," despite
being aware of his belatedness. What is more important, she
argues, is that this was an act similar to patronymy and patri-
mony, "an insistence on marking 'the product of copulation with
his own name' stems from the uncertainty of the male's relation
to origins."[83] In fact, "America" was not thus named *in situ* by
the Italian navigator, who by doing so supposedly resolved his
excitement of sexual possession and fear of emasculation. Mc-
Clintock might have ascribed too much power to Vespucci. Although his collection of letters in which he proposed the idea of
a "New World" is entitled *Mundus Novus* (1503), he did not go
so far as naming the *mundus novus* after his own name. Historically, it was Martin Waldseemüller who suggested such a name,
in honor of Amerigo Vespucci, not Vespucci himself.

McClintock's swift interpretation unintentionally erects
Vespucci as a heroric "discoverer" who colonizes the "feminized" other, probably out of his "desire of adventure and individual improvement," which, as the *Columbia Encyclopedia*
wanted us to believe, is often the cause of such endeavors. Since
the renaming and the invention of America is a gradual process, from *Novus Orbis* to *Terra Nova,* and then to *America,*[84]
the misreading of Amerigo–America, which turns the historical

---

81 Quijano, "Colonialidad del poder y clasificación social," has analyzed that
    the categorization of the world in European modernity conveys a hierarchy
    which keeps Europe and European men at the highest level.
82 "Americus rediscovers America. He called her but once and thenceforth she
    was always awake."
83 McClintock, *Imperial Leather*, 29.
84 Mignolo, *The Darker Side of the Renaissance*, 269.

process into a *fiat lux* instance, can be seen as still under the spell of *creatio ex nihilo*.

0.2 Gendering *Creatio ex Nihilo*

At the Akron Woman's Rights Convention in 1851, Sojourner Truth, an antislavery activist addressed the public with the question, "Ar'n't I a woman?" She also pointed to her physical strength to challenge the stereotype of women being feeble, as well as other gender stereotypes. This speech has been read as a manifesto demanding the recognition of her membership in the "woman party." Sojourner Truth has been represented either distortedly as an angry black woman embodying the "fervor of Ethiopia, wild, savage, hunted of all nations but burning after God in her tropic heart" by her contemporary biographer,[85] or coercively as the *black* feminist challenging the universal assumption of "sisterhood" actually dominated by her white counterparts. "Ar'n't I a woman" has often been (mis)read as "Ain't I *also* a woman?" Truth's interrogative pronouncement, predating the social-constructivist account of gender by 20th-century "second wave" feminism, is therefore still not read as a general question. Her sound critique of gender stereotypes is consistently misplaced as an outcry against racial prejudice in the United States.

0.2.1 A Brief Review of the Debates on "Gender"
One of the central issues discussed and theorized in feminist and gender studies is the concept of gender, its usefulness or uselessness and (in)applicability in different contexts. As soon as the concept of gender was introduced in feminist theorization of "sex," it could be said, critics already began to problematize it. Critiques likely take two forms: reconstructing gender or refusing it. The former does not question the concept of "gender"

---

85 Harriet Beecher Stowe, quoted in Nell I. Painter, "Sojourner Truth in Life and Memory: Writing the Biography of an American Exotic," *Gender & History* 2, no. 1 (1990): 3–16, at 9.

itself, but hopes to correct the problems of its blindness to racial and class difference, or to its heteronormative assumptions.

Black feminist theory, theorizing black women's experience as being at the same time racialized and gendered, perceives that "some ideas that Africanist scholars identify as characteristically 'Black' often bear remarkable resemblance to similar ideas claimed by feminist scholars as characteristically 'female.'"[86] Black feminists insist on the intersectional oppressions of gender and race *rather than* an additive account of oppressions often expressed as "further repressed by."[87] That is to say white women are *not* exempted from the issue of race. Gender always already intersects with race, sexuality, class, ability, religion, and other categories.

Elizabeth Spelman challenges in particular the tendency of those feminist theorists who use the "additive method," assuming that "gender is indeed a variable of human identity independent of other variables such as race and class, that whether one is a woman is unaffected by what class or race one is."[88] The danger of such theoretical separatism is that it reproduces "all the women are white, all the blacks are men," which renders visible the racism of the women's movement and sexism of the civil rights movement in the context of the United States. Additive methods, in short, assume that "identities" are separate and separable entities, that one is either *only* a woman or *only* a black. In this categorical logic of modernity/coloniality, María Lugones contends, "black woman" becomes an impossible concept.[89] Put in Spelman's words, "additive analyses" still have

---

86 Patricia H. Collins, *Black Feminist Thought: Knowledge, Consciousness, and the Politics of Empowerment* (New York: Routledge, 2000), 269.

87 See Kimberle Crenshaw's "Demarginalizing the Intersection of Race and Sex: A Black Feminist Critique of Antidiscrimination Doctrine, Feminist Theory and Antiracist Politics," *University of Chicago Legal Forum* (1989): art. 8 and "Mapping the Margins: Intersectionality, Identity Politics, and Violence against Women of Color," *Stanford Law Review* 43, no. 6 (1991): 1241–99.

88 Elizabeth V. Spelman, *Inessential Woman: Problems of Exclusion in Feminist Thought* (London: The Women's Press, 1988), 81.

89 Lugones, "Toward a Decolonial Feminism," 742.

"the effect of obscuring the racial and class identity of those described as 'women,' [and] make it hard to see how women not of a particular race and class can be included in the description."[90]

Black feminists' emphasis on individual and particular experience "fosters a fundamental paradigmatic shift [...] by] embracing a paradigm of intersecting oppression of race, class, gender, sexuality and nation."[91] It promotes a situated and contextualized truth, and consequently criticizes prevailing knowledge, representative of a universalist claim for truth. This implied universalism is often found in white, middle-class feminism, which habitually speaks for all and as if from nowhere (*ex nihilo*). Adrienne Rich calls it "white solipsism," that is, "to think, imagine, and speak as if whiteness described the world."[92]

The blindness to race relative to the formation of gender hierarchy replicates what Hélène Cixous calls "patriarchal binary thought." Cixous follows Jacques Derrida's critique of the Western metaphysical tradition to emphasize that hierarchical binary oppositions always regard the male/masculine as superior to the female/feminine and all the terms associated with it, for example, in the typical opposition between the (masculinized) Culture and (feminized) Nature.[93]

"Patriarchal binary thought" can be summed up as phallogocentrism, a combination of "logocentrism," a philosophy that privileges the *logos*, the presence in speech/truth, especially in the Western metaphysics[94] criticized by Derrida, and "phallo-

---

90 Spelman, *Inessential Woman,* 115.
91 Collins, *Black Feminist Thought,* 273.
92 Adrienne Rich, "Disloyal to Civilization: Feminism, Racism, Gynephobia," in *On Lies, Secrets, and Silence* (New York: W.W. Norton & Company Inc., 1978), 299.
93 Toril Moi, *Sexual/Textual Politics: Feminist Literary Thought,* 2nd edn. (London: Routledge, 2002), 103.
94 Gayatri Spivak points out in the "Translator's Preface" to the English translation of Jacques Derrida, *Of Grammatology* (Baltimore: Johns Hopkins University Press, 1997) that "almost by a reverse ethnocentrism, Derrida insists that logocentrism is a property of the West" (lxxxii). Zhang Longxi, *The Tao and the Logos: Literary Hermeneutics, East and West* (Durham: Duke University Press, 1992) analyses the "taocentrism" which shows a sim-

centrism," a system "that privileges the phallus as the symbol or source of power."[95] However, Hélène Cixous here seems to have forgotten that this hierarchical binarism infinitely intersects with race, or, more precisely, with racial categorization and hierarchization, an invention of Western modern "rational thought" as part of its colonial legacy. Anibal Quijano relates the coloniality of (rational) knowledge to a "fundamental presupposition" that regards "knowledge as a product of a subject-object relation."[96] Needless to say, in this paradigm of rational knowledge, the White male takes up the position of the "subject," preparing himself to conquer by appropriating, occupying, naming, or even "reinventing" the "objects." Toril Moi is right to point out, following Cixous, that the masculine value system is an "economy of the proper," meaning "property — appropriate: signaling an emphasis on self-identity, self-aggrandizement and arrogative dominance."[97] Yet one should remember that the masculine "economy of the proper" is constructive of the logic of colonialism.

If Hélène Cixous and the *écriture feminine* seek to undo this hierarchical binarism by asserting the other-than-masculine spectrum while typically ignoring the question of race, black feminists have theorized the intersectionality of gender and race as a more radical criticism of the system of domination through an emphasis based on experience, "defin[ing] our own realities *on our own terms*."[98] If "being Black is a source of pride, as well as an occasion for being oppressed,"[99] blackness or femininity for that matter should not be understood only in terms of oppression. The additive method of analysis that adds "blackness"

---

ilar preoccupation/suspicion of written language in the Chinese tradition, similar to Derrida's analysis of Western metaphysics, through a comparison of *tao* and *logos*. He argues that both *tao* in Chinese and *logos* in Greek mean "truth" and "speech" at once.

95 Moi, *Sexual/Textual Politics*, 191n5.

96 Quijano, "Coloniality and Modernity/Rationality," 172.

97 Moi, *Sexual/Textual Politics*, 109.

98 Collins, *Black Feminist Thought*, 274.

99 Spelman, *Inessential Woman*, 124.

or "color" as a form of further, *additional* burden to the universalist "all women" who are said to be already oppressed by the "patriarchal binary opposition," operates on a strong conviction of those identities' separability.

What is more, the additive method conceals "racism pure and simple"[100] by assuming that "there is nothing positive about having a Black history and identity," as if the elimination of "blackness" also eliminated the "extra burden" for black women. At the same time, both the additive method and the color-blind *écriture féminine* have not only generalized the issue of "patriarchy," which decolonial feminists and feminists of color have shown to be a historico-culturally specific concept universally projected,[101] but they have also overlooked the historical contingency of what is accounted for or accountable as "woman." We will see, through the two ancient cases this book studies, that both cosmologies belie the "additive method," particularly in the case of Nahua cosmology and its writing/painting system *tlacuilolli,* discussed in Part II.

We should not forget that historically black women were violently thrown out of the category of "woman" by European scientists. Sarah Baartman, the South African Khoikhoi woman brought to be exhibited in London in 1810 and some years later, in 1814, sold to Réaux, a businessman who was involved in animal trade with the Musée National d'Histoire Naturelle in Paris. Against her will, she was closely examined, especially her supposedly "abnormal" genitalia, after her death by the professors of the museum, Henri de Lainville and Georges Cuvier. Cuvier published an article, "Extraits d'observations faites sur le cadavre d'une femme connue à Paris et à Londres sous le nom de Vénus Hottentot" (1817), asserting his thesis that Sarah Baartman represents "a living missing link connecting animals and humankind."[102] This abhorrently racist "scientific truth," in the

---

100 Ibid.

101 I shall draw on the decolonial feminist critique of the first issue of the complicity between gender and colonialism later.

102 Clifton Crais and Pamela Scully, *Sara Baartman and the Hottentot Venus: A Ghost Story and a Biography* (Princeton: Princeton University Press, 2009),

form of a plaster cast of Baartman's body parts, continued to be shown in the Musée de l'Homme in Paris until 1976. It was only in 2002 that her bodily remains, stored in the museum, were returned and buried in South Africa. The case of Sarah Baartman "has become synonymous with the pain and sufferings of a black woman of a colonized people" and "a prime example of the creation of the 'Other.'"[103]

Monique Wittig, in "One Is Not Born a Woman" provocatively claims that a lesbian is not and cannot be a woman, and that "a lesbian has to be something else, a not-woman, a not-man, a product of society, not a product of nature." She further argues that "women are a class [… and] the category 'woman' as well as the category 'man' are political and economic categories not eternal ones."[104] Wittig questions not only the "gendered" aspect of "woman," but also the supposedly unquestionable biological predisposition of the category: "[I]t is civilization as a whole that produces this creature [i.e., the human female], intermediate between male and eunuch, which is described as feminine."[105] She rejects the kind of feminist theorization which is based on biological explanation, "since it assumes that the basis of society or the beginning of society lies in heterosexuality."[106] Furthermore, she correlates the category of "sex" and the category of "race." Following Colette Guillaumin, who shows that "race" was a concept directly linked to "the socioeconomic reality of black slavery" before which it did not exist, Wittig argues that "sex," like "race," is later "taken as an 'immediate given' […] 'physical features', belonging to a natural order."[107] This brings us back to the case of Sarah Baartman. It is not difficult to discern the complicity between scientific knowledge production in the West

---

154.

103 Ibid., 155.

104 Monique Wittig, "One Is Not Born a Woman (1981)," in *The Straight Mind and Other Essays* (Boston: Beacon Press, 1992), 9–20, at 13.

105 Ibid., 10.

106 Ibid.

107 Ibid., 11.

and its global colonial/capitalist interests through the regulation of heteronormative gendering.

Similar to Wittig's critique of the binary division of the human population — be it along gender or sex lines — into male and female, Judith Butler, in her groundbreaking work *Gender Trouble,* attacks the heteronormative assumption that sustains such a division. Butler argues that given the historicity of sex, that is to say, the understanding that this supposedly immutable, anatomic, and natural "given" is not always the same, but changes over time and across different geographies, we must ask if "the ostensibly natural facts of sex discursively produced by various scientific discourses [are] in the service of other political and social interests."[108] The answer is a definite "yes," and the most direct of those "political and social interests" is heteronormativity, or as Wittig ironically puts it, "when thought by the straight mind, homosexuality is nothing but heterosexuality."[109] In the preface to the reprint of *Gender Trouble* from 1999, Butler recounts her reasons for writing the book back in the 1980s, namely "to criticize a pervasive heterosexual assumption in feminist literary theory."[110] She reads this heterosexual assumption, or what she terms "heterosexual matrix," as a discursive or epistemic hegemony through which bodies, genders, and desires are dualistically, oppositionally, and hierarchically naturalized into male/masculine/man and female/feminine/woman.

Butler also criticizes the "radical disjunction" between heterosexuality and homosexuality inherent in Wittig's account, which is based on the problematic assumption of a "systematic integrity of heterosexuality," as it "replicates the kind of disjunctive binarism that she herself characterizes as the divisive philosophical gesture of the straight mind."[111] We should add here that this is not only a gesture of the "straight mind" or heteronormativity, but also that of modern/colonial categorical logic. Butler

---

108 Butler, *Gender Trouble,* 10.
109 Monique Wittig, "The Straight Mind," in *The Straight Mind and Other Essays* (Boston: Beacon Press, 1980), 21–32, at 28.
110 Butler, *Gender Trouble,* vii.
111 Ibid., 154–55.

further complicates the critique of heteronormativity by pointing out the contingent psychic boundaries between seemingly
coherent groupings, and proposes we understand heterosexuality as "both a compulsory system and an intrinsic comedy, a constant parody of itself, as an alternative gay/lesbian perspective."[112]

Butler and Wittig criticize the gender/sex division primarily
from the point of view of a concern for sexuality, which has been
overlooked or simply presumed to be heterosexual. They like-
wise have shown that sexuality is intrinsically linked to how we
understand sex, which itself is already a gendered category. In
her influential "Thinking Sex: Notes for a Radical Theory of the
Politics of Sexuality," published in 1984, Gayle Rubin demon-
strates the complex social reality of sexuality, especially when it
is considered to be "perverse," for example, such as lesbian sad-
omasochism, gay leather fetishism, and pornography. Though
sharing similar concerns as Wittig and Butler with sexuality,
Rubin proposes to establish an autonomous field that studies
sexuality "against the grain of much contemporary feminist
thought, which treats sexuality as a derivation of gender."[113] She
argues that "feminist conceptual tools [which] were developed
to detect and analyze gender-based hierarchies [... become] irrelevant and often misleading [... for assessing] critical power
relations in the area of sexuality."[114]

This call for independent research on sexuality, however,
has been misread as a call for the repudiation of gender and
the separation of feminism from the field of lesbian/gay studies, who "restrict the proper object of feminism to gender, and
[...] appropriate sexuality as the proper object of [lesbian/
gay studies]."[115] Judith Butler criticizes lesbian/gay studies' de-
contextualization of Gayle Rubin's article. She also warns that

---

112 Ibid., 155.
113 Gayle Rubin, "Thinking Sex: Notes for a Radical Theory of the Politics of
     Sexuality," in *Pleasure and Danger: Exploring Female Sexuality,* ed. Carole S.
     Vance (Boston: Routledge & Kegan Paul, 1984), 276–319, at 308.
114 Ibid., 309.
115 Judith Butler, "Against Proper Objects: Introduction," *differences: A Journal
     of Feminist Cultural Studies* 6, nos. 2–3 (1994): 1–26, at 8.

lesbian/gay studies should not ignore the important contribution of feminist scholarship on sexuality by reducing feminist theorizations to gender only. We should also not overlook the diversity of debates and voices within feminism, notably feminists of color who theorize the intersection of gender and race; working-class feminists who think class and gender together; or continental European feminist studies of "sexual difference" as irreducible "neither to a biological difference nor to a sociological notion of gender."[116]

0.2.1.2 *Localizing and Decolonializing Gender*
If Gayle Rubin opens a way of thinking beyond the concept of gender, while at the same time preserving its validity within Anglo-American feminism, other groups of feminists tend to question the very usefulness of gender as an analytical term for their locally embedded experiences. For example, some continental European feminists of "sexual difference" reject the usefulness of gender in the linguistic context of Romance languages. Decolonial feminists writing from the experiences of colonized cultures, notably in Africa and the Americas, argue that the imposition of the (heteronormative) gender system is constitutive of modern colonialism. These theorizations emphasize the coloniality of gender and see heteronormative gendering as a modern/colonial design imposed on colonized cultures.

Écriture féminine pays special attention to the role played by language, the semiotic and symbolic aspects that structure sexual differences. Allied with the French feminists' emphasis on sexual differences, Toril Moi criticizes the opposition of "gender" to "sex," which, for her, results in "women [being] divorced from their bodies, and […] 'woman' [being] turned into a discursive and performative effect."[117] She is especially critical of the performative account of "gender" proposed by Judith Butler and believes that avoiding essentialism should not lead to claiming "that there are no women, or that the category 'woman'

---

116 Ibid., 16.
117 Moi, *Sexual/Textual Politics*, 178.

in itself is ideologically suspect."[118] Moi unjustly accuses Butler's critique of the heterosexual assumption sustaining feminism, which is reflected in the question of "woman," of discarding or suspending "woman." In this sense, Moi treats "woman" as an ahistorical concept exempted from cultural differences and the workings of race and sexuality. She clearly does not agree that "the creation of 'women' as a category was one of the very first accomplishments of the colonial state" in post-colonial Africa.[119] She would not appreciate either what Wittig calls "our first task [as radical lesbian feminists, which] is to always thoroughly dissociate 'women' (the class within which we fight) and 'woman', the myth."[120] We see another example of "the historical and the theoretico-practical exclusion of nonwhite [and non-heterosexual] women from liberatory struggles in the name of women."[121]

Rosi Braidotti takes distance from the concept of "gender" as a useful concept mainly out of two concerns. First, "as a vicissitude of the English language, [...gender] bears little or no relevance to theoretical traditions in the Romance languages" like French, Spanish, or Italian. Second, adopting "gender studies" instead of "feminist studies" or "women's studies" in universities "has resulted in a shift of focus away from the feminist agenda toward a more generalized attention to the social construction of differences *between* the sexes," which broadens but also narrows down the political agenda, to the extent that "gender studies" promote the illusion of symmetry between the sexes whose difference should be regarded "as a powerful factor of dissymmetry."[122] Braidotti argues that "this binary way of thinking is in keeping with Beauvoir's Cartesian assumptions, which

---

118 Ibid.
119 Oyèrónké Oyèwùmí, *The Invention of Women: Making an African Sense of Western Gender Discourses* (Minneapolis: University of Minnesota Press, 1997), 124.
120 Wittig, "One Is Not Born a Woman (1981)," 15.
121 Lugones, "Heterosexualism and the Colonial/Modern Gender System," 188–89.
122 Rosi Braidotti, *Nomadic Subjects: Embodiment and Sexual Difference in Contemporary Feminist Theory* (New York: Columbia University Press, 1994), 151.

lead her to separate mind from body and build the gender/sex distinction on a binary foundation."[123]

María Lugones follows those who have become known as "decolonial feminists," suggesting that gender is inseparable from coloniality and needs to be engaged critically. First, she counterintuitively points out that the colonial answer to Sojourner Truth's question "ain't I a woman?" is an emphatic "no," because "the semantic consequence of the coloniality of gender is that 'colonized woman' is an empty category: no women are colonized; no colonized females are women."[124] She draws this conclusion from a close reading of the categorical logic of modernity and argues, "if *woman* and *black* are terms for homogenous atomic and separable categories, then their intersection shows us the absence of black women rather than their presence."[125]

Lugones advocates a radical reading of the modern categorization of gender/sex alongside the distinction of human/non-human and heteronormativity. She emphasizes that "turning the colonized into human beings was not a colonial goal," and that attaining gendering would be a way of transforming from non-human to human. As a consequence, "sex was made to stand alone in the characterization [i.e., bestialization] of the colonized."[126] Without rejecting "gender" as a relevant concept, Lugones cautions against its blind application without an acknowledgment that imposing a hierarchical gender dichotomy is part of the colonial project of subjugating and dehumanizing the colonized. She suggests that we should carefully use "the terms *woman* and *man* and bracket them when necessary."[127] In her excellent account of the way gendered identities customarily assumed to be universal were formed through European colo-

---

123 Ibid., 262.

124 Lugones, "Toward a Decolonial Feminism," 745. Lugones here refers to Sojourner Truth's question, "Ar'n't I a woman?" which we encountered earlier and will discuss further below.

125 Ibid., 742.

126 Ibid., 743–44.

127 Ibid., 749.

nization in Yorùbáland, Oyèrónké Oyèwùmí contends that "in precolonial Yorùbá society, body-type was not the basis of social hierarchy […] there were no *women* — defined in strictly gendered terms — in that society."[128]

Besides analyzing colonial formation and the imposition of Western gender binaries, decolonial feminisms engage with the resisting strategies of the colonized, whose proper cosmologies and ways of organizing the world, including human "genders" incompatible with the modern man/woman dichotomy, have survived and been woven into an oppression-resistant relationship with modernity/coloniality. This active engagement with resistance, "the tension between subjectification (the forming/ informing of the subject) and active subjectivity" is to be understood as a process of

> adaptation, rejection, adoption, ignoring, and integrating [which] are never just modes of isolation of resistance as they are always performed by an active subject thickly constructed by inhabiting the colonial difference with a fractured locus [… and] the multiplicity in the fracture of the locus [is] both the enactment of the coloniality of gender and the resistant response from a subaltern sense of self, of the social, of the self-in-relation, of the cosmos, all grounded in a peopled memory.[129]

In a broader sense, colonial modern history, for those whom Silvia Rivera Cusicanqui calls "oppressed but not defeated," is "simultaneously an arena of resistance and conflict, a site for the development of sweeping counter-hegemonic strategies, and a space for the creation of new indigenous languages and projects of modernity."[130] The point of decolonial feminism is neither suggesting to go back to a precolonial, "original" system of embodi-

---

128 Oyèwùmí, *The Invention of Women,* xii–xiii.
129 Lugones, "Toward a Decolonial Feminism," 753–54.
130 Silvia Rivera Cusicanqui, "Ch'ixinakax Utxiwa: A Reflection on the Practices and Discourses of Decolonization," *South Atlantic Quarterly* 111, no. 1 (2012): 95–109, at 95.

ment, nor proposing a generalizable remedy or another univer-
salized truth. It urges us first and foremost to unlearn modern/
colonial categories with which we operate seemingly inevitably
by *learning to learn* from the diverse experiences of resistance
(as sites of continuous repression), which rely on cosmologies
and gender systems that do not always presume the universal
validity of "binary opposition," "hierarchical categorization,"
"sexual difference found in language," or "patriarchy."[131] The importance of the postmodern and postcolonial critique of "origin" notwithstanding, it is extremely problematic and dubious
when any attempts to look at the "precolonial" are deemed to be
an impossible task, or worse, a nativist nostalgia. In other words,
Judith Butler's caution of the "feminist recourse to an imaginary
past [… in order] not to promote a politically problematic rei-
fication of women's experience in the course of debunking the
self-reifying claims of masculinist power"[132] needs a decolonial
twist through which the seemingly self-evident notions of "feminist," "women," and "masculinist" need to be qualified within
the realm of modern/colonial West and perhaps its aftermath.

0.2.2 Against Proper Objects and Against Coercive Mimeticism
The "pluralist turn" in critical theory, acknowledging localized,
gendered, racialized, culturally specific differences, has been
a great achievement in the humanities. However, these posi-
tionings, both from within and without different "identitarian
groups," run the risk of becoming part of a property economy.
This risk involves at least two issues, that of insisting on the
"proper objects of study," in Judith Butler's words, and that of
ghettoizing the "ethnic" enunciation in the form of "coercive

---

131 See Oyèwùmí, *The Invention of Women*; Cecelia F. Klein, "None of the
   Above: Gender Ambiguity in Nahua Ideology," in *Gender in Pre-Hispanic
   America: A Symposium at Dumbarton Oaks,* ed. Cecelia F. Klein (Washington, DC: Dumbarton Oaks, 2001), 183–254; Pete Sigal, "Latin America and
   the Challenge of Globalizing the History of Sexuality," *American Historical
   Review* 114 (2009): 1340–53.
132 Butler, *Gender Trouble,* 48.

mimeticism," to use Rey Chow's term.[133] In the first case, it suggests a cultural relativism that works discreetly, with essentialism requiring, for example, that in order to be a genuine feminist, one has to be a lesbian or that one has to be "of color" in order to speak about the issue of race. This kind of theoretical position perpetuates the police system of discipline and punishment. What is more, it suggests that whatever a supposedly "minority" or "ethnic" group theorizes is only valid within that identity group, while those who habitually speak for all retain the right and ability to be universally applicable.

The debates over gender from different standpoints within feminism and gender studies have invaluably complicated our understanding of the issue. However, problematic receptions of these different positions, particularly those "other positions," are also prevalent. Going back to the case of Sojourner Truth, "Ar'n't I a woman?" would make a 20th-century reader experience *déjà vu*. Speaking at the women's convention in Ohio in 1851, Sojourner Truth asks the audience to question their assumptions about women:

That man over there says that women need to be helped into carriages, and lifted over ditches, and to have the best place everywhere. Nobody ever helps me into carriages, or over mud-puddles, or gives me any best place! And ain't I a woman? Look at me! Look at my arm! I have ploughed and planted, and gathered into barns, and no man could head me! And ain't I a woman? I could work as much and eat as much as a man — when I could get it — and bear the lash as well! And ain't I a woman? I have borne thirteen children, and seen most all sold off to slavery, and when I cried out with my mother's grief, none but Jesus heard me! And ain't I a woman?[134]

---

133 Butler, "Against Proper Objects"; Rey Chow, *The Protestant Ethnic and the Spirit of Capitalism* (New York: Columbia University Press, 2002).

134 Sojourner Truth, "Ain't I a Woman?" speech delivered in December 1851 at the Women's Convention, Akron, Ohio. See "Sojourner Truth: 'Ain't I a

In a nutshell, it sums up the social construction theory of gender said to have begun only during the "second wave" feminism of the 1960s. For example, in her classical introduction to feminist theories, Rosemarie Tong introduces the sex/gender system under the rubric of radical-libertarian feminism, quoting from Herster Eisenstein's *Contemporary Feminist Thought* (1983):

> [R]adical-libertarian feminists rejected patriarchal society's assumption there is a necessary connection between one's sex (male or female) and one's gender (masculine or feminine) [...] they claimed that gender is separable from sex and that patriarchal society uses rigid gender roles to keep women passive [...] and men active.[135]

Truth's compelling questioning is often read as a black feminist's contestation of the colorblind fake sisterhood of white feminists. As such, it has been interpreted consistently as "Ar'n't I *also* a woman?" Her statement is very sharp in terms of its denunciation of the gender/sex fallacy, "exposing a concept [e.g. "woman"] as ideological or culturally constructed rather than as natural or a simple reflection of reality."[136]

Despite this, Truth has almost always been read as part of the negotiation or critique of white feminists' blindness towards black women in the suffrage and abolition movement. Tong introduces Sojourner Truth in the rubric of the suffrage and abolition movement and affirms at the outset that "working-class white women and black women did contribute to the 19th-century women's rights movement,"[137] against a common idea that 19th-century suffragists were a white middle-class-women-only movement. However, Tong automatically racializes Truth's

---

Woman?' December 1851," *Modern History Sourcebook*. https://sourcebooks. fordham.edu/halsall/mod/sojtruth-woman.asp

135 Rosemarie Tong, *Feminist Thought: A More Comprehensive Introduction*, 3rd edn. (Boulder: Westview Press, 2009), 51.

136 Collins, *Black Feminist Thought*, 15.

137 Tong, *Feminist Thought*, 22.

statement by visualizing and focalizing on Truth's skin color in her problematic representation of the event:

> Demanding the audience look at her black body, Sojourner Truth proclaimed that her "womanhood," her "female nature," had never prevented her from working, acting, and yes, speaking like a man.[138]

Truth asks, "look at me!" She didn't say, "look at me, who is black!" Nor did she say "as a black woman." The fictive account of the event in which Truth demands the scrutiny of her "black body" perpetuates a colonial gaze obsessed with the "skin color," as well as a racist idea that equates black femininity with a different female nature that needs to be contained in scare quotes.

Nell Painter, who has written a biography of Sojourner Truth (1994), has shown the extremely problematic reception history of Truth, in which her own words and photographic portraits were often "shadowed" (a word used by Truth herself). Harriet Beecher Stowe, for example, wrote a biography entitled *Libyan Sibyl* (1863) in which Truth is portrayed as embodying the "fervor of Ethiopia, wild, savage, hunted of all nations but burning after God in her tropic heart."[139] Truth's representation of herself as a middle-class, educated woman with eyeglasses who "does not look as though she would speak in dialect"[140] in her photographic portrait utterly contrasts the "fictive, hybrid cameo of [...] an angry Sojourner Truth, who snarls, 'And ain't I a woman?' then defiantly exhibits her breast."[141]

This unfortunate reading of Truth is not an isolated case. Her words are continuously viewed as having "commented ironi-

---

138 Ibid., emphasis mine.
139 Stowe quoted in Painter, "Sojourner Truth in Life and Memory," 9.
140 The then presiding officer of the Women's Rights Convention Frances Dane Gage rewrote Sojourner Truth's speech fully in dialect. To compare the different versions of the speech, see "Compare the Two Speeches," *The Sojourner Truth Project,* https://www.thesojournertruthproject.com/compare-the-speeches/.
141 Painter, "Sojourner Truth in Life and Memory," 464.

cally, and pointedly, on the failed sisterhood that sought to silence her within and exclude her from the very movement that women like her inspired, enabled, and initiated."[142] Certainly, as an abolitionist activist and feminist, her political agenda is indeed intersectionally conscious, embracing the complexity of race, class, and gender (as well as religion). She opens her speech by stating "I think that 'twixt the negroes of the South and the women at the North, all talking about rights," and later she asks, "What's that got to do with women's rights or negroes' rights?"[143] However, she is not being "intersectional" here in her critique: "Intersectionality is important when showing the failures of institutions to include discrimination or oppression against women of color."[144] The demand that Sojourner Truth speaks of black woman (only) shows what "intersectional analysis" often goes wrong: that of demanding people of color and them only to account for intersectionality.[145] It is striking to notice that throughout reception history, Sojourner Truth has been primarily presented as a black woman who *only* speaks (or *can only* speak) in terms of her *blackness,* not because her recorded speech has directly addressed the question of race, but because her blackness automatically prevents (white) audiences (those in the conventions where she spoke and those who read and represented her afterwards) from allowing her to be heard as speaking about "the women issue," and therefore claiming the universalist position of white feminists. Consequently, her contribution to the contestation of gender essentialism "in general" is denied.

---

142 Ann Ducille, "On Canons: Anxious History and the Rise of Black Feminist Literary Studies," in *The Cambridge Companion to Feminist Literary Theory,* ed. Ellen Rooney (Cambridge: Cambridge University Press, 2006), 29–52, at 37.
143 "Sojourner Truth: 'Ain't I a Woman?' December 1851."
144 Lugones, "Toward a Decolonial Feminism," 757–58n9.
145 For an astute critique of intersectionality, see Jasbir K. Puar, "'I Would Rather Be a Cyborg than a Goddess': Intersectionality, Assemblage, and Affective Politics," *Transversal Texts by* EIPCP — *European Institute for Progressive Cultural Policies,* January 2011, http://eipcp.net/transversal/0811/puar/en/.

It is interesting to recall here an anecdote from a feminist conference that took place a century later, in the 1980s, as Michael Kimmel retells it. The story goes that a black woman responded to a white woman who "asserted that the fact that they [the black woman and the white woman] were both women bonded them." She points out that in the morning, looking in the mirror, instead of seeing "a woman" as her white interlocutor reportedly did, "I see a *black* woman. To me, race is visible every day, because race is how I am not privileged in our culture. Race is invisible to you, because it's how you are privileged."[146] The readings of "Ar'n't I a woman?" that change it to "Ain't I *also* a woman,"[147] resonate with this anecdote in the sense that Sojourner Truth, or any other woman of color, or lesbian/queer woman, or disabled woman, or working-class woman, or any one with an "extra," can be seen in the mirror/eyes of others only in terms of their differences. Whatever they may have to say can only be read through the lens of these identities, which are socially constructed, historically contingent, and ultimately abstractions.

I find it useful to further examine the reception history of Sojourner Truth through the concept of "coercive mimeticism" as theorized by Rey Chow, a kind of mimeticism in which "the original that is supposed to be replicated is no longer the white man or his culture but rather an image [of the ethnic subject]."[148] This mimeticism is different from the imperialist and imperative one that urges the colonized to be judged against or to imitate the white man, even though they will never reach the standard, or, as Homi Bhabha argues, to be "almost the same but not quite."[149] Chow criticizes Bhabha and cultural theorists alike for

---

146 Michael Kimmel, "Toward a Pedagogy of the Oppressor," *Tikkun* 17, no. 6 (2002): 42.
147 Nell I. Painter, "Representing Truth: Sojourner Truth's Knowing and Becoming Known," *The Journal of American History* 81, no. 2 (1994): 461–92, at 464, points out that the phrase "Ar'n't I a woman" "is sometimes rendered more authentically Negro as 'Ain't I a woman?'"
148 Chow, *The Protestant Ethnic and the Spirit of Capitalism*, 107.
149 Bhabha, *The Location of Culture*, 86.

having neglected the fact that "the ethnic person is expected to come to resemble what is recognizably ethnic [...] 'Asianness,' 'Africanness,' 'Arabness,' and other similar kinds of [stereotyped] nativenesses" and that this expectation is what "coercive mimeticism" denotes:

> [A] process (identitarian, existential, cultural, or textual) in which those who are marginal to mainstream Western culture are expected [...] to resemble and replicate the very banal preconceptions that have been appended to them, a process in which they are expected to objectify themselves in accordance with the already seen and thus to authenticate the familiar imaginings of them as ethnics.[150]

Truth's case, if I may conclude with Chow's words, is that "ethnic subjects and texts, even when they are not necessarily speaking about their so-called ethnic difference per se, are habitually solicited in this manner by the public in the West and the world at large."[151] The predominant readings of Sojourner Truth are distorted in a way that places her "natively" in her place as the black feminist and simultaneously excludes her contribution from speaking to the woman question "in general," which can only be enunciated from the position of the white, straight, able-bodied, middle-class woman, even when it is a critique of that universalist positioning.[152]

In the conclusion of her article "Against Proper Objects," Judith Butler proposes a "queer strategy" that I find useful to emphasize, because it exposes all the different perspectives and positions on the question of "gender(ing)" that seem too overwhelming and almost cacophonic. She argues that

---

150 Chow, *The Protestant Ethnic and the Spirit of Capitalism,* 107.
151 Ibid., 116.
152 For example, is it possible to allege Sojourner Truth's (universal) question on the stereotype of women to be universalist? Or is it possible to read "one is not born a woman" as speaking about White women only?

it is that complexity and complicity that call to be thought most urgently, which means thinking against the institutional separatisms which work effectively to keep thought narrow, sectarian, and self-serving [...], resisting the institutional domestication of queer thinking.[153]

Feminists of color have long shown that identities produced intersectionally exceed modern categorical logic, which "organizes the world ontologically in terms of atomic, homogenous, separable categories."[154] Nurturing ways of thinking that embrace transversal and pluriversal queer non-fixities would provide us a way out of the theo-political, monotheistic *creatio ex nihilo*. Monotheism, universalism, fixity, truth all seem to depart from a conviction summarized by Keller as "truth is either One, or None,"[155] a capitalized Truth miraculously exempted from any contamination of history, location, perspective, language, gender, race, class, ability, sexuality, and so on.

Rejecting *one* ultimate truth in a linear logic of progression is linked to a so-called postmodern nihilism as a negative response to modernity. Despite the fact that such an accusation is helplessly conservative, it is also extremely ethnocentric (again), because so-called "nihilism" is to be found in Buddhism, Daoism, Nahua philosophy, Zapatista political theory, Judaic Midrash hermeneutics, or even the Bible, especially the Elohist Genesis. The position of rejecting pluriversality as postmodern nihilism is Eurocentric in the sense that it assumes the epistemic zero point along a linear logic, in which the West is the only conceivable center of legitimate knowledge and its critique. That is to say, even as a critique and despite the existence of previous or parallel non-Western philosophies with similar concerns and arguments, Europe still believes itself to have created those similar pronouncements as if out of nothingness. The continuity of the

---

153 Butler, "Against Proper Objects," 16.
154 Lugones, "Toward a Decolonial Feminism," 742.
155 Keller, *Face of the Deep,* 39.

theo-political doctrine of *creatio ex nihilo* in its colonial guise works especially well in the realm of knowledge production.

0.2.3 Decolonizing Gender(ing)
or Advancing the Decolonial with the Queer

Engaging the queer strategy of constantly bringing down conventional boundaries and the decolonial insistence on pluriversal truths (rather than truth in the singular as an abstract universalism), this section will deal with the issue of gender/sex to the specific contexts this book has set out to examine. First, I ask what we mean by the "historicity of sex." Then I proceed to ask how thinking about gender might influence or change our interpretations of the two myths and, above all, their modern/colonial reception.

First let us go back to the feminist debates on the gender/sex system and focus on the historicity of sex and gender in the context of Western culture. Historians have shown that "female" was not always understood as being in ontological opposition to "male" throughout Western history. Indeed, as Thomas Laqueur famously argues, from ancient Greece to the 18th century, sex was understood through the "one sex model," in which the male body was considered to be the norm while the female body was seen as the less-male, the inversion or deformation.[156] That is to say, for a long time "woman didn't exist," to paraphrase Jacques Lacan.

In her 1993 article "The Five Sexes: Why Male and Female Are Not Enough," feminist biologist Ann Fausto-Sterling asks a similar question to the one posed by Michel Foucault in his discussion of "the true sex."[157] She shows the existence of bodies that cannot be reduced to male or female and further points out that "hermaphrodites," or "intersex" people as they are usually called, can be divided further into at least three different

---

156 Laqueur, *Making Sex*.
157 Michel Foucault, "Le vrai sexe," in *Dits et écrits IV, 1980–1988* (Paris: Gallimard, 1994), texte no. 287.

groups.[158] As she observes, medical interventions that claim to "correct" the intersex bodies to fit into the rigid binary male/ female are very common, which is also the reason why intersex bodies are largely unknown to normative society. She relates this coercive disciplining of "unruly" bodies to "a cultural need to maintain clear distinctions between the sexes, […] the great divide [… and also because] they raise the specter of homosexuality."[159]

Fausto-Sterling's research brings together gender and sexuality into a mutually constructive relation underwritten by the "straight mind" (Wittig) or the "heterosexual matrix" (Butler) underlying the coercive separation of the human population into *only* two sexes, male and female. That is to say, the human body is not "naturally" divided into two sexes, rather, it is the imperative of gender roles coerced through heterosexist hegemony that regulates our understanding of it, at least from the 18th century onwards in the Western context.

The above-cited studies are primarily concerned with the understanding of sex/gender/sexuality in modern Western society. It is reasonable to suspect that in the two ancient cultures studied in this book, Babylonian and Nahua, sex/gender was understood in very different ways. Once one looks carefully into the myths, the common division of deities into either god or goddess seems too simplistic, to say the least.

In Part I, we witnessed the ambiguous and ever-changing genders of the primordial waters and their divine personifications through the *deep* history of the region. In the Sumerian myth of *Enki and Ninmah* (ancestral to the Babylonian *Enuma Elish*), Nammu, the primordial *mother* personifies the *abzu,* where human beings are said to be first formed. While Nammu, originally a facet of the primordial water Apsu, "reappears" later in *Enuma Elish* and becomes Tiamat, Apsu (now Tiamat's "husband") retains its semantic connection to the primordial sea as the fresh-water ocean and the watery womb-like birth place of

---

158 Fausto-Sterling, "The Five Sexes."
159 Ibid., 24.

Marduk, the rival god who later kills Tiamat, who in that very battle resumes the masculine gender. The rigidly gendered deities — Apsu/god/husband and Tiamat/goddess/wife — only appear in the modern/colonial reception of the myth. Their extremely fluid and "confusing" ways that queerly commingle inside the epic and throughout history, while at the same time easily separating and merging with clearly demarcated "identities" in the cosmic battles, are enough to defy modern/colonial categorization and even questions like, "who *is* Apsu and what is 'his' gender?"

In Part II, we will explore the creation myths of the Nahuas in Central America. We will investigate the "strange case of Tlaltecuhtli." Often translated as "goddess of the earth," Tlaltecuhtli in fact literally means "*lord* of the earth" in Nahuatl, as *tlal(li)* means "earth" and *tecuhtli* "lord." The mother-of-all, Coatlicue, from a sheer grammatical point of view, has no gender, since Nahuatl does not have grammatical gender for nouns. Coatlicue is often translated as "*she* who has the serpent skirt" or "snakes-her-skirt."[160] Although some argue that the Nahua "gender system" uses sartorial differences to indicate differences of gender/sex, suggesting that, in this case, *cueitl* "skirt" might refer to femaleness,[161] the complexity (or, in fact, the simplicity) of its Nahua enunciation is lost (or silenced) in translations that rigidly gender "it" as "she." The issue becomes even clearer when we introduce Coatlicue Mayor, believed to be an artistic representation of Coatlicue, which does not convey exclusive association with the feminine. While Coatlicue, a genderless word, is feminized, Tlaltecuhtli, a clearly marked masculine title of the earth deity that appears on the underside of Coatlicue Mayor, is also feminized to fit into the imaginary of a "universal archetype" of the earth as the *vagina dentata.*

---

160 E.g., Cecelia F. Klein, "A New Interpretation of the Aztec Statue Called Coatlicue," *Ethnohistory* 55, no. 2 (April 2008): 229–50.

161 Pete Sigal, "Imagining Cihuacoatl: Masculine Rituals, Nahua Goddesses and the Texts of the Tlacuilos," *Gender & History* 22, no. 3 (2010): 538–63, at 549.

It is not surprising to notice a similar colonial logic in the two creation myths under consideration. Marduk is said to have created the world, despite generations of gods being born to Tiamat and Apsu, the drama of Apsu's murder, the revolt of Tiamat, and all the battles that ensue. Although the *Enuma Elish* account does not deliberately neglect the role that Tiamat (now reduced to pure, primordial chaos) plays in the creation credited to Marduk, it nevertheless makes an effort to erase the importance of that which did exist before Marduk's creation, so much so that it becomes chaos-*qua-nihil. Creatio ex nihilo* is deliberately conflated with *creatio ex materia.*

In the Nahua creation myth, we can find two similar accounts that resemble *creatio ex nihilo* or the attempt to do so. One is the creation of the world by the "brother-gods" Quetzalcoatl and Tezcatlipoca by killing the so-called "goddess"[162] Tlaltecuhtli, who dwells in the primordial ocean after the end of the fourth cosmic era.[163] The other one is the creation of the universe by Huitzilopochtli, the patron god of the Aztecs, who has guided them to the promised land of Tenochtitlan, a place already inhabited by various indigenous tribes. Huitzilopochtli is the one credited with having created the universe by killing his sister Coyolxauhqui, whose head becomes the moon and whose allies become the "four hundred southern stars." While this does not qualify as *creatio ex nihilo,* similar to Marduk's "creation," the worlds that existed before or parallel to their "creations" do not seem to matter.

Besides the strategy of complete erasure, i.e., reduction to nothingness, the reduction of the conquered world to a feminized *materia* allegedly void of meaning, a *terra nullius* without inhabitants, is also a common tactic. It is the cosmic womb, the

---

162 In Chapter 3 I will contest the association of Tlaltecuhtli with "goddess," a "strange issue" in scholarship that seems to ignore the semantic meaning of the Nahua name Tlaltecuhtli, the literal meaning of which is "Earth Lord" (*tlal,* earth; *tecuhtli,* lord). For the moment, I will use scare quotes to remind the reader to dissociate Tlaltecuhtli from "goddess of the earth."

163 Alfonso Caso, *El pueblo del sol* (México D.F.: Fondo de Cultura Económica, 1994).

penetrable void of the feminine body from a heteronormative and sexist imagery. Not surprisingly, read in the light of contemporary critical, especially feminist theories, the creation myths become typical phallocentrisms, with the familiar scenario of a masculine/colonial power penetrating the feminine/colonized space. When analyzing the conflated colonial and masculine control of the feminized/colonized bodies/spaces, I find it more useful to problematize the clear-cut dichotomy between the colonial/masculine and colonized/feminine.

While we need to retain the useful arguments that critiques of phallocentrism and modern colonialism have to offer, we should also read the non-modern cosmologies and complexities from which these creation myths have emerged as being in tension with their modern/colonial receptions which have inevitably simplified and essentialized the "genders" of these mythical beings.

Is the critique of phallocentric violence penetrating the feminine "body" really useful or even relevant in the case of the Nahua creation myth about the killing of the "goddess" Tlaltecuthli by the "brothers" Quetzalcoatl and Tezcatlipoca, when we acknowledge the gender complementarity of Nahua cosmology, but also, more strikingly, when we know that Tlatecuhtli is the lord (*tecuhtli*) of the earth (*tlal*) and that both Quetzalcoatl and Tezcatlipoca have rather ambiguous genders — to the extent that Tezcatlipoca has even been called an effeminate faggot (or *puto* in Spanish) by the Franciscan friar Sahagún?[164]

Will a critique that assumes the ontological separability of the gendered "rivals," the masculine hero and the feminine monster (or victim, depending on where one stands), be too reductive and restrictive once we read *Enuma Elish* closely, and realize that Marduk, who kills Tiamat, the once benevolent "mother" (so that the "monster" rendering of Tiamat can at best be a "monstrification"), was never been born out of her omnipresent "stomach?" Tiamat's stomach, the pervasive watery space, min-

---

164 Pete Sigal, "Queer Nahuatl: Sahagún's Faggots and Sodomites, Lesbians and Hermaphrodites," *Ethnohistory* 54, no. 1 (2007): 9–34.

gles with another personified and masculinized watery space/ deity, Apsu, her "husband," killed earlier by Marduk's father Ea, but remains as an "unanimated" watery dwelling inside which Marduk is said to have been born.

Although it is extremely unlikely that anyone would naively believe that we could return to a place of the "origin" or "essence" of non-modern cultures, a conceptual cousin of the one untainted Truth, it is a quite a different thing to question the usefulness of modern/colonial gender/sexuality categories by highlighting the complementary and often fluid modes of embodiment, especially in the mythical realm, in non-modern cultural texts and imaginaries, in a way that is below the logic of either/or, as we have seen in Part I and will discuss further in Part II.

We need to insist, however, that this so-called fluidity does not automatically assure less violence (both in ancient Babylonia, especially during its regional dominance, and in 14th–16th-century Cemanahuac, especially during the Aztec's expansion). This is itself a caution against the facile celebration of terms such as "fluidity" in contemporary critical discourses. The non-dichotomous systems have different nuances and power relations, as we have learned and shall continue to learn from the following chapters with and against their modern/colonial receptions.

PART II

—

THE EARTH

3

The Strange Case of Tlaltecuhtli

*Tezcatlipoca: ynin vel teutl ipan machoia, noujian
ynemjian: mictla, tlalticpac, ylhujcac.*

*el Dios, llamado tezcatlipuca: era tenido por verdadero dios, y inuisible:
el qual andaua, en todo lugar: en el cielo, en la tierra, y en el infierno.*[1]
— Bernardino de Sahagún, *Códice florentino*[2]

Michael E. Smith introduces one of the Nahua creation myths, concerning the cosmic battle between Quetzalcoatl, Tezcatlipoca, and Tlaltecuhtli, as follows:

The giant earth monster Tlaltecuhtli ("Earth Lord"), a crocodile-like creature, swam in the sea searching for flesh to eat. The gods turned themselves into serpents, entered the sea, and tore Tlaltecuhtli in half. The upper part of her body be-

---

1   "The god called Tezcatlipoca was believed to be a real god and was invisible. He walks in all places: in *mictlan,* the place of the dead, on the earth and in *ilhuicac,* the 'sky.'" My translation here is based on both the Nahua and the Spanish texts. For a comparison between the two, see later discussions in this chapter.

2   The *Códice florentino* was written in Spanish and transcribed into Nahuatl by the Franciscan Friar Bernardino de Sahagún with the help of numerous Nahuatl-speaking scholars at the Tlatelolco school. Because of the different ways in which Nahua pronunciation was transcribed, there are different spelling conventions for the Nahuatl language.

came the land, and the lower part was thrown into the sky to become the stars and heavens.[3]

What exactly is the gender of this earth monster, Tlaltecuhtli, who, in this short paragraph, first appears as "lord," then as a crocodile-like creature of an unspecified gender, and finally as a female body that is cut in half by the two gods Quetzalcoatl and Tezcatlipoca?

In this chapter, we will discuss the "strange case" of Tlaltecuhtli in the colonial/modern reception history of Nahua deities. We will review Tlaltecuhtli's "four types of representation," defined by the Mexican archeologist Eduardo Matos Moctezuma, which allows us to conclude that Tlaltecuhtli *could* be identified as a feminine deity, given a specific context and representational style. We continue, however, to ask how an "Earth *Lord*" (which is the literal translation of the Nahua name Tlaltecuhtli) has come to be known only as the "goddess" or "lady" of the earth through its reception. We will analyze this question from two different but related points. First, we will insist upon the "power to signify" of the Nahua language, a power that it has been denied in modern scholarship and museum curatorship, where Tlaltecuhtli is consistently mistranslated as "Earth Lady." Second, we will explore how the Nahua form of complementary "dualism" has been dichotomized into a masculine celestial sphere and a feminine terrestrial sphere. This critique of the heteronormatively gendered reception history of Tlaltecuhtli and Nahua cosmology reflects on larger problems concerning the issue of "coloniality," especially the coloniality of gender, or what I call the "heteronormative dichotomous cut." Finally, we propose to read the case of Tlaltecuhtli, or precisely its "ambiguity," by learning to learn from the "grammatology" of the Nahua language, that is, its particular form of "writing/painting" (*tlacuilolli*), as well as the absence of the copular verb "to be." This will lead to an onto-epistemological concern that is radically dif-

---

3   Michael E. Smith, *The Aztecs* (Oxford: Blackwell, 1996), 206, emphasis mine.

ferent from the quest of Western philosophy: "what is…." This will be further explored in the next chapter through the statue (a form of *tlacuilolli*) Coatlicue Mayor.

3.1 The Classification and Feminization of Tlaltecuhtli

Tlaltecuhtli appears on many occasions and in a wide variety of places, often represented as having an intimate relationship with the earth. For example, on the underside of the colossal statue Coatlicue Mayor, Tlaltecuhtli is represented as facing the earth. Thanks to a replica of the relief placed next to the statue, we are able to see this earth deity, who is not supposed to be seen by the uninitiated viewer. In Nahua mythology, Tlaltecuhtli represents the earth and the characteristics associated with it, understood by the Nahuas as a powerful combination of life and death, similar to the figure of a *vagina dentata* that simultaneously gives and devours life.[4] In Nahuatl, the name "Tlaltecuhtli" combines *tlal,* meaning "earth," and *tecuhtli,* meaning "lord" or "god." Strikingly, the combination of strong feminine characteristics, especially the life-generating power associated with the earth, and the name, Tlaltecuhtli, or "Earth *Lord,*" appears discordant.

Eduardo Matos Moctezuma, the prominent Mexican archeologist who leads the excavation team working closely with Nahua artifacts and art works at Templo Mayor (Mexico City), summarizes four different types of representation of Tlaltecuhtli.[5] We will introduce this complex deity by referring to Matos Moctezuma's account, and, at the same time, we will analyze the underlying heteronormative assumptions that have resulted in the problematic gendering of this deity.

In "Tlaltecuhtli: Señor de la tierra" (1997), published almost ten years before the 2006 excavation of a giant disk, identified as Tlaltecuhtli in Templo Mayor, Matos Moctezuma identifies

---

4   Jill Raitt, "'Vagina Dentata' and the 'Immaculatus Uterus Divini Fontis,'" *Journal of the American Academy of Religion* 48, no. 3 (2011): 415–31.

5   Eduardo Matos Moctezuma, "Tlaltecuhtli: Señor de la tierra," *Estudios de Cultura Náhuatl* 27 (1997): 15–40.

four types of representation of Tlaltecuhtli: group A — anthropomorphic and masculine figures; group B — anthropomorphic and feminine figures; group C — zoomorphic and feminine figures; and group D — figures with the face of Tlaloc, the god of rain. At no point in the article does Matos Moctezuma identify "Tlaltecuhtli" exclusively as a *diosa* (goddess), and indeed he suggests that "all the representations of the god correspond to specific moments and the diverse functions that he has."[6] Referring to Mircea Eliade's *Traité d'histoire des religions,* Matos Moctezuma confirms that "many deities of the earth and those related to fertility," such as Nahua earth deity Tlaltecuhtli, "are bisexual."[7] Thus, his study seeks to analyze Tlaltecuhtli's "bisexual" figuring.[8] In the article, Matos Moctezuma does not mean "bisexuality" in the sense of one's sexual orientation, but rather as the presence of both sexes, male and female, identifiable in the representations of this deity of earth. We will come back to this interesting conflation of concepts below.

Matos Moctezuma suggests that the figures from group A face the earth and therefore represent the male aspect, while the figures from group B and group C (though zoomorphically represented) lie on the earth facing the sky and therefore represent the female aspect.[9] Unlike many researchers who hastily silence the literal meaning of Tlaltecuhtli and feminize it as "Lady of the Earth,"[10] Matos Moctezuma does not reject the masculine aspect of the deity. From him, we learn that Tlaltecuhtli means "Earth Lord" from two quotations by different authors. Friar Diego Durán claims that "Tlaltecuhtli, composed of two names, *tlalli* and *tecuhtli,* which means 'great lord', together means, 'the

---

6   Ibid., 36: "todas estas representaciones del dios corresponden a determinados momentos y a las diversas funciones que tiene." All translations to English from non-English sources, unless stated otherwise, are mine.

7   Ibid., 24: "muchas divinidades de la tierra y relacionadas con la fecundidad son bisexuales."

8   Ibid., 16.

9   Ibid., 25–30.

10   See, for example, Elizabeth Baquedano and Michel Graulich, "Decapitation among the Aztecs: Mythology, Agriculture and Politics and Hunting," *Estudios de Cultura Náhuatl* 23 (1993): 163–77.

great lord of the earth."[11] And Manuel Orozco y Berra confirms that "Tlaltecuhtli, of *tlalli,* earth and *tecutli,* lord, was a male god."[12] However, despite this being the masculine grouping, we sense that the masculine type is hovering outside of the possible significations of the "earth deity," as Matos Moctezuma himself argues: "This group [A, masculine-identified] turns out to be very special and is essentially different from the other three [groups]."[13] The "particularity" of group A is even more accentuated, if the earth is believed to be exclusively a feminine sphere, in a so-called female position awaiting insemination.[14]

Even a complex and rich study such as Matos Moctezuma's is not immune to the dichotomous classification and hierarchization of sexual differences accompanied by a reading that ultimately reduces the existing nuances. This "categorical logic of modernity," complicit with heterosexual normativity or "heterosexualism,"[15] as María Lugones names it, seems to have prevented Matos Moctezuma from accepting what ought to have been clear to him: the semantic meaning of the Nahua name Tlaltecuhtli — Earth Lord. He accurately translates Tlaltecuhtli in the title of his paper, "Tlaltecuhtli: Señor de la tierra." However, he has never suggested or explained why, if the earth is identified with femininity to such a great extent, if the main function of the earth is to wait to be fertilized, and if the deity is represented pervasively in the act of laboring with a *vagina dentata* (a motif that simultaneously suggests death),[16] the Nahuas

---

11 Friar Diego Durán, quoted in Matos Moctezuma, "Tlaltecuhtli," 20: "Tlaltecuhtli, el cual vocablo se compone de dos nombres, que es tlalli y tecuhtli, que quiere decir 'gran señor' y, así quiere decir 'el gran señor de la tierra."

12 Manuel Orozco y Berra, quoted in ibid., 24. "Tlaltecuhtli, de tlalli, tierra, y tecutli [*sic*], señor, era el dios varón."

13 Ibid., 27: "este grupo [A, masculino] resulta muy particular y en esencia diferente a los otros tres]."

14 Ibid., 36.

15 María Lugones, "Heterosexualism and the Colonial/Modern Gender System," *Hypatia* 22, no. 1 (2007): 186–209.

16 The death-threatening aspect of *vagina dentata* imagery is *not* directly associable with the feminine. However, as we have shown in Part I of this volume through the case of the battle between Tiamat and Marduk, in a

should still call Tlaltecuhtli *tecuhtli,* a lord. Deeply embedded in this blindness to the apparent discrepancy between "name" and "nature" is the heteronormative gendering according to which "to have a gender means to have entered already into a heterosexual relationship of subordination."[17] For example, Matos Moctezuma identifies the ones facing the earth as being in a penetrating position, thus male; while those lying on the earth facing the sky are seen as "able to be sexually possessed."[18] The superior position is not only equated with the penetrating one, but the penetrated, inferior one is immediately feminized, "possessed."

Through this reading of different representations of the earth deity as inhabiting penetrating and penetrated positions, we understand that by "bisexual" Matos Moctezuma actually means heterosexual (intercourse). The "bisexual" deities are not only heterosexual, but are even heteronormatively coupled in the most authentic missionary position for the sole purpose of reproduction.[19] By the same token, not only are the zoomorphic representations of the deity included in the feminine grouping, but a lying position of those representations of Tlaltecuhtli

---

phallocentric culture, feminization and monstrification are an inseparable process of construction that not only serves to keep the "phallus/penis" dominant, but also to justify "phallic" violence in the name of order.

17 Catherine MacKinnon in Judith Butler, *Gender Trouble: Feminism and the Subversion of Identity* (London: Routledge, 1999), xiii.

18 Matos Moctezuma, "Tlaltecuhtli" 36: "para poder ser poseídas sexualmente."

19 "Reproductive heteronormativity" signifies not only the compulsory interpretation of *all* types of sexuality in terms of heterosexuality, as Monique Wittig succinctly points out ("when thought by the straight mind, homosexuality is nothing but heterosexuality"), but also a coercion that compels sexual activities to "reproduce." See Monique Wittig, "The Straight Mind," in *The Straight Mind and Other Essays* (Boston: Beacon Press, 1980), 21–32, at 28. Calvin Thomas extends the concept of "reproduction," and argues interestingly that "people who fuck in the name of identity, who make an identity out of who they fuck, who fuck to reproduce 'the person', are fucking heteronormatively [...] even if 'the person' or 'identity' thereby reproduced is 'homosexual'" (Calvin Thomas, *Straight with a Twist: Queer Theory and the Subject of Heterosexuality* [Chicago: University of Illinois Press, 2000], 33).

identified as feminine is also read as an invitation "to be sexually possessed."

We can find similar examples in other sources. The slippage
in Smith's sentence, quoted at the beginning of this chapter,
transforms Tlaltecuhtli from lord to monster, and then suddenly feminizes the lord/monster at the precise moment when the
deity is "torn apart," in an act readable as violent penetration.
Smith's ultimate conclusion that this is a female deity is not an
isolated one. This would not have become visible as a problem,
had Smith not "unnecessarily" added an accurate translation of
the Nahua name Tlaltecuhtli. Many other researchers and museum presentations have rendered the problem itself invisible
by presenting the deity as a "Goddess of the Earth" called Tlaltecuhtli, without suggesting that the name has a different inherent meaning. For example, French scholar Michel Graulich explains that this is the "mother Tlaltecuhtli (Lady of the Earth)."[20]
In a discussion on "Finding the Goddess in the Central Highlands of Mexico," Tlaltecuhtli is also identified as "the goddess"
from whom "the earth was created."[21] Examples are also numerous outside of academic circles, for instance, the giant disk exca-
vated in 2006 is displayed in the Museo de Templo Mayor under
the title "Tlaltecuhtli: Diosa de la tierra" ("Tlaltecuhtli: Goddess
of the Earth"). Some media, such as *La Jornada* and *Arqueología
Mexicana,* as well as several introductory articles published by
the Instituto Nacional de Antropología e Historia, univocally
represent Tlaltecuhtli as *la diosa de la tierra.*[22]

---

20 Michel Graulich, "Aztec Human Sacrifice as Expiation," *History of Religions*
    39, no. 4 (2000): 352–71, at 362.
21 Cecilia M. Corcoran, "Finding the Goddess in the Central Highlands of
    Mexico," *Feminist Theology* 8, no. 24 (2000): 61–81, at 68.
22 See Ana Mónica Rodríguez, "El hueco central de Tlaltecuhtli, misterio a de-
    batir cuando se muestre al público," *La Jornada,* March 23, 2010, http://www.
    jornada.unam.mx/2010/03/23/cultura/a05n1cul; Eduardo Matos Mocte-
    zuma and Leonardo López Luján, "La diosa Tlaltecuhtli de la Casa de las
    Ajaracas y el rey Ahuítzotl," *Arqueología Mexicana,* https://arqueologia-
    mexicana.mx/mexico-antiguo/la-diosa-tlaltecuhtli-de-la-casa-de-las-ajaracas-
    y-el-rey-ahuitzotl; and Instituto Nacional de Antropología e Historia, "Se
    cumplen 10 años del descubirmiento del monolitode la diosa Tlaltecuh-

Certainly, we might suppose that those journalists who equate Tlaltecuhtli with *diosa de la tierra* are merely reporting what scholars and archeologists have already officially agreed on, without necessarily being suspicious about what that "unpronounceable"[23] Nahua word might mean. But it is difficult to imagine that experts in Nahua culture would be totally ignorant of the language, one of the most widely spoken languages in Mesoamerica before Spanish colonization and one of the numerous indigenous languages still extensively spoken in Central America.[24] Tlaltecuhtli can be literally translated as "Earth

tli," October 1, 2016, http://www.inah.gob.mx/boletines/5623-se-cumplen-10-anos-del-descubrimiento-del-monolito-de-la-diosa-tlaltecuhtli.

23 For example, in a Spanish radio broadcast which invited the Mexican anthropologist Marco Antonio Cervera to talk about Nahua mythology, the host asked "¿Cómo era el lenguaje de los mexicas, porque claro los dioses y los nombres son como bárbaros [...] son complicadísimos de pronunciar?" ("What was the language of those Mexicas, because, of course, the gods and their names are like barbarians [...] are extremely complicated to pronounce?"). See "Los dioses de los Mexicas," *ABC Punto Radio*, April 29, 2012, http://www.ivoox.com/dioses-mexicas-audios-mp3_rf_1195682_1.html.

24 Serge Gruzinski, *La colonisation de l'imaginaire: Sociétés indigènes et occidentalisation dans le Mexique espagnol XVIᵉ–XVIIIᵉ siècle* (Paris: Éditions Gallimard, 1988), 353, points out, "la diffusion du castellan fut de tout temps un objectif qui hanta la Couronne espagnole. Elle y voyait le moyen d'étendre son emprise sur les populations indigènes et de raffermir sa domination" ("the diffusion of castellan was all the time an objective that haunted the Spanish Crown. It saw there the way to extend its influence on the indigenous populations and to consolidates its domination"). The Nahua language dwells in the ambiguous status of a less-than-official language, regarded as a language of the Aztec past even though it is still widely spoken (almost two million speakers, according to León-Portilla), and therefore deprived of its official status as one of the many languages spoken in Mexico (Miguel León-Portilla, "El destino de las lenguas indígenas de México," in *De historiografía lingüística e historia de las lenguas,* eds. Ignacio Guzmán Betancourt, Pilar Máynez, and Ascensión H. de León-Portilla [Mexico D.F.: Siglo XXI, 2004], 51–70). Only in 1992 did the Mexican Constitution suggest that awareness of the coexistence of other indigenous languages had been totally ignored legislatively. It was only in 2003 that the Ley general de derechos lingüísticos de los pueblos indígenas recognized legal rights for indigenous languages equal to Spanish. For example, article 7 states: "Las lenguas indígenas serán válidas, al igual que el español, para cualquier asunto o trámite de carácter público, así como para acceder plenamente a

Lord" without much space for ambiguity. While we might expect that referring to *señor de la tierra* using the pronoun *ella* ("she") would cause consternation — unless it were for poetic juxtaposition or something like the biblical *Elohim bara* — Tlaltecuhtli is in fact continually referred to as such without causing as much as a raised eyebrow or needing the excuse of "poetic justification."[25]

Let us take a look at another example from an encyclopedia entry, where we read: "the feathered-serpent god QUETZALCOATL and the smoking mirror god TEZCATLIPOCA [...] saw Tlaltecuhtli and grabbed her by her legs."[26] Though linguistically Quetzalcoatl and Tezcatlipoca do not automatically assume or convey any "masculinity," because the Nahua language has no grammatical gender and their names, "plumed serpent" (Quetzalcoatl) and "smoking mirror" (Tezcatlipoca), don't indicate a specific gender, it is not uncommon for them to be called "gods." Especially when the cosmic battle against the feminized Tlaltecuhtli is recounted, Quetzalcoatl and Tezcatlipoca are presented as masculine deities, despite, as Pete Sigal shows, the "androgynous" or "bisexual" characteristics of both "gods."[27] Certainly, I

---

la gestión, servicios e información pública" ("Indigenous languages will be valid as Spanish for any public issues or administrative process, as well as for the access to any management, service and information pertaining to the public sector") ("Ley General de Derechos Lingüísticos de Los Pueblos Indígenas," 2003, https://www.inali.gob.mx/pdf/ley-GDLPI.pdf). Nevertheless, Castilian Spanish remains dominant and the de facto monolingual status of Mexico has not been shaken. This domination of Spanish over other indigenous languages can be read in parallel with "internal colonialism," born at the shift "from the colonial regime ruled from the metropolis to a national regime ruled by the Creoles," reflected in a nutshell in the "Latinity" of "Latin America" its erasure of the indigenous and Afro-descendant population. See Walter Mignolo, *The Idea of Latin America* (Oxford: Blackwell, 2005), 65.

25 See Chapter 2 in this volume for a discussion of the poetic function of the grammatical discrepancy in the case of the Elohist Genesis.

26 Ann Bingham, *South and Meso-American Mythology A to Z* (New York: Facts on File, 2004), 109.

27 See Pete Sigal, "Queer Nahuatl: Sahagún's Faggots and Sodomites, Lesbians and Hermaphrodites," *Ethnohistory* 54, no. 1 (2007): 9–34, and Pete Sigal,

am not suggesting an insistence on the language–gender relation, pretending that no other linguistic or ideological apparatus would suggest the gendering of certain words and expressions. Much less would I argue that a genderless language conveys a more egalitarian or less biased view on sexual or gender differences. Rather, I am asking how a clearly masculine-gendered name like Tlal*tecuhtli* could become automatically feminized in the process of translation, while the "neutral," grammatically genderless, and culturally "androgynous" Quetzalcoatl and Tezcatlipoca become masculinized.

According to Matos Moctezuma's study, the earth embodies the following functions: 1) the fertilized earth; 2) the earth as *vagina dentata* that devours dead bodies; 3) the earth as the transformer who gives birth to the dead into the Mictlan, place of the dead; 4) the earth as the central point of the universe, linking the celestial and the terrestrial; and 5) the earth that rests upon the primordial water.[28] The only exclusively "masculine" feature, according to this study, is the one related to "the center of the universe,"[29] while the one related to "femininity" is the "fertilized earth." The "center of the universe" therefore becomes masculinized while the feminine continues to be reserved solely for the purpose of reproduction, to be fertilized or inscribed with meaning from above.

According to this particular creation myth, the "brothers" Tezcatlipoca and Quetzalcoatl transform into giant serpents, dive into the primordial water, and slaughter the earth monster Tlaltecuhtli who is eating human bones, a quintessential element for the re-creation of human beings at the beginning of the fifth cosmic age. They subsequently create the earth and heaven, using the slaughtered body parts of Tlaltecuhtli. If we assume that the Quetzalcoatl-Tezcatlipoca duo is masculine and Tlaltecuhtli is feminine (as in the expression of *diosa de la*

"Imagining Cihuacoatl: Masculine Rituals, Nahua Goddesses and the Texts of the Tlacuilos," *Gender & History* 22, no. 3 (2010): 538–63.

28 Matos Moctezuma, "Tlaltecuhtli," 36.

29 Ibid., 35: "el centro del universo."

tierra), the myth can be easily read as a masculine control of the feminine/monstrous (m)other through violent killing and the appropriation of the female body, as in the case of Marduk's slaughter of Tiamat analyzed in Part I. In the Babylonian case, the feminization of Tiamat is complicit with her monstrification inside *Enuma Elish,* whose colonial undertone is repeatedly underpinned by sexist mytho-political propaganda during the period of the Babylonian Empire and reinforced by equally gender-stereotypical readings in its modern reception history. The feminization of Tlaltecuhtli, by contrast, is largely exaggerated in its modern/colonial receptions, through the silencing of the Nahua language and the cosmology expressed in it.

The aim of my critique here is neither a "correction" of what archaeologists have wrongly identified, nor a proposal of a "truer" answer to the question "What is Tlaltecuhtli?" In fact, the problem and confusion might well stem from this particular question, which tries its best to delimit and control the meaning(s) of Tlaltecuhtli through the seemingly inevitable verb "to be" (I will return to this question below). Tlaltecuhtli, far from being merely a name, has a semantic meaning clear enough for any Nahuatl speaker: "Earth Lord." Similarly, for a Hebrew speaker, *'adam* in Genesis would clearly mean "the human" rather than the male name Adam.[30] While *'adam* becomes widely translated as Adam, always and certainly not coincidentally gendered male, Tlaltecuhtli has been widely represented also as merely the name of an earth deity, de-gendered (the *tecuhtli* part marking masculinity ignored or maybe "castrated") and re-gendered as feminine. In both cases, the inherent meanings of the Hebrew and Nahuatl words are neglected.

Smith's and Matos Moctezuma's cases are somehow special, as they indeed translate the word correctly, but then immediately appear to forget or ignore the gendered implications of that

---

30 See Robert Alter, *Genesis: Translation and Commentary* (London: W.W. Norton & Company Inc., 1996), 5, and my essay "*'adam* Is Not Man': Queer Body before Genesis 2:22 (and After)," in *Unsettling Science and Religion: Contributions and Questions from Queer Studies,* eds. Whitney Bauman and Lisa Stenmark (Lanham: Lexington Books, 2018), 183–97.

translation in the same sentence. What we want to ask is how Tlaltecuhtli became known as a goddess and how an exhibition title such as "Tlaltecuhtli: diosa de la tierra" became possible. I argue that both scholarly works and museum presentations are not free from the colonial matrix of power and knowledge. Because of this, even when the meaning of the silenced language is made clear, its cosmological and philosophical specificity cannot have a place in the interpretations of the mythologies conceived in it. The modern gender system, with heteronormative sexuality and universalistic "archetypes" as the epistemic monopoly, where other knowledges and forms of being are overlooked, only permits the understanding of the earth deity as "goddess" or the feminization of any deity related to the earth.

At the same time, we need to further complicate the issue by acknowledging the fact that Tlaltecuhtli *can* be, and often is, identified as feminine. That is to say, a "correct" translation of Tlaltecuhtli as the "Earth Lord" would be equally inadequate in conveying all the possible meanings, representations, and metamorphoses of this earth deity. The next section will scrutinize the coercive modern gendering founded on (biological) dichotomous dimorphism through a critique of the classification of Nahua deities into the so-called celestial and terrestrial ones, not surprisingly gendered as, respectively, masculine and feminine ones.

3.2 Performing "Castration" for Tlaltecuhtli

Scholarly research and museum curatorship do not provide merely constative "observations" about what there is and how things are represented. They are also performative and constructive forces that inscribe normative discourses into what the observed "objects of study" are said to represent. Put differently, the readings of Smith and Matos Moctezuma, among others, which I have shown are imbued in heterosexualist assumptions, construct a particular normative discourse that gains validity and intelligibility precisely through repetition or reiteration.[31]

Such discourse construction implies a double process of naturalization and exclusion. Naturalization takes the form of asserting "how s/he/it naturally is"[32] and is accompanied by an exclusion of other possible readings that would, for example, take the *tecuhtli*-ness of Tlaltecuhtli seriously without censoring this particular disruptive element. In this section, we will analyze how modern scholarship performs "sex assignment" for Tlaltecuhtli through the castration (in the sense of cutting off the penis/phallus), that is to say, the silencing of the inherent meaning of *tecuhtli*. We will accentuate the disruptive voice that strives to be heard at the surgical moment of castration, when Tlaltecuhtli is translated/transformed into "Earth *Lady*," who is to be slaughtered by the masculinized deities in order to fit into the heterosexualist myth of the feminine earth and the monstrous *vagina dentata*. This symbolic/phallic meaning of *tecuhtli* has to be repeatedly castrated in order to feminize the "monster" (which, of course, always also serves to monstrify the feminine at the same time), so that the haunted phallocentric sexual dissymmetry can still work to define its very centrality. This "phallus castration," we need to notice, is performed on a colonized language, Nahuatl, and by the modern/colonial knowledge system written in European languages. Such feminization of the colonized is not a new story.[33] Certainly, these discursive operations function under a naturalized idea that

---

31 See Butler, *Gender Trouble*, 11.

32 Certainly, even using "s/he/it" has to be constrained within the possibilities language offers, which would in a similar manner reiterate the "natural" division between she and he, between s/he and it, etc. The Nahuas do not have this linguistic problem, as there is only one pronoun regardless of gender. For example, see James Lockhart, *Nahuatl as Written: Lessons in Older Written Nahuatl, with Copious Examples and Texts* (Stanford: Stanford University Press, 2001), 1.

33 See Part O and Anne McClintock, *Imperial Leather: Race, Gender and Sexuality in the Colonial Contest* (New York: Routledge, 1995), and María Lugones, "Toward a Decolonial Feminism," *Hypatia* 25, no. 4 (2010): 742–59, among others.

there are two "opposite sexes." In the following sections, we will revisit some discussions around the coercive sex assignment of intersex subjects in modern society, and see how it reveals both the uncertainty and the violence of modern/colonial dimorphic system of gender (and sex).

3.2.1 Modern Sex Assignment Surgery on Intersex Subjects

The idea of intersex functions as abjection, which is necessary for the emergence of the two supposedly oppositional sexes. Intersex thus marks the liminality of this dimorphic division. What happens if we take "gender" into consideration? By gender, we mean the discursive practice that performatively constructs the very bodies onto which gender is said to have imposed its "constructions."[34] The constructiveness of gender does not leave the idea of sex untouched. We follow Butler to further argue that "sexual differences are indissociable from discursive demarcations" and are never simply a "fact or static condition of a body" but materialize "through a forcible reiteration of [... regulatory] norms."[35] Taking these considerations into account, intersex points to the instabilities that are both inherent in and resistant to the materialization complying with a regulatory norm that "is never quite complete."[36] In modern normative societies, intersex people are mostly treated as abnormal, in need of "correction" in order to satisfy normative sexual dimorphism. Their fate clearly shows the power and violence of modern heteronormative hegemony, but, at the same time, reveals its innate instability. This is where the possibilities of subverting heteronormativity lie.

Modern society continues to assume that there are only two sexes despite a considerable part of the world population being intersex.[37] Julie Greenberg shows that US legal institutions "have

---

34 Butler, *Gender Trouble,* passim.
35 Judith Butler, *Bodies That Matter: On the Discursive Limits of "Sex"* (London: Routledge, 1993), 1–2.
36 Ibid., 2.
37 Four percent accroding to John Money in Anne Fausto-Sterling, "The Five Sexes: Why Male and Female Are Not Enough," *The Sciences* (March/April 1993): 20–25.

the power to assign individuals to a particular racial or sexual category."[38] She argues that the assumption behind such sexual and racial assignments is the binarism of race and sex, as well as the belief that "race and sex can be biologically determined [...] despite scientific evidence to the contrary."[39]

The deep anxiety provoked by the existence of intersex people becomes evident in the practice of the surgical "corrections" of their bodies. We call this intervention "sex assignment," in which the pathologized intersex subject's sex is altered to align with normative expectations soon after birth. This anxiety is similar to the "colonial anxiety" analyzed by Bhabha and reviewed in Part O. It is a result of modern categorical logic. This brings us back to the issue of race. Greenberg reviews the "one-drop" policy in US legal policy, which classifies an infant with "one drop" of blood from a black parent or ancestor as "black" rather than "white." The racial puritanism and anti-miscegenation undertone cannot be clearer. However, it shows that white men's fear of racial "pollution," and of feminization in general, is an effect of the realization that the very concept "white man" is inherently unstable and contestable.

Butler argues that "castration could not be feared if the phallus were not already detachable, already elsewhere, already dispossessed."[40] Transposing her deconstruction of castration fear to the case of race, we soon realize that the very purist concept of "white man" is not prior to the event of "corruption" or fear of the encounter with the monstrified "other," which is usually claimed to happen "later," but it is in fact constructed at the very moment of that encounter, as a *result* of the fear of feminization/racialization.

Unwanted surgical intervention on intersex bodies is a brutal one, literally inscribed on the flesh. It reiterates the normativity

---

38 Julie Greenberg, "Definitional Dilemmas: Male or Female? Black or White? The Law's Failure to Recognize Intersexuals and Multiracials," in *Gender Nonconformity, Race, and Sexuality: Charting the Connections,* ed. Toni Lester (Madison: University of Wisconsin Press, 2002), 102–24, at 102.

39 Ibid., 103.

40 Butler, *Bodies That Matter,* 101.

and authority of gender dimorphism at the expense of the lives inconceivable by such a norm. By inconceivable, I mean that a certain body that does not confirm the regulatory norm is not regarded as livable or legitimate and is in danger of either being altered or killed.

What is at stake here is the realization of the very contingency and inconsistency within the regulatory rule of reproductive heteronormativity. Without making this clear, the illusory fantasy of heterosexualism will lure us into believing that "gender trouble" is a modern fuss, strictly alien to a non-modern, pre-colonized culture, like the Nahua's. And if the illusion of heterosexualism fails to be recognized, the colonized indigenous cultures might be dangerously assumed to be in a "natural state" of "heterosexuality," because the straight colonizing mind "takes for granted that what founds society, any society, is heterosexuality."[41] Readings that split the organic and transformative Nahua theology (and sometimes, the same deity, like Tlaltecuhtli) into coupling gods and goddesses reiterate the sexist cliché of the passive feminine who invites penetration, as if heterosexuality and the missionary style were truly ahistorical and cross-cultural.

3.2.2 "Correcting" the Sex of Tlaltecuhtli

The reference to modern surgical interventions is pertinent to our discussion of the Nahua deity of the earth, because scholarship and museum curatorship similarly continue to perform "sex assignment" on Tlaltecuhtli, whose "gender" and "sex" do not seem to correspond to each other neatly. The sex assign-

---

41 Wittig, "The Straight Mind," 24. The straight colonizing mind is actually not as *straight*-forward as one would want to believe. Today, homosexuality, or more precisely the so-called "tolerance toward homosexuals," has become evidence of the deviance of a given culture. While 19th-century British travellers condemn the "immoral" sexuality of sodomy in Muslim society as proof of its decadence, contemporary neo-liberal discourse uses the same rhetoric to feed the Islamophobic imagination. See Joseph Andoni Massad, ed., *Desiring Arabs* (Chicago: University of Chicago Press, 2008) and Jin Haritaworn, *Queer Lovers and Hateful Others: Regenerating Violent Times and Places* (London: Pluto Press, 2015).

ment is performed through "castration" in order to fit the heterosexualist expectation of the earth, a monstrous, destructive yet productive symbol, as *exclusively* feminine. The discourse is well protected by the rhetoric of "exception"[42] when evidence of the contrary is revealed to the researcher. This is why I believe, as in the case of US legal policy on racial and sexual assignment, that showing "scientific evidence to the contrary"[43] alone could not adequately prevent the imposition of normative gender law.

Cixous summarizes how phallogocentrism works through hierarchical dualisms, and argues that in Western philosophy, woman is always on the side of "passivity."[44] Zainab Bahrani, in her exploration of gender and representation in Babylonian art, similarly observes that "woman serves to define the masculine in the Symbolic, and whatever is excess or lack can be located in her as Other: thus anxiety, threat, extremes of good and evil all come to be localized at the body of woman, as the site of alterity."[45]

Curiously, in our "strange case," the masculine symbolic centrality is attained not because of the possession of a "phallus," but as a result of the castration of the Nahua phallus/*logos*. If we compare the troublesome *tecuhtli* part of the Earth Lord Tlaltecuhtli to the phallus or the symbolic power to signify, *tecuhtli* itself has to be castrated, that is to say, silenced and eradicated of meaning. Only then is it possible for the masculine-identified "creation gods" Quetzalcoatl and Tezcatlipoca to be regarded as the central figures. More interestingly, a heteronormative understanding that associates the earth (or the "terrestrial sphere") as exclusively feminine with the position of awaiting penetra-

---

42 For example, as previously mentioned, Matos Moctezuma, "Tlaltecuhtli," 27, believes that the masculine-identified Group A of representations of Tlaltecuhtli "turns out to be very special and is essentially different to the other three [groups]."

43 Greenberg, "Definitional Dilemmas," 103.

44 Hélène Cixous and Catherine Clément, *La jeune née* (Paris: Union Générale d'Éditions, 1975), 116–17: "la pensée a toujours travaillé par opposition, Parole/Écriture [… par] oppositions duelles, hiérarchisées [… et] dans la philosophie la femme est toujours du côté de la passivité."

45 Zainab Bahrani, *Women of Babylon: Gender and Representation in Mesopotamia* (London: Routledge, 2001), 36.

tion by the consequently masculinized heavenly (or "celestial") gods, is, paradoxically, bought at a price: that of castrating Tlaltecuhtli's phallus.

Matos Moctezuma argues that the masculine *aspect* of Tlaltecuhtli represents the "center of the universe."[46] If he is right, the desirable masculine centrality, which we can call its phallocentrism, is actually haunted by the very *tecuhtli*-phallus. That is because Tlaltecuhtli's symbolic, that is, phallic power to signify shows nothing more than the fact that the earth deity is a *tecuthli*, a "lord," not a feminized "goddess" as the heteronormative gendering would have it. In his eyes, the phallus *tecuhtli* becomes simultaneously the abhorrent symbol that resists at every moment of appearance any direct association with the earth (and thus the so-called terrestrial deities) and the feminine. Paradoxically, the semantic phallus of *tecuhtli* has to be castrated in order to keep the colonial phallus of masculine power in/as the center of the universe.

This "castration" is often performed secretly in the equations of Tlaltecuhtli with the "*goddess* of the earth," while explicitly, but very quickly, in some other cases.[47] Elizabeth Baquedano and Michel Graulich, for example, invite us to imagine "how exactly Tlalteotl was killed" through the "decapitation" allegedly represented by Coatlicue Mayor, which we will discuss in detail in the next chapter. They refer to Tlaltecuhtli as Tlalteotl and translate the Nahua word as "Earth Deity," that is to say, genderless. The cosmic slaughter of Tlalteotl is, however, recounted with a clear gendering: "[A]t the beginning of time Quetzalcoatl and Tezcatlipoca brought from the heavens a 'savage beast' with *her* joints filled with eyes and mouths, Tlalteotl ('Earth Deity') and put *her* in the primordial water."[48] In a nutshell, the slaughtered deity is feminized.

---

46 Matos Moctezuma, "Tlaltecuhtli," 35: "centro del universo."

47 Baquedano and Graulich, "Decapitation among the Aztecs"; Smith, *The Aztecs*. I will return to Banquedano and Graulich's article in the next chapter.

48 Baquedano and Graulich, "Decapitation among the Aztecs," 164, emphasis mine.

Matos Moctezuma's take is more complex. In the separate analysis of each of the four groups of his classification, he states that group D (representations of Tlaltecuhtli with the face of Tlaloc, the rain deity) is clearly feminine, yet has the typical features of the figures from group A, i.e., the masculine one. He concludes, quoting Bonifaz, though with reservations, that Tlaltecuhtli-Tlaloc is "feminine and masculine, as it would like to be seen; the two are the same: Tlaloc is Tlaltecuhtli, Tlaltecuhtli is Tlaloc."[49] However, when it comes to deciding the essential functions, the author attributes exclusive masculinity to the Tlaloc group because the "rain" or celestial water/semen is believed to fall down from above to fertilize the earth (group B and C, the "feminine" and "zoomorphic"). Put another way, group A (masculine) and group D (with the face of the rain deity Tlaloc) suddenly ascend to the masculinized celestial level in order to fertilize groups B and C, the feminized ones (of course by overlooking group C's zoomorphism).[50] Being subjected to an allegedly penetrative position, these different representations of the same "Earth Lord" unavoidably slip into the penetrating males and the feminine ones who are "facing up, in the position of [maternal] labouring, but also in the position of being fertilized."[51]

In a nutshell, the hierarchized, dichotomous sexualization/gendering of representations of the same deity becomes naturalized spatially and symbolically as the separation between heaven and earth. We have argued several times, following Lugones, that heteronormativity is intersected with coloniality, for which she coined the word "heterosexualism." The highly problematic

---

49 Matos Moctezuma, "Tlaltecuhtli" 29–30: "Feminino y masculinos, como quiera que se vistan, ambos son lo mismo: Tlaloc es Tlaltecuhtli, Tlatecuhtli es Tlaloc."

50 When I say overlooking I don't simply mean ignoring, but conveying another interesting point to explore, that is, the relationship between femininity and animality. However, engaging with this critique goes beyond the scope of this book.

51 Matos Moctezuma, "Tlaltecuhtli," 30: "personajes femeninos que están boca arriba, en posición de parto, pero también en posición de ser fecundadas."

grouping of Tlaltecuhtlis around the idea of "vaginal penetration" should be analyzed through this lens of heterosexualism. In his discussion of the challenge that Latin American sexualities pose to the globalization of the History of Sexuality, Pete Sigal creates the concept of "the colonialism of vaginal intercourse." He explains:

[B]oth Catholic priests and Hispanized people from all walks of life provided a culture framework in which the most intimate carnal relations between people were supposed to center around the penetration of the vagina by the penis. [… However, the] Moche pottery and the Nahua ritual suggest that centering sexuality on vaginal intercourse was a fundamentally *colonial maneuver* that did epistemic violence to the relationship between sexuality and history in non-Western societies.[52]

The coercive mimeticism of "vaginal intercourse" also relates to the simplistic categorization of the Nahua cosmos into the celestial and terrestrial spheres, which, unsurprisingly, are respectively masculinized (the celestial) and feminized (the terrestrial). In order to contest this coercive division and gendering, we return to Nahua cosmology and to Ometeotl, the supposed terrestrial deity. With the feminine Omecihuatl and the masculine Ometecuhtli, Ometeotl *in tlalxicco ónoc* — "spreads from the navel of the earth."[53] According to León-Portilla's explanation, based on the *Códice florentino* by Bernardino de Sahagún, the supposedly celestial Ometeotl and their two gendered aspects, Ometecuhtli and Omecihuatl, dwelling on the highest level of the thirteen skies, also originate (*ono*) from the navel of the earth (*tlalxicco*: *tlal*, "earth"; *xictli*, "navel"). Surprisingly, we also find that the lord and lady of the "underworld" (more

---

52 Pete Sigal, "Latin America and the Challenge of Globalizing the History of Sexuality," *American Historical Review* 114 (2009): 1340–53, at 1341.

53 Miguel León-Portilla, *Aztec Thought and Culture: A Study of the Ancient Nahuatl Mind,* trans. Jack Emory Davis (Norman: University of Oklahoma Press, 1963), 32.

precisely, "place of the dead"), Mictlantecuhtli and Mictlanci-huatl (or Mictecacihuatl),[54] dwell on the sixth level of the thir-teen "skies," supposedly reserved only to the "celestial" deities.[55] For example, in the 16th-century French manuscript *Histoyre du Mexique,* possibly a translation of the lost book *Antigüedades Mexicanas* by the Franciscan friar André de Olmos,[56] we find the following description:

> The Mexicans and many of their neighbors believed that there were thirteen skies, […] in the sixth [sky lived] Mict-lantentli, who is the god of hell [… and in] the eighth Tlalo-catentli, god of the earth.[57]

According to this account, not only Mictlantecuhtli, the deity of "underworld," but also Tlaltecuhtli, live on one of the thirteen levels of the "sky." Coatlicue, as we will see in the next chapter, is often regarded as an *Earth* Goddess belonging to the terrestrial sphere. For example, under the grouping of "The Earth Gods," Alfonso Caso argues that "three goddesses, who apparently are only three different aspects of the same deity, portrayed the

---

54 There is no scholarly explanation available for the different versions of the "lady of the place of the dead," but in terms of etymology, *mictlan* means the "place of the dead," while *micteca* means "people from the place of the dead" (as with geographical terms: Tepozteca are people or things from Tepozt-lan). So I suggest that the difference between Mictecacihuatl and Mictlan-cihuatl seems to be only a linguistic variation. Here, in order to show her relation to Mictlantecuhtli, I opt for the version "Mictlancihuatl."

55 For a detailed discussion on the question of the "thirteen levels" of the Na-hua universe, see Alfredo López Austin's "La verticalidad del cosmos," *Estu-dios de Cultura Náhuatl* 52 (2016): 119–50.

56 For more information on this issue, see the editor's "Introduction" in M. Éd-ouard de Jonghe, ed., "Histoire du Mechique, manuscrit français inédit du XVIᵉ siècle," *Journal de la Société des Américanistes, nouvelle série* 2 (1905): 1–41, at 1–8.

57 Ibid., 22: "Croioyent les Mechiquiens et beaucoup de ses circunvoisins qu'il y avoyt treze cieux, […] au sixiesme Mictlantentli, qui est dieu des enfers [… et à] l'huictiesme Tlalocatentli, dieu de la terre." "Mictlantentli" in the manuscript refers to Mictlantecuhtli or "Mictlanteutli," as it is written in the editor's note (ibid., 22n7); "Tlalocatentli" refers to Tlaltecuhtli or "Tlalocan teutli," as it is written in the editor's note (ibid., 22n9).

earth in its dual function of creator and destroyer: Coatlicue, Cihuacóatl, and Tlazoltéotl."[58] "She" is also regarded as one of these "other nocturnal, terrestrial and underworld deities (like Mictecacíhuatl, Coatlicue, the *cihuateteo,* Itzpapálotl, and the other *tzitzimime*)."[59] Meanwhile, the "terrestrial" Coatlicue is also the mother of Huitzilopochtli (representing the sun), Coyolxauhqui (the moon), and Centzonhuitznahuac (the four-hundred southern stars), all celestial deities, and actually the entire universe.

Ometeotl, the genderless/beyond-gender divinity who manifests both masculine and feminine aspects, has been reduced to a "him" (both linguistically and ideologically) in the same way that Gruzinski and others render the Nahua word *teotl* as masculine.[60] On the one hand, the celestial sphere, masculinized through modern representation, excludes Coatlicue (mother of the universe), Coyolxauhqui (goddess of the moon), or any other "goddess." On the other hand, the simultaneously feminized terrestrial sphere can accommodate Earth *Lord* Tlaltecuhtli only under the condition that he (the deity and the word *tecuhtli*) is castrated and becomes a mere name without meaning the "*goddess* of the earth."

In order to find possible clues to these puzzles, I would like to return to the *Códice florentino,* quoted at the beginning of this chapter. In Book I, Chapter 3 of the *Códice,* we read a description of the deity Tezcatlipoca in Spanish, on the left side: "el Dios, llamado tezcatlipuca: era tenido por verdadero dios, y inuisible: el qual andaua, en todo lugar: en el cielo, en la tierra, y en el infierno"; and in Nahuatl, on the right side: "Tezcatlipoca:

---

58 Alfonso Caso, *The Aztecs: People of the Sun,* trans. Lowell Dunham (Norman: University of Oklahoma Press, 1958), 53.

59 Leonardo López Luján and Vida Mercado, "Dos esculturas de Mictlantecuhtli encontradas en el recinto sagrado de México-Tenochtilan," *Estudios de Cultura Náhuatl* 26 (1996): 41–68, at 50: "otras deidades nocturnas, terrestre y del inframundo (como Mictecacíhuatl, Coatlicue, la cihuateteo, Itzpapálotl y las demás tzitzimime)."

60 For a detailed discussion of the "gender" of Ometeotl, Ometecuhtli, and Omecihuatl, and the masculinization of this deity in modern scholarship, see the next chapter.

ynin vel teutl ipan machoia, noujian ynemjian: mictla, tlalticpac, ylhujcac." The Spanish text reads: "The god called tezcatlipuca was taken as the real god and invisible: the one (who) was marching in all places: in the sky, in the earth and in hell." The Nahuatl text reads: "Tezcatlipoca: this old god in every part he walked: the place of the dead, the earth and the 'sky'."[61]

The Spanish text shows Tezcatlipoca's path as if he walks from heaven, through the earth, to hell, a sequence that is conceivable within and compatible with the Spanish/Catholic cosmology. The Spanish text thus presents the Nahuatl text in a reversed order. It is not necessary to exaggerate or stress the different sequence of these places, because, after all, Tezcatlipoca is able to walk wherever they want. However, León-Portilla asserts that "[t]he original Nahuatl texts […] are not the work of Sahagún, but of his elderly native informants from Tepepulco and Tlateloco (sic)."[62] We can at least sense a tension between the Spanish and Nahuatl texts put side by side in the manuscript. Then we can infer that Sahagún, in his Spanish text, which certainly followed the Nahua one rather than the other way around, felt the necessity to make the "sky" (even if it is the Nahua sky, ilhuicatl[63]) appear first, while his informants, the Nahua painters/ writers (tlacuilo), naturally assumed the priority of mictlan and tlalticpac, because the earth plays a central role in the Nahua cosmology.[64]

---

61 Strictly speaking, the word ylhujcac does not mean "sky" in the sense we understand it, but the space above the earth. See Katarzyna Mikulska Dąbrowska, "El concepto de Ilhuicatl en la cosmovisión nahua," Revista Española de Antropología Americana 38, no. 2 2008): 151–71.

62 León-Portilla, Aztec Thought and Culture, 9.

63 Ilhuicatl, ylhujcac, or ilvicac are variations of the same word, translated as "sky." Following the Nahuatl spelling convention we choose to follow, unless it is quotations from original texts, I will use the spelling of ilhuicatl.

64 See Sylvia Marcos, "Mesoamerican Women's Indigenous Spirituality: Decolonizing Religious Beliefs," Journal of Feminist Studies in Religion 25, no. 2 (2009): 25–45, and José Rabasa, Tell Me the Story of How I Conquered You: Elsewheres and Ethnosuicide in the Colonial Mesoamerican World (Austin: University of Texas Press, 2011).

Another issue emerges when we compare the two versions of the same text in translation. *Mictlan* is translated in the Spanish as *infierno,* a Christian concept, "hell," and is also often translated as *inframundo* or "underworld." While in the Christian cosmology *infierno* and *inframundo* are interchangeable, *mictlan,* or the place (*tlan*) of the dead (*micto*), is not exactly situated "beneath the earth." *Ilhuicatl* (the Nahua "sky") and *mictlan* (the Nahua "hell") might not be in the same spatial relation as Christian heaven and earth. Otherwise, it would have been absurd for the celestial Ometeotl to "spread from the navel of the earth," while the terrestrial Tlaltecuhtli, or even infra-terrestrial Mictlantecuhtli and Mictlantecihuatl, dwell on different levels of the "sky."

In *La filosofía nahuatl,* first published in 1956, Miguel León-Portilla analyzes the Nahua expression *topan, mictlan,* which he believes is one of the fundamental "quests" of the wise man *tlalmatini.* León-Portilla translates *topan, mictlan* as "knowing what is beyond us (and) the place of the dead."[65] He explains that *topan* means "what is beyond us" and *mictlan* "the place of the dead."[66] We can find a similar expression in the *Códice florentino,* for example, *in topan in mictlan in ilvicac* which means "beyond us (in) the *mictlan,* (in) the *ilhuicatl.*"[67] Indeed, as Mikulska Dąbrowska argues, both *in mictlan* (the place of the dead) and *in ilvicac* (the "sky") "appear to be situated *topan,* 'beyond us', which suggests a location 'above', where one would imagine it to be the opposite of 'Mictlan.'"[68] That is to say, the "sky" (*ilhuicatl*) is not necessarily above (*topan*) and "hell" (*mictlan*) is not necessarily below. León-Portilla's careful translation "topan, mict-

---

65 Miguel León-Portilla, *La filosofia nahuatl: Estudiada en sus fuentes* (México D.F.: Universidad Nacional Autonoma de México, 1956), 70: "Conoce lo (que) está sobre nosotros (y), la región de los muertos."

66 Ibid.: "lo que nos sobrepasa"; "la región de los muertos."

67 I'd like to remind the reader that *in* in Nahuatl means "the," not "in."

68 Mikulska Dąbrowska, "El concepto de Ilhuicatl en la cosmovisión nahua," 154: "aparecen situado topan, 'sobre nosotros', lo cual sugiere una ubicación 'arriba', donde uno se imaginaría que debería de estar el lugar opuesto a Mictlan."

lan (lo sobre nosotros, lo que se refiere al más allá, a la región de los muertos),"[69] suggesting not only the spatial but also the metaphysical "beyond" (*topan*), however, has become spatialized as up and down in the English version as "*topan, mictlan,* what is above us and below us, in the region of the dead" by its translator Jack Emory Davis.[70] Suddenly the Nahuas seem indecisive on whether the "region of the dead" is "above us" or "below us." But what the Nahua philosophers were pondering is the question of *topan,* that is, "the metaphysical beyond."[71] León-Portilla translates *topan mictlan* as *más allá* or *au-delà* of *mictlan* for that matter. However, the English translation expresses the necessity to add a spatial preposition that cannot suggest any metaphysical speculation, "below us," to fit the expectation that *mictlan,* the region of the dead, should be down there.

Pete Sigal argues that Nahua mythology "alludes to a set of powerful deities that asserted a feminine earth and a masculine sky."[72] However, they did not stop there; deities were able "to change genders and identities in order to access relevant levels of the cosmos [and the] actual substances that made up these gods could be exchanged when the god willed it."[73] How is this "changeability" maintained? In order to answer this question, we need to look closely at Nahua cosmo-philosophy, which will be the focus of the next chapter. Before we can learn to learn from Nahua cosmo-philosophy, and therefore its "queer" divinities, we need to unlearn certain epistemic habits so entrenched in colonial modernity.

---

69 "topan, mictlan (what is beyond us, which refers to the au-delà, in the region of the dead)."

70 Jack Emory Davis, quoted in León-Portilla, *Aztec Thought and Culture,* 15.

71 Marcos, "Mesoamerican Women's Indigenous Spirituality," 33.

72 Pete Sigal, *The Flower and the Scorpion: Sexuality and Ritual in Early Nahua Culture* (Durham: Duke University Press, 2011), 3.

73 Ibid.

3.3 The Question of Writing

Tlaltecuhtli, Lord of the Earth, has been consistently translated as Lady of the Earth in scholarly works and curatorial texts. Despite the fact that Tlaltecuhtli, as we have already seen, *can* be regarded as a feminine figure, "earth mother," or *vagina dentata,* a title that takes into account the deity's gender complexity does not seem to exist. As we have already seen, there are not only feminine representations of Tlaltecuhtli, but also masculine, zoomorphic, and Tlaloc-faced ones. According to Matos Moctezuma, the categorizations that do not fit into the general naturalized "nature" of Tlaltecuhtli, one that intimately links the deity with the earth, such as the masculine group A and, to some extent, the masculinized Tlaloc-faced group D, should therefore be treated as special or exceptional ones. On the one hand, this "exception," also assumed in other research and curatorial presentations, is performed through what I called "sex assignment by castration," under the rubric of "Tlaltecuhtli: Diosa de la tierra." On the other hand, despite the attempt to disavow any interpretation associable with heteronormativity, we have to accept the fact that one feminine function of the earth, namely, its birth-giving function, is undeniable. Being an earth deity, Tlaltecuhtli ~~is~~ Tonantzin, our benevelonet mother, and Tlaltecuhtli ~~is~~ feminine.[74]

Surprised to learn that Tlaltecuhtli is not "*Lady* of the Earth," I began the investigation of the strange case of Tlaltecuhtli. My unease at seeing the Nahua language silenced even in some very sophisticated research in the field made me wonder about the reason behind this. In previous sections, I offered an "archaeological" examination of how the modern/colonial heterosexualist gender system has imposed a "sex assignment" on Tlaltecuhtli whose "sex" (*tecuhtli* being masculine) and "gender" (the earth and the related imagery of *vagina dentata* being feminine) do not seem to be in accordance with each other. This coercive

---

74 I return to the usage of "~~is~~" (a technique known as *sous rature* or "under erasure") in the next section.

modern "correction" happens at the expense of Nahuatl's power to signify.

In this section, I want to problematize the ontological questions — "who *is* Tlaltecuhtli?" and "what is their 'true sex'?"[75] I will do so by turning first to Jacques Derrida's critique of Western metaphysics or logocentrism and Hélène Cixous's further critique of phallogocentrism. I am, however, suspicious of the universal applicability of Derrida's work, and Cixous's work for that matter. Unlike Gordon Brotherston, who in his early work states that "no literary approach to the texts of the New World can avoid the problem of 'grammatology' raised by Derrida in his book of that title,"[76] I mention these important critiques of Western metaphysics not because they are in any way universal, but precisely because they show that neither phallogocentric metaphysics nor critiques of it should be blindly applied to the Nahua context. As Elizabeth Boone suggests, the "need to record speech is not universally felt."[77] Let us therefore first understand how Nahua cosmology functions. Pete Sigal aptly summarizes it as

a complex amalgam of different concepts in which deities had the ability to transform themselves into virtually any-

75 Michel Foucault, "Le vrai sexe," in *Dits et écrits IV, 1980–1988* (Paris: Gallimard, 1994), text no. 287.

76 Gordon Brotherston, "Towards a Grammatology of America: Lévi-Strauss, Derrida and the Native New World Text," in *Literature, Politics and Theory: Papers from the Essex Conference, 1976–1984,* eds. Francis Barker et al. (London: Methuen & Co.Ltd, 1986), 190–209, at 190. Mignolo reports that Brotherston "dropped his claim for a 'grammatology' of the Americas and replaced it, instead, with a long discussion on the social role of the Mesoamerican scribes and the sign carriers" (Walter Mignolo, "Writing and Recorded Knowledge in Colonial and Postcolonial Situations," in *Writing without Words: Alternative Literacies in Mesoamerica and the Andes,* eds. Elizabeth Hill Boone and Walter Mignolo [Durham: Duke University Press, 1994], 293–313, at 310n5).

77 Elizabeth Hill Boone, "Writing and Recording Knowledge," in *Writing without Words: Alternative Literacies in Mesoamerica and the Andes,* eds. Elizabeth Hill Boone and Walter Mignolo (Durham: Duke University Press, 1994), 3–26, at 20.

thing [… with an underlying] set of beliefs about the inter-connections among the earth, the heavens and the land of the dead.[78]

This extremely flexible cosmology and certainly also its comple-mentary gender system are reflected in and constructive of its very form of "writing," *tlacuilolli,* which means both "to write" and "to paint," a concept to which we will return in more de-tail in the subsequent chapter. The fact that the Nahuas have not developed a writing system to record speech word by word suggests that Nahua philosophical and cosmological concerns are very different from the European metaphysical tradition, which regards speech as the presence of truth best recorded by alphabetic language. In this context, we will focus on the im-portance and absence of the verb "to be" in Western and Nahua philosophies respectively. Finally, we will return to our concern regarding gender(ing) and discuss how Tlaltecuhtli and other Nahua deities in general resist modern gender categories. We should not forget that in pre-Conquest Mexico-Tenochtitlan, Tlaltecuhtli, the name of this important earth deity, was not "written" in the way that we have come to pronounce and know it, that is, in Latin characters. Rather, it was recorded in the writ-ing/painting system *tlacuilolli* of pre-Conquest Nahuatl.

3.3.1 *The Instituting Question of (Western) Philosophy*
The ontological quest for "what is?" of the Western metaphysi-cal tradition is not shared, or at least not shared in the same way, by the Nahuas. Their language, Nahuatl, does not attach any importance to that quintessential verb of Western philos-ophy, *to be.* The question "what *is* Tlaltecuhtli?" or the state-ment "Tlaltecuhtli *is…*" is already trapped in a particular kind of philosophical quest that prefigures its possible answers. Cix-ous rightly relates the question of "what is?" to the philosophical construction of masculinity and argues, "As soon as the ques-tion 'What is it?' is posed, from the moment a question is put, as

---

78 Sigal, *The Flower and the Scorpion,* 3.

soon as a reply is sought, *we are already caught up in masculine interrogation.*[79] In order to adequately explore this question, I follow Cixous's suggestion to perform a linguistic analysis: "We must take culture at its word, as it takes us into its word, into its tongue [*langue*]. You'll understand why I think that no political reflection can dispense with reflection on language [*langage*], with work on language [*langue*]."[80]

The Nahuas have a different philosophical concern, which constructs the very materiality of their language as a non-alphabetic one. Whereas Western metaphysics deems it necessary to record speech as a kind of presence of truth, the Nahuas do not approach the world in this way. At least, it appears that their *tlacuilolli* does not seek to record speech word by word.

Derrida points out that "the instituting question of philosophy [is]: 'what is…?'"[81] This question can be understood as a preoccupation with "Being" and an ontological quest for an ultimate God, Truth, or Meaning immune to worldly "distortions," whose underlying influence is that of the theo-political concept of *creatio ex nihilo* as discussed in Part 0. Alphabetic writing is believed to be able to perfectly imitate speech, and speech *entendu(e)* (heard and understood) is believed to be "closest to the self as the absolute effacement of the signifier."[82] Of course, the Eurocentrism of this belief becomes clear once we deprive the so-called "instituting question of philosophy" of its universalist assumption, and situate it as local to Western philosophy

---

79 Hélène Cixous, "Castration or Decapitation?," trans. Annette Kuhn, *Signs: Journal of Women in Culture and Society* 7, no. 1 (1981): 41–55, at 45, originally published as "Le sexe ou la tête," *Les Cahiers du GRIF* 13 (1976): 5–15, at 7: "dès qu'on pose la question de 'qu'est-ce que c'est?', dès qu'on pose une question, dès qu'on demande une réponse, […] on est déjà pris dans l'interpellation masculine."

80 Cixous, "Castration or Decapitation?" 45 [7]: "il faut prendre la culture au mot, comme elle nous prend dans son mot, dans sa langue […et] une réflexion politique ne peut pas se dispenser d'une réflexion sur le langage, d'un travail sur la langue."

81 Jacques Derrida, *Of Grammatology*, trans. Gayatri Chakravorty Spivak (Baltimore: Johns Hopkins University Press, 1997), 19.

82 Ibid., 20.

and the logocentric tradition. And yet, even Spivak's postcolonialist explanation of the Heideggerian/Derridian technique of *sous rature,* a rebellion against logocentrism, falls into a universalistic trap:

> Heidegger crosses out the word "Being," and lets both deletion and word stand. It is inaccurate to use the word "Being" here, for the differentiation of a "concept" of Being has already slipped away from that precomprehended question of Being. Yet it is necessary to use the word, *since language cannot do more.*[83]

A quick contestation of Spivak's belief in the absolute necessity of the word "being" in "language [that] cannot do more" can be found in Nahuatl, in which this word simply does not exist. Previously, we stated that "Tlaltecuhtli ~~is~~ Tonantzin and therefore Tlaltecuhtli ~~is~~ feminine." Here, the technique of *sous rature* or "under erasure," used first by Martin Heidegger and then Jacques Derrida, is adopted. Spivak concisely explains this technique: "[W]rite a word, cross it out, and then print both word and deletion. (Since the word is inaccurate, it is crossed out. Since it is necessary, it remains legible)."[84] Since Nahuatl does not use the verb "to be" and allows every noun to function as a stand-alone nominal predicate, the Nahua expression *tlaltecuhtli tonantzin* should best be translated into English as "Tlaltecuhtli ~~is~~ Tonantzin," if we are to respect the internal logic of the language.

Moving around or beyond the logocentric question "what is Tlaltecuhtli?" requires a critical overview of logocentrism and of the different philosophical preoccupations of Western metaphysics and Nahua cosmo-philosophy. A comparative discussion of the verb "to be" in Western languages and its absence in Nahuatl will then help us to explore further Nahuatl's "writing

---

83 Gayatri Chakravorty Spivak, "Translator's Preface," in Derrida, *Of Grammatology,* xv, emphasis mine.

84 Ibid., xiv.

without words." Its pictorial representation and linguistic function provide the fluidity that allows the feminine rendering of Tlaltecuhtli, Lord of the Earth.

Derrida calls the philosophical quest in Western metaphysics for *logos* the "metaphysics of presence." He contends that "there has to be a transcendental signified for the difference between signifier and signified to be somewhere absolute and irreducible."[85] Through his grammatological scrutiny, Derrida suggests that this metaphysical tradition is characterized by "logocentrism," a theory that privileges speech over writing following the logic of binary opposition. Logocentric philosophers deem written language an inferior mode of conveying truth, as opposed to speech, which is believed to be a non-mediated expression of thought and truth. Following the same hierarchical line of thought, different written languages are ranked in such a way that alphabetic languages are placed on top, believed to be the most developed ones. Alphabets are privileged because they are believed to be the best way to register speech. As a result of this hierarchization, writing systems such as Nahua *tlacuilolli* are discarded as "primitive writings," still in an early period of development from pictographic to alphabetic system, if they are given the privilege of being considered writing at all.

The evolutionary model in studies of writing systems posits a linear logic. All non-alphabetic writing systems are believed to inevitably develop from so-called "primitive" pictography to ideograms and finally reaching the front line of development, that of alphabetic writing. Even some highly knowledgeable scholars in non-alphabetic language systems fall into the trap of this evolutionary model constructed within the logocentric tradition. For example, in his influential *The Chinese Language: Fact and Fantasy* published in 1984, John DeFrancis suggests that the Chinese character-based writing system has failed in terms of mass literacy and subsequently calls for a linguistic reformation (indeed alphabetization) of the Chinese language. DeFrancis's argument about the feasibility of alphabetization is

---

85 Derrida, *Of Grammatology*, 20.

based on his theory that "Chinese characters are a phonetic, not an ideographic, system of writing."[86]

On the other side of the Pacific, American indigenous languages such as Nahuatl, Maya, and Quechua, to name but the most widely spoken ones, are believed to be undeveloped not because they did not develop a writing system, but because colonial prejudice holds that they are not able to develop one. In his influential *A Study of Writing,* Ignace Gelb expresses a typical ethnocentrism without much reservation:

Would it not be surprising […] if the pre-Columbian Indians, who produced a culture frequently compared with the fully developed cultures of the ancient Near east, did not have a writing of the same stature as the systems found in the Orient? The answer I would give is that the Amerindian cultures cannot properly be compared with the cultures of the Near East. […] The highly developed calendar system is the most conspicuous feature of the Amerindian cultures and it stands out as a unique achievement among the dearth of other culture accomplishments. Such a high level of development in a specialized field is surprising, but not unique. […] Furthermore, even a superficial knowledge of the inscriptions of the Aztecs and Mayas is enough to convince oneself that they could never have developed into real writing without foreign influence. The features of the written forms, stagnant for about seven hundred years, the creation of the grotesque head-variant forms with their characteristic superabundance of unnecessary details — a cardinal sin in writing from the point of view of economy — are all indications of a decadent, almost baroque, development.[87]

---

86 John DeFrancis, *The Chinese Language: Fact and Fantasy* (Honolulu: University of Hawai'i Press, 1984), 133.

87 Ignace J. Gelb, *A Study of Writing* (Chicago: University of Chicago Press, 1974), 57–58.

"Pre-Columbian Indians" (as he calls the sum of the diverse groups of indigenous peoples, condemning them to the inevitability of the temporal linearity expressed in "pre-Columbian") did not develop "writing" because, according to the circular logic of the author, they were culturally decadent. Their cultural decadence or impotence, according to Gelb, would have kept their writing stagnant and grotesque, "almost baroque." No effort whatsoever is made to understand the philosophical, cultural, and historical reasons for the possible disinterest in developing a writing system comparable to the "oriental" ones. Nor has the author investigated the importance of, precisely, "the baroque" in the formation and resistance of the colonial Americas. Certainly, it does not occur to Gelb to compare Maya writing to other known writing systems. Another interesting paradox is that, while writing is condemned as unreliable and inferior within the Western metaphysical tradition, forms of writing other than alphabetic ones, or languages without certain "written" forms, are condemned as indicators of the inferiority of those cultures, peoples, and "races."

Although Gelb and others claim that the Aztecs had no "real writing," they did have a concept for it in Nahuatl, *tlacuilolli*. *Tlacuilolli* derives from the verb *icuiloa,* which roughly means "to write" and "to paint." What is more, according to Marc Thouvenot, *tlacuilolli* in fact encompasses a wide range of other meanings that are beyond text or painting, for example: sculptures made of wood or stone, or even tattoos.[88] In contrast to the condescending idea that Nahua writing is made of mnemonic "little drawings," the Nahua scribes developed a complex system of conveying meaning and sound that is both logographic and logosyllabic, "written" with "scribal resources such as rebus and phonetic complementation, the conventions of transliteration and transcription, [and] the composition of signs in

---

88 Marc Thouvenot, "Imágenes y escritura entre los nahuas del inicio del xvi," *Estudios de Cultura Náhuatl* 41 (2010): 169–77.

glyphic blocks."[89] For example, the Nahua sign resembling a human hand is a representation of *atl* (water). And the sign *atl* does not only convey the meaning "water" but is also sign of one of the 20 calendar days. On the other hand, although there is a mnemonic representation of *xochitl* (flower) as the figure of a flower, the sign has different functions. It can designate a flower or one of the 20 calendar days like *atl* does. What is more, the image of a flower might only serve as a phoneme, forming part of a glyph that might or might not convey the meaning of a flower or a calendar day. A glyph that reads *Xochimilco* (name of a place) is formed using the figures of "flower" (*xochitl*) and "cultivated field" (*milpa*). Brotherston rightly argues, "we should be aware of denying some inner systemic principle to even the most primitive-seeming graphie [*sic*]."[90]

3.3.2 ~~Being~~
I shall take a detour through a similar case with its own nuances, namely the reception of Chinese writing in the West. Rey Chow summarizes the "Chinese hallucination" (a term coined by Derrida) as follows:

> Chinese "writing" has been a source of fascination for European philosophers and philologists since the eighteenth century because its ideographic script seems (at least to those who do not actually use it as a language) a testimony of a different kind of language — a language without the mediation of sound and hence without history.[91]

"People without history" is an idea rooted in the Eurocentric theory "according to [whose] concept of history as defined in the Western world from ancient Greece to twentieth-century

---

89 Alonso Lacadena, "Regional Scribal Traditions: Methodological Implications for the Decipherment of Nahuatl Writing," *The PARI Journal* 8, no. 4 (2008): 1–22, at 8.

90 Brotherston, "Towards a Grammatology of America," 200.

91 Rey Chow, *Writing Diaspora: Tactics of Intervention in Contemporary Cultural Studies* (Bloomington: Indiana University Press, 1993), 18.

France, every society that did not have alphabetic writing [...] did not have History."[92] Hegel made a similar assertion about the unsuitability of Chinese for logical thinking without bothering himself to study the Chinese language at all. For example, he claims that only the German language is capable of having two contrary meanings in a single word, an attribute even Latin does not have.[93] Qian Zhongshu, in his seminal work 管錐編 (*Limited Views: Essays on Ideas and Letters*) exposes Hegel's prejudice:

> As we know, the German philosopher Hegel wrote disparagingly about the Chinese language, saying that it was unsuited for logical reasoning. He boasted at the same time, that German had the ability to capture ineffable truths, and adduced "*Aufheben*" as an example, observing that it combined two contrary meanings in a single word [*ein und dasselbe Wort für zwei entgegengesetzte Bestimmungen*], and asserted that even Latin does not have such semantically rich concentrations.[94]

Quoting Hegel in German, Qian proposes a similar example to *Aufheben* and shows that the word 易 (*yi*), as in the classic 易經 (*The Book of Changes*), simultaneously means "simple," "to change," and "unchanging":

> Compared to "unchanging" and "simple," *yi* 易 in the sense of "to change" is an antonymous meaning, whereas "unchanging" and "simple" are distinct but synonymous mean-

---

92 Mignolo, *The Idea of Latin America,* xii. For a more radical take on this, see: José Rabasa, *Without History: Subaltern Studies, the Zapatista Insurgency, and the Specter of History* (Pittsburg: University of Pittsburgh Press, 2010).

93 Hegel in Zhongshu Qian, *Limited Views: Essays on Ideas and Letters,* trans. Ronald Egan (Cambridge: Harvard University Asia Center/University Press, 1998), 203.

94 Ibid., 203, originally published as 管錐編, vol. 1 (Beijing: Sanlian Shudian Press, 2007), 5: "黑格爾嘗鄙薄吾國語文，以為不宜思辨；又自誇德語能冥契道妙，舉"奧伏赫變"（Aufheben）為例，以相反兩意融會於一字(ein und dasselbe Wort für zwei entgegengesetzte Bestimmungen), 拉丁文中亦無意蘊深富爾許者."

ings of *yi*. The statement that "the one name of *yi* contains three meanings" thus refers jointly to antonymous and synonymous meanings, as well as the fact that all are used simultaneously.[95]

It comes as no surprise that those who desperately disparage other cultures do not even consider it necessary to consult some basic knowledge about these cultures.[96] However, ignorance does not always result in direct denigration, as in the case of Gelb or Hegel, who condemn languages that they do not know. It also sometimes leads to exotic fantasies. Derrida points out, for example, that "the concept of Chinese writing […] functioned as a sort of European hallucination [which] translated less an ignorance than a misunderstanding [and] was not disturbed by the knowledge of Chinese script."[97] Reading on the surface of an unknown language, especially when it is alleged to be "pictorial," is common practice.

A famous case is Ezra Pound's "translation" of Chinese poems under the influence of Ernest Fenollosa, who believed that Chinese "ideograms" were "shorthand pictures of the operations of nature."[98] Contrary to Derrida's claim that Pound's "invention of Chinese poetry" should be regarded as "the first break in the most entrenched Western [logocentric] tradition,"[99] Zhang Longxi's analysis of the Pound–Fenollosa case suggests that

---

95 Ibid., 204 [12]: "'變異'與'不易','簡易'背出分訓也;'不易'與'簡易',並行分訓也。'易一名而含三億'者,兼背出與並行之分訓而同時合訓也." For a trans/queer reading of *yi*, see my essay "Transdualism: Towards a Materio-Discursive Embodiment," *TSQ: Transgender Studies Quarterly* 5, no. 2 (2018): 425–42.

96 Qian excuses Hegel for being ignorant of Chinese with a mild, diplomatic criticism: "Now, Hegel cannot be blamed for not knowing Chinese. To flaunt one's ignorance carelessly, making it the basis of a grand pronouncement, is also something that scholars and specialists do all the time, and this too can hardly be held against him" (Qian, *Limited Views,* 203).

97 Derrida, *Of Grammatology,* 80.

98 Ernest Fenollosa, *The Chinese Written Character as a Medium for Poetry* (San Francisco: City Lights Books, 1969), 8.

99 Derrida, *Of Grammatology,* 92.

they should [not] be regarded as free from the sort of Chinese prejudice Derrida has detected in Leibniz, because for them [...] "what liberates Chinese script from the voice is also that which, arbitrarily and by the artifice of invention, wrenches it from history and gives it to [poetry]."[100]

The debates over the "ideographicality" of the Chinese language are numerous. Although they are not the major concern of the current study, a quick survey will help our discussion of the Nahua case. After all, it is not uncommon for me to be asked questions, such as "isn't your language made up of little drawings?" echoing Fellonosa's theory of the Chinese language. The misunderstanding of Nahua *tlacuilolli* and Maya hieroglyphs as silent "pictures" also aligns with this theory. DeFrancis even asserts that "there never has been, and never can be, such a thing as an ideographic system of writing."[101]

Whether or not these so-called pictorial or pictographic writings convey sound is an irrelevant question. In fact, they might well *not* convey sound. Of course, anyone who knows Chinese knows that the script does record sound, but is not reducible to sound. As Shang Wei puts it: "[O]ne-to-one correspondence between script and sound and overall congruence between writing and speech, [...] did not exist in early modern and premodern China."[102] Shang's observation does not include the act of read-

---

100 Longxi Zhang, *The Tao and the Logos: Literary Hermeneutics, East and West* (Durham: Duke University Press, 1992), 25.

101 DeFrancis, *The Chinese Language*, 133. Several pages later, after surveying the rather ethnocentric theories of Gelb and Mallery regarding "Amerindian" writings as "merely mnemonic," he argues that to "lump together the writing of the American Indians and the early Chinese and Egyptians because of some similarity in graphic forms is to fall victim to the kind of befuddled thinking that is indicated by calling all of them pictographic or ideographic" (ibid., 137–38).

102 Wei Shang, "Writing and Speech: Rethinking the Issue of Vernaculars in Early Modern China," in *Rethinking East Asian Languages, Vernaculars, and Literacies, 1000–1919*, ed. Benjamin A. Elman (Leiden; Boston: Brill, 2014), 254–301, at 256. Shang continues: "the very fact that a given word or morpheme is often associated with more than one pronunciation and that the same text can be subject to different vocalizations inevitably complicates,

ing. We can find in Hegel some ungrounded assertions that "the reading of hieroglyphs is for itself a *deaf* reading and a mute writing."[103] Zhang Longxi responds to this prejudice with some common sense:

[R]eading any […] language is a linguistic act of comprehending the meaning of a succession of signs, either with silent understanding or with utterance of the sounds [and] it is not an archaeological act of digging up some obscure etymological roots from underneath a thick layer of distancing abstraction.[104]

Let us now return to the Nahua case to survey how *tlacuilolli,* the most salient form of writing of the Nahuas, as well as other surrounding groups, is read (out). Elizabeth Boone, an expert in Nahua writing, explicates that

these pictorial histories did not remain mute. Aztec historians did not just consult them quietly in libraries or offices, nor did they read the histories to themselves […]. [Instead], the pictorial histories are closer to being scripts, and their relation to their readers is closer to being that of a play's script to its actors.[105]

By the same token, Pete Sigal situates the discussion of the writing/painting activity within the religio-ritual setting, where Nahua priests "'read' these documents out loud in a variety of cer-

---

if not entirely defeats, the effort to find the exact equivalent of European vernaculars in the Chinese writing system. In other words, it is misleading to raise the issue of vernacularization in discussing Chinese writing, as Chinese writing is almost always at variance with the spoken language and thus stands in a different relationship with speech than Latin does."

103 Hegel, in Zhang, *The Tao and the Logos,* 25.

104 Ibid., 25–26.

105 Elizabeth Hill Boone, "Aztec Pictorial Histories: Records without Words," in *Writing without Words: Alternative Literacies in Mesoamerica and the Andes,* eds. Elizabeth Hill Boone and Walter Mignolo (Durham: Duke University Press, 1994), 50–76, at 71.

emonies by expanding on the images presented on the page."[106] These "images" were *tlacuilolli,* which were not meant "to be read as transparent assertions of a reality that they had witnessed [or] as complete narratives."[107] *Tlacuilolli* was not a widely practiced activity but was reserved to the professional scribes called *tlacuilo*: "[A] good tlacuilo contrasts with the bad, not in what we might call his ability to represent accurately a given reality but rather in his artistic merit. Thus a bad tlacuilo is said to be 'dull' and one who 'paints without reflection.'"[108] What Gelb considers the "cardinal sin" of their "almost baroque" writing is clearly an asset.

In Nahuatl, no equivalent to the verb "to be" exists. "I am a person" would be *nitlacatl* with the first person singular prefix *ni-* attached to the noun *tlacatl* ("person"). In case of the third person singular, such as "s/he is Tlaltecuhtli," one only needs to say *tlaltecuhtli*. James Lockhart explains this particularity that "each noun in an utterance is at least potentially a complete equative statement in itself," with the example of the "word for 'house' in its dictionary form, *calli,* [which] has a third person subject and by itself means 'it is a house,' or since in many cases no distinction exists between singular and plural, 'they are houses.'"[109] Put in another way, the relationship between the subject and predicate in Nahuatl does not presuppose fixity. In the words of Gaston Bachelard: "It is not being that illustrates relation, far from that; it is relation that illuminates being."[110]

This grammatical relationality is reflected in the pervasive connectedness between earth and heaven, man and woman, good and bad in every aspect of Nahua cosmology, especially in its concept of the divine.[111] As a mutually dependent relationship,

---

106 Sigal, *The Flower and the Scorpion,* 33.

107 Ibid.

108 Ibid., 40.

109 Lockhart, *Nahuatl as Written,* 1.

110 Gaston Bachelard, *Le nouvel esprit scientifique* (Paris: PUF, 1971), 148: "loin que ce soit l'être qui illustre la relation, c'est la relation qui illumine l'être."

111 Sylvia Marcos, *Taken from the Lips: Gender and Eros in Mesoamerican Religions* (Leiden: Brill, 2006), 36.

it gives the possibility for "humans and animals under certain circumstances [... to] become gods"[112] and vice versa. We only need to see how many rulers named themselves Quetzalcoatl, imagining themselves to be the "incarnations" of this supreme deity. Again, this is different from an idea of the transcendental God (capitalized, singular, but perhaps not the pluri-singular *elohim*) who created the world *ex nihilo,* and the human individual as a projection of God's image. Keller coins the formula "Genesis 1 + omnipotence + ontology = *creatio ex nihilo,*" which can be played back as *creatio ex nihilo* conditioned by Christian doctrine leading to "ontology": "What is?"[113]

The very contradiction between Tlal*tecuhtli* and *Goddess* of the Earth does not exist in Nahuatl, not because the noun *tecuhtli* might *be* "goddess" or "lady" but because from its very root, the gender of Tlaltecuthli is uncertain. As one of the most important deities in Nahua cosmology, given their direct association with the earth, Tlaltecuhtli is not confined to any one "sex." The Nahuas have produced a coherent system in which complementarity, relationality, and communality, rather than opposition, ontology, and individuality, are emphasized and enacted through *tlacuilolli* writing/painting and its highly mutable pantheon. For these reasons, the Nahuas seem to be perfectly comfortable calling the Earth Lord: Tonantzin Tlaltecuhtli, "Our Mother: The Earth Lord," in the *Song of Teteoinnan.*[114] That "the earth lord is our mother" might at least cause speculation or unease for a modern English speaker (just as Smith's quotation with mesmerizing gender-blending at the beginning of this chapter has generated all the speculations for us throughout). "Tonantzin Tlaltecuhtli," however, could be translated also as "Our Mother ~~is~~ the Earth Lord" or "the earth lord is our (benevolent) mother." Without the fixation of the verb "to be,"

112 Sigal, *The Flower and the Scorpion,* 3.
113 Catherine Keller, *Face of the Deep: A Theology of Becoming* (London: Routledge, 2003), 64.
114 Sigal, *The Flower and the Scorpion,* 152–53.

Tlaltecuhtli becomes Tonantzin, which is perfectly legitimate in Nahuatl.

Nahua cosmology asserts that a feminine earth is not contra-dictory to the masculine name of the earth deity, Tlaltecuhtli. In grammatical terms, "the Nahuatl way of saying that a thing 'is' another thing is the verbless conjunction or reciprocal ref-erence of two nouns of the same person and number."[115] How-ever, the creativity of Nahuatl appears to go further than that. The coexistence of masculinity, femininity, zoomorphism, and Tlaloc-rendering in the representations of one deity, Tlaltecuh-tli, can be read as a possibility of conveying what I have termed elsewhere the logic of "either…and."[116] Tlaltecuhtli is (either) feminine (and) masculine. And because neither *tonantzin* nor *tlaltecuhtli* was locked in alphabets and the compatible grammar of subject-predicate linked with "to be," the monolithic fixation is even less palpable. They are all entangled, through the earth, through the "mother figure," through Ometeotl. This strong sense of connectedness or entanglement of Nahua philosophy, without surprise, determines and is reproduced in its syntax:

> [I]n the absence of case or a fixed word order, it is often hard to determine the function of third person nouns in Nahuatl, particularly when there are several in a sentence. Object and subject are particularly hard to tell apart. […] In cases like these we must hope that the context will settle the question for us.[117]

A language philosophy that relies on context would only answer the question "what is Tlaltecuhtli?" with a quasi-postmodern "relativism" — *it depends.* Peter van der Loo believes that what he calls the Mesoamerican "pictorial notating system"[118] has the privilege of being read "not only by the actual painter but

---

115 Lockhart, *Nahuatl as Written,* 11.
116 Xiang, "Transdualism."
117 Lockhart, *Nahuatl as Written,* 11–12, emphasis mine.
118 Not only the Nahuas but also other indigenous peoples such as Zapotecos have developed similar writing/painting systems.

also by many other Mesoamerican peoples who may have spoken very different languages."[119] Within the conventional limits (that is to say, *not* everything goes), it allows "regional and also personal interpretations of the important elements of the religion [… and] the necessary flexibility for regional and personal adaptation."[120] Furthermore, "the implication of the name, the images, and the partnerships of Tlaltecuhtli all suggest an identity that […] cannot be only female. Rather, Tlaltecuhtli signified a figure, a deity whose gender cannot be named."[121]

"Who is Tlaltecuhtli?" is eventually a misleading question to ask, especially when they are isolated from the ritualistic, mythological, philosophical, and linguistic contexts of the Nahuas. Like Tezcatlipoca, the one who kills Tlaltecuhtli in the beginning of the Fifth Era, they also *noujian ynemjian: mictla, tlalticpac, ylhujcac*, "walk in any place: in *mictlan*, the place of the dead, on the earth and in *ilhuicac*, the 'sky'."

Tlaltecuhtli ~~is~~ immensely free.

119 Peter L. van der Loo, "Voicing the Painted Image: A Suggestion for Reading the Reverse of the Codex Cospi," in *Writing without Words: Alternative Literacies in Mesoamerica and the Andes,* eds. Elizabeth Hill Boone and Walter Mignolo (Durham: Duke University Press, 1994), 77–86, at 84.
120 Ibid., 85.
121 Sigal, *The Flower and the Scorpion,* 304n68.

4

Coatlicue Mayor:
Or, Other Ways of Rereading
the World

Me quitaran a quererte Llorona,
Pero olvidarte nunca[1]
— "La Llorona," Mexican Popular Song

William Bullock wrote in his 1824 travelogue, *Six Months' Residence and Travels in Mexico,* about witnessing the exhumation of Coatlicue Mayor, the colossal statue of the Aztecs attributed to Coatlicue or "the one with serpent skirts," in the court of the Real y Pontificia Universidad de México. Bullock considered Coatlicue, the "Tonantzin" (our benevolent mother) of the Nahuas, a "horrible deity, before whom tens of thousands of human victims had been sacrificed, in the religious and sanguinary fervor of its infatuated worshippers."[2] The English collector recounted how the "Indians" reacted to the "decided anger and contempt" of the university students when the statue was exposed:

---

1   "They stopped me from loving you, Llorona / But, (I will) never forget you." This is one of the various versions of the folk song "La Llorona." For an excellent interpretation by Chavela Vargas, see http://www.youtube.com/watch?v=t4OV7Rw8OVM.

2   William Bullock, *Six Months' Residence and Travels in Mexico* (London: John Murray, 1824), 338.

I attentively marked their countenances; not a smile escaped them, or even a word — all was silence and attention [...]. In reply to a joke of one of the students, an old Indian remarked, "It is true we have three very good Spanish gods, but we might still have been allowed to keep a few of those of our ancestors!" and I was informed that chaplets of flowers had been stolen thither, unseen, in the evening for that purpose; a proof that, notwithstanding the extreme diligence of the Spanish clergy for three hundred years, there still remains some taint of heathen superstition among the descendants of the original inhabitants.[3]

In the account, the serious "Indians" were distinguished from the contemptuous students, who apparently found their beliefs ridiculous and laughable. The Mexican natives were carefully kept away from the Catholic university students, not in terms of space — for they were all present in the same crowd — but in terms of cosmology and religion. While descendants of the original Nahuatl-speaking inhabitants of Mexico-Tenochtitlan continued their pagan worship, the students either got angry or made jokes about the native faith and *Weltanschauung* evidenced by Coatlicue Mayor. We do not know whether Bullock simply invented this story to reinforce the idea of the indigenous people's stubborn clinging to their "heathen superstition," but it is certainly true that he took the side of the angry or amused students, whose own ethnic background remains unknown.

In this chapter, I will try to explore a profoundly different way of understanding the world, through a decolonial learning-to-learn from Nahua cosmo-philosophy. This "learning" first requires a process of unlearning, a process of suspending the certainty of modern and colonial categories through which we mostly operate. I am not content, however, to merely "critique" what has allegedly gone wrong. Instead, in the second half of this last chapter, I will read from within what could be called "Nahua cosmo-philosophy," specifically with the help of reading

---

3   Ibid., 341–42.

Coatlicue Mayor as a form of *tlacuilolli*, rather than as a mere artistic representation. Ultimately, I seek to show that the "pictorial writing" of the Nahuas is an adequate and efficient system of "writing" for their cosmology and philosophy.

4.1 Coatlicue and Coatlicue Mayor

From about 1540, soon after the fall of Tenochtitlan and the Aztec Empire in the year 1521, the Franciscan friar Bernardino de Sahagún began composing the *Códice florentino*[4] in the form of the Aztec pictorial historiographic account known as *códices,* helped by trilingual (Nahuatl, Spanish, and Latin) Nahua *tlacuilos* (scribes, historiographers, and illustrators). The *Códice florentino* is also referred to as *Historia general de las cosas de Nueva España*[5] (henceforth, *Historia*). The three-volume *Códice* describes at length many aspects of the Aztec society recently conquered and renamed as New Spain (*Nueva España*). Most pre-*Conquista* codexes were destroyed by the Spanish colonizers who deemed them pagan idolatry. Sahagún laments: "They and their things were so abused and destroyed that nothing is left to them the same as it was before."[6] It has become a widely accepted thesis that our knowledge about pre-Hispanic Mexico is inevitably intertwined with (if not only knowable through) post-conquest ethnographic and historiographic writings such as the *Códice florentino*.

The *Historia* is one of the two colonial ethnographies where the mythic figure Coatlicue appears. Book 3 of the *Historia* tells

---

4 This particular codex is called *Códice florentino* because the earliest copy (1577) is held in the Biblioteca Medicea Laurenziana in Florence, Italy.

5 For a discussion of the different versions of *Códice florentino* and *Historia* see José Luis Martinés, *El "Códice florentino" y la "Historia general" de Sahagún* (México D.F.: Archivo General de la Nación, 1989).

6 Bernardino de Sahagún, *Historia general de las cosas de Nueva España* (México D.F.: Imprenta del Ciudadano Alejandro Valdés, 1829), 2: "fueron tan atropellados y destruidos ellos y todas sus cosas, que ninguna apariencia les quedó de lo que eran antes." All translations to English from non-English sources, unless stated otherwise, are mine.

the story of the birth of Huitzilopochtli, one of the most important deities of the Aztecs:

According to what the old natives have said and known about the birth of the devil Huitzilopochtli to whom the Mexicans devoted honour and respect, it is that there is a mountain called Coatepec next to the village Tula, where there lives one woman called Coatlicue who was the mother of some Indians called Centzonhuitznahuac who had a sister called Coyolxauhqui.[7]

The *Historia* designates Coatlicue as *una muger,* "a woman," who is mother of "some Indians" with the name of Centzonhuitznahuac (meaning "400 southerners," representing the southern stars in Nahuatl). They also have a sister, Coyolxauhqui, who is the goddess of the moon. It is said that one day Coatlicue takes a feathered ball that falls from the sky and puts it next to her belly when she is sweeping the temple. Touching this feathered ball gets her pregnant with Huitzilopochtli.[8]

---

7 Ibid., 234: "Segun lo que dijeron y supieron los naturales viejos del nacimiento y principio del Diablo que se decia Vitzilopuchtli, al cual daban mucha honra y acatamiento los mexicanos es: que hay una sierra que se llama Coatepec, junto al pueblo de Tulla, donde vivia una muger que se llamaba Coatlycue que fue madre de unos indios, que se decia Centzon-xitznaoa, los cuales tenían una Hermana que se llamaba Coyolxauhqui." Note: in the translated version, I have changed some of the old spellings of Nahuatl names to versions that are more common. For example, "Vitzilopuchtli" has been changed to "Huitzilopochtli."

8 The Christian influence in seeing this miraculous pregnancy as a virgin birth cannot be overstated. Bierhorst John Bierhorst has argued that there is a rich and discreet symbolism of different elements such as *xochitl,* flower, which can connote sexual power. See John Bierhorst, *Cantares Mexicanos: Songs of the Aztecs* (Stanford: Stanford University Press, 1985). I also want to point out that we should not be too quick to equate the event with a Catholic repertoire of the "virgin birth." Both "feather" and "sweeping the temple" have strong sexual connotations in Nahua rituals. See Pete Sigal, *The Flower and the Scorpion: Sexuality and Ritual in Early Nahua Culture* (Durham: Duke University Press, 2011), and Pete Sigal, "Imagining Cihuacoatl: Masculine Rituals, Nahua Goddesses and the Texts of the Tlacuilos," *Gender & History* 22, no. 3 (2010): 538–63.

This unexpected pregnancy allegedly annoys her 400 sons and her daughter Coyolxauhqui, who incites her 400 brothers to kill their mother. But Huitzilopochtli, then still in Coatlicue's womb, overhears their plan. Huitzilopochtli is the patron god of the Aztecs, who, according to legend, led the nomadic Aztec tribe to conquer the Mexican Valley and build the capital Tenochtitlan on an island of the Texcoco Lake, where they encountered a divine revelation: an eagle devouring a snake on top of a nopal cactus. Also the god of sun and war, Huitzilopochtli is born at the very moment when the group led by Coyolxauhqui arrives at Coatepec to prepare for their matricide. Huitzilopochtli is born fully armed, and kills his sister and the majority of his brothers, the 400 southerners.

We can observe the political meaning of this particular story, mainly dedicated to recording the mythical birth of Huitzilopochtli, as it was told and retold in Tenochtitlan. Archaeologists have discovered that the myth was repeatedly performed in the form of human sacrifice in the Templo Mayor.[9] Not unlike the Babylonian New Year Festival where *Enuma Elish* and the victory of Marduk over Tiamat was recited, the Aztec sacrifice based on the myth of Huitzilopochtli's victory over Coyolxauhqui and Centzonhuiznahuac can be read as a discourse that reiterated and justified Aztec colonial subjugation of the native inhabitants.

We can further conclude from this account that Coatlicue is the mother of the sun (represented by Huitzilopochtli), the moon (represented by Coyolxauhqui), and the stars (represented by Centzonhuiznahuac). Although she is often referred to as the earth mother since her name, Coatlicue, contains the terrestrial animal *coatl*, "snake" in Nahuatl, she seems to have given birth to the whole universe.

Friar Diego Durán provides a more detailed story about Coatlicue in his *Historia de las Indias de Nueva-España y Islas de Tierra Firme,* roughly written at the same time as Sahagún's

---

9   See Eduardo Matos Moctezuma, *Vida y muerte en el Templo Mayor* (México D.F.: Editorial Océano, 1986).

Historia. Here, Coatlicue appears to be a semi-mythical and semi-historical figure.

In chapter XXVII, we are told that Montezuma, the great king of Mexico-Tenochtitlan, commands his coadjutant Tlacaelel to find out where their ancestors lived and specifically to look for the mother of their patron god Huitzilopochtli, Coatlicue, who is said to still be alive. An old historian named Çuauhcoatl informs King Montezuma that the ancestors come from a place called "Aztlan," which is also the origin of their name, "Aztec," people of Aztlan. Tlacaelel then sends several magicians or wizards to look for Coatlicue in this legendary place. They carry with them the most precious treasures to their patron god's mother.[10] Upon arrival at Coatepec, the servant of Coatlicue tells them that poor Coatlicue is still sadly waiting for the return of her son, Huitzilopochtli, since he promised her he would return with glory.

Coatlicue appears to be very old and "the ugliest and dirtiest one could think and imagine."[11] She tells those young men that she has not washed her face nor combed her hair nor changed her clothes for the mourning of her son Huitzilopochtli, and that such mourning and sadness will not end unless he returns. She is then told that Huitzilopochtli is already dead. The wizards show her the treasures they bring to her and tell her that Huitzilopochtli was the king of all these. She calms down, but then begins to complain about all the sadness and solitude her son has caused her.[12]

---

10 Diego Durán, *Historia de las Indias de Nueva España y Islas de Tierra Firme, Tomo I* (1867; rpt. Alicante: Biblioteca Virtual Miguel de Cervantes, 2005), 220: "y mandó luego sacar gran cantidad de mantas, de todo género dellas, y de vestiduras de muger y de piedras ricas de oro y joyas muy preciosas, mucho cacao y teonacaztli, algodon, rosas de vainillas negras, muchas en cantidad, y plumas de mucha hermosura, las mejores y mas grandes; en fin, de todas las riqueças de sus tesoros, lo mejor y mas precioso."

11 Ibid., 223: "la mas fea y sucia que se puede pensar ni imaginar."

12 She tells them that Huitzilopochtli also anticipated the war and conquest in the Mexican Valley: "en el qual tiempo tengo de hacer guerra á todos las prouincias y ciudades, villas y lugares, y traellos y sujetallos á mi seruicio; pero por la mesma órden que yo los ganare, por esa mesma órden me los an

The wizards return to Tenochtitlan and repeat to Montezuma the curse of Coatlicue:

[A]t a certain moment it [the Mexican people] will be thrown out of the land and return to that place [Aztlan] because for the same order it had subjugated the other people, it will be kicked out and [stripped of] the dominance it had over others.[13]

After hearing this, the king and his coadjutant burst into tears. Thus, Diego Durán's account brings the mythical figure Coatlicue to history. Coatlicue seems to have predicted the fall of the Tenochtitlan. Durán continues the story of conquest in the next chapter, XXVIII: "[A]lready at that time it [the curse] was becoming true, there were signals and comets that predicted the arrival of the Spaniards."[14] It is very likely that the story was told

---

de quitar y tornar á ganar gentes estrañas, y me an de echar de aquella tierra; entonces me vendré acá y me voluevé á este lugar, porque aquellos que yo sujetare con mi espada y rodela, esos mesmos se an de voluer contra mí y an de empeçar desde mis piés a echarme caueça abaxo, y yo y mis armas irémos rodando por el suelo: entonces, madre mia, es cumplido mi tiempo y me volueré huyendo á vuestro regaço, y hasta entonces no hay que tener pena; pero lo que os suplico es que me deis dos pares de çapatos, los unos para ir y los otros para voluer" ("as in such time, I will wage war on all the provinces and cities, villages and places, and bring them down and subject them to my service; but for the same order that I will win over them, for that same order foreigners will get rid of and return to win over me and throw me away from that place. Then I will come back here to this place, because those whom I have subjugated with my sword and shield, those same [people] will turn back against me and begin with my feet to throw my head down, and I with my weapons will be turning around down to the ground. As a result, my mother, when my time arrives I will come back escaping to your lap and until then please don't be sad; but what I beg of you are two pairs of shoes, one pair to go and the other pair to come back") (ibid., 225).

13 Ibid., 227–28: "cierto tiempo auia de ser echado desta tierra y que se auia de volver á aquel lugar, porque por la mesma órden que auia de sujetar las naciones […] le auian de ser quitadas y priuado del dominio y señorío que sobre ellas tenia."

14 Ibid., 229: "en aquel tiempo [la maldición] se iba cumpliendo, uvo señales y cometas que pronosticaron la venida de los españoles."

in order to justify the Spanish *Conquista* as a kind of predetermined fate. However, the theme of the "return of the repressed" already seems to haunt the Aztecs way before it starts to haunt the Spaniards.

Coatlicue returns in a different form two centuries later. In 1790, an accidental discovery revealed the monolithic statue Coatlicue Mayor, which has since then been recognized as representing Coatlicue, Huitzilopochtli's mother, at the Plaza Mayor near Templo Mayor in Mexico City. Just two years later, archaeologist Antonio León y Gama published a study, *Descripción histórica y cronológica de las dos piedras* (1792), with detailed descriptions of this colossal statue, as well as the Piedra del Sol (also known as the Aztec calendar stone). In fact, León y Gama thought that the statue represented not Coatlicue, but Huitzilopochtli's wife, Teoyamiqui. Later, the German humanist Alexander von Humboldt, who read León y Gama's work, also believed that this was a statue of Teoyamiqui.[15] Both Coatlicue Mayor and the Piedra del Sol are emblematic art works of Aztec civilization and are now housed next to each other in the Sala Mexica of the Museo Nacional de Antropología in Mexico City, as important symbols of the glorious Aztec past of Mexico.

Being buried and exhumed several times during its stay at the university, Coatlicue Mayor was first transferred to the Galería de Monolitos as part of president Benito Juárez's campaign to "form a sense of Mexican National identity" by fomenting "an interest in the pre-Hispanic past."[16] In the end, it was moved to the newly built Museo Nacional de Antropología. Coatlicue Mayor has undergone a turbulent reception history ever since it was exhumed for the first time.

In order to unearth something, it has to be buried first. We are not sure why exactly the statue was buried in the first place. It is reasonable to speculate that Coatlicue Mayor was deliberately buried to protect it against barbaric acts of the conquer-

---

15   Ann de León, "Coatlicue or How to Write the Dismembered Body," *Modern Language Notes* 125 (2010): 259–86, at 269.

16   Ibid., 260.

ing Catholic Church. In the museum today, we can see the "sister" sculpture of Coatlicue, Yolotlicue (the one with the skirt of hearts), which was heavily damaged during that disastrous vandalism in the name of God. Some 200 years after the Spanish *Conquista,* the viceroy of the then Viceroyalty of New Spain, Revillagigedo, called the newly rediscovered Coatlicue Mayor "a monument of American antiquity" and sent it to the Real y Pontificia Universidad de México. However, the friars and professors of the university soon regarded the statue as a demonic presence of Aztec paganism with "some secret religious motivation"[17] so dangerous that the "idol" might contaminate the Mexican youth.[18] For this reason, this "satanic symbol" was soon buried again. The fact that the "devilish monster" was never destroyed, but constantly exhumed and reburied leads one to speculate that those who were reportedly disgusted or threatened by it were at least to some extent also subjected to a certain fear of that "secret religious motivation."

Some years later, in 1803, Alexander von Humboldt travelled to Mexico City and was permitted to unearth the *demonio* to examine it before it was quickly buried again because "the presence of the terrible statue was unbearable."[19] Humboldt believed that the statue was an "incorrect representation" of the human body, which in turn proved the barbarity of the conquered people.[20] Twenty years after Humboldt, the English collector William

17 Moxó y Francoly in Eduardo Matos Moctezuma, *Las piedras negadas: De la Coatlicue al Templo Mayor* (México D.F.: Consejo Nacional para la Cultura y las Artes, 1998), 39: "algún secreto motivo religioso." The "invocation of the ghost" might be read as a countercolonial strategy. See José Rabasa, *Tell Me the Story of How I Conquered You: Elsewheres and Ethnosuicide in the Colonial Mesoamerican World* (Austin: University of Texas Press, 2011). To a certain extent, the university friars and professors were right about this "secret motivation."

18 Matos Moctezuma, *Las piedras negadas,* 41.

19 Octavio Paz, "Diosa, demonia, obra maestra," in *México en la obra de Octavio Paz III: Los privilegios de la vista* (México D.F.: Fondo de Cultura Económica, 1977), 39–52, at 40: "la presencia de la estatua terrible era insoportable."

20 Alexander von Humboldt, *Vues de Cordillères et monuments des peuples indigènes de l'Amérique* (Paris: Librairie Grecque–Latine–Allemande, 1816).

Bullock had the chance to make a copy of the exhumed statue in 1823, and transferred it to his exhibition in the Egyptian Hall in London. Similar to the bewildered Europeans preceding him, Bullock seized the opportunity to debunk the statue as a way to argue against those who "have accused the Spanish authors of exaggeration in their accounts of the religious ceremonies of this, in other respects, enlightened people." His argument was that "a view of the idol [Coatlicue Mayor] under consideration will of itself be sufficient to dispel any doubt on the subject."[21] He further interpreted the statue as a reflection of the horror that Hernán Cortéz and his troops faced at the "Noche Triste":

[T]he adventurous Cortez, and his few remaining companions in arms, were horror-stricken by witnessing the cruel manner in which their captive fellow-adventurers were dragged to the Sacrificial stone, and their hearts, yet warm with vitality, presented by the priests to the gods; and the more the separated seat of life teemed with animation, the more welcome was the offering to the goddess.[22]

The conqueror is presented as an "adventurous" hero subjected to unbearable horror in front of the sanguinary, almost cannibalistic, Aztec barbarians. The scene echoes Jan van der Straet's painting, *America* (c. 1575), of the early days of the "discovery" of America, as well as the definition of colonialism by the *Columbia Encyclopedia* as a result of "more or less aggressive humanitarianism, and a desire for adventure or individual improvement," as we have seen in Part O.[23]

In contrast to the overt disgust with and fear of a pagan "monster" expressed by Catholic friars and the two 19th-century European travellers, Humboldt and Bullock, Octavio Paz praises the statue as a masterpiece of art. In his introduction to Mexican

---

21 Bullock, *Six Months' Residence and Travels in Mexico*, 339–40.

22 Ibid., 339.

23 Barbara A. Chernow and George A. Vallasi, eds., *The Columbia Encyclopedia*, 5th edn. (New York: Columbia University Press, 1993), 600–601.

Art written for the catalogue of the *Exposición de Arte Mexicano en Madrid* (1977), Paz dedicated one special section entitled "Diosa, demonia, obra maestra" ("Goddess, Demon, Masterpiece") to a review of the reception history of Coatlicue Mayor. The 1990 Nobel Prize laureate of literature argues that Coatlicue Mayor is a supernatural presence, a "dreadful mystery" (*misterio tremendo*) for both the Aztec priests and the Spanish Catholic friars. According to him, the intellectual and aesthetic speculations from the 18th and 20th centuries have abandoned the magnetic territory of the supernatural "[by] leaving the temple for the museum, [the statue] has changed nature but not appearance."[24] Later in this short essay, Paz reads the changing attitudes towards the statue as a reflection of what European consciousness has experienced before the so-called "discovery of America."[25] Like Coatlicue Mayor, he argues, "those civilizations of America were not older than the European one; they were different. Their difference was radical, a genuine otherness."[26]

There are numerous works on Coatlicue Mayor. While most have taken into account the statue's complexity, which encapsulates the whole of Nahua cosmology, a point we will discuss in more depth in the next sections, few have thoroughly questioned the strict feminine rendering of the statue. Through a discussion of the "decapitation" allegedly represented by Coatlicue Mayor, I hope to show that, like the straightforward feminine rendering, the assumption that the statue represents a decapitated human body derives from a Eurocentric expectation of mimetic representation.

---

24 Paz, "Diosa, demonia, obra maestra," 40–41: "[al] dejar el templo por el museo, [la estatua] cambia de naturaleza ya que no de apariencia."

25 Ibid., 42: "descubrimiento de América."

26 Ibid., 43: "las civilizaciones de América no eran más antiguas que la europea: eran diferentes. Su diferencia era radical, una verdadera otredad." Some years later, the Franco-Bulgarian philosopher Tzvetan Todorov proposes a similar thesis regarding the question of the Other. See Tzvetan Todorov, *La conquête de l'Amérique: La question de l'autre* (Paris: Éditions du Seuil, 1982).

In Elizabeth Baquedano and Michel Graulich's article on decapitation among the Aztecs, Coatlicue Mayor is listed as material evidence of the important role decapitation played in Aztec religious culture and practice. As the authors contend, "several famous Aztec statues of the earth goddess, in particular the colossal so-called Coatlicue and Yollotlicue, represent a beheaded woman with eyes and mouth at every joint."[27] The authors also refer to the story we reviewed above concerning the "virgin birth" of Huitzilopochtli by Coatlicue and his decapitation of Coyolxauhqui, which means that they are aware that Coyolxauhqui, not Coatlicue was decapitated. What is more, the decapitation of Coyolxauhqui by Huitzilopochtli, according to the account given by Sahagún, is meant to protect his mother Coatlicue, and not to kill her. Simply put, an interpretation of Coatlicue Mayor as "decapitated" is in fact not compatible with the mythical story.

Elizabeth Boone is aware of this discrepancy between the representation of the allegedly decapitated Coatlicue Mayor and the myth in which it is her daughter Coyolxauhqui who is decapitated. In order to work out this puzzle, she suggests that both "decapitated" statues, Coatlicue Mayor and Yolotlicue, belong to "the broad category of powerful, potentially dangerous, supernatural women [...] that Huitzilopochtli, as the sun god, must forestall and render impotent."[28] This speculation is not convincing either, as Cecelia Klein points out that "according to the *Anales de Quauhtitlan* [...] Huitzilopochtli was among the deities who sacrificed themselves to put the sun in motion, a role that would have made him their [Coatlicue's and Yolotlicue's] collaborator rather than their enemy."[29]

---

27 Elizabeth Baquedano and Michel Graulich, "Decapitation among the Aztecs: Mythology, Agriculture and Politics and Hunting," *Estudios de Cultura Náhuatl* 23 (1993): 163–77, at 165.

28 Elizabeth Hill Boone, "The 'Coatlicues' at the Templo Mayor," *Ancient Mesoamerica* 10, no. 2 (1999): 189–206, at 204.

29 Cecelia F. Klein, "A New Interpretation of the Aztec Statue Called Coatlicue, 'Snakes-Her-Skirt'," *Ethnohistory* 55, no. 2 (April 2008): 229–50, at 243.

Klein proposes an alternative interpretation, namely that Coatlicue Mayor might represent "one of a group of heroic women whose collective death not only enabled the creation and survival of the universe but the government as well."[30] She goes on to read the coded symbolism of the braided skirt, and argues that "these skirts not only figuratively spelled out their names but also epitomized their feminine powers of creation."[31] She then draws the conclusion that

> Coatlicue is here not (just) Huitzilopochtli's mother, but rather a grand creatrix, the mother of all beings and objects that inhabited the Aztec universe. [...] Coatlicue and its companion statues celebrate primordial women as the self-less donors of everything the Aztecs had cause to treasure. [...] If this reading of the Coatlicue statue is correct, women's powers to generate new life on every level were, among the Mexica, very great indeed.[32]

Coatlicue Mayor indeed represents more than just Huitzilopochtli's mother, the mythical and historical Coatlicue, recorded in Sahagún's and Durán's ethnographies. Klein's interpretation however, simplifies the complexity of Nahua gender, which the author herself argues belies modern/colonial dichotomous gender.[33] A sole "feminine" creation power generated by martyred "women," however tempting or familiar that might sound to a (feminist) modern reader, is not likely to be an adequate account of the Nahua cosmo-philosophy. Even if one can temporarily read the statues as representations of self-sacrificing female warriors, this cannot convincingly explain Coatlicue and Yolotlicue's allegedly "dismembered and decapi-

---

30 Ibid.
31 Ibid., 244.
32 Ibid., 245.
33 See Cecelia F. Klein, "None of the Above: Gender Ambiguity in Nahua Ideology," in *Gender in Pre-Hispanic America: A Symposium at Dumbarton Oaks,* ed. Cecelia F. Klein (Washington, DC: Dumbarton Oaks, 2001), 183–254.

tated appearance."[34] Even if decapitation is important in sacrificial rituals, as Baquedano and Graulich have argued, no evidence shows that the sacrificed deities have self-decapitated or self-dismembered at the beginning of the Fifth Era.

In a more recent study published in 2010, Ann de León also assumes that Coatlicue Mayor represents a "goddess" and that this "goddess" Coatlicue is decapitated. Although she does not cite Boone's earlier article, we have reason to suspect that de León would agree with her, as she also told a slightly mismatched story of matricide: "Coatlicue's body as mutilated [...] as occurred with the statue, [... is designed] to narrate how Coatlicue's children killed her."[35] Except for Sahagún's account, in which Coatlicue's children led by the sister merely intend to kill the mother, we do not have any account in which Coatlicue is actually killed. What is more, if we compare Sahagún's account to Durán's, we should assume that Coatlicue is immortal and remains alive in Coatepec.

The alleged matricide in de León's article and Klein's interpretation of the statue as a representation of a self-sacrificing woman, set out to explain the reason why Coatlicue Mayor represents a "dismembered and decapitated" body.[36] Ann de León makes a compelling point in that regard. By tracing the reception history of Coatlicue Mayor in post-Conquest Mexico, she criticizes the colonial European receptions of Mexico that portray its indigenous past as barbaric on the basis of two major accusations, the lack of (alphabetic) writing and the incapacity for mimetic representation.[37] In the case of Humboldt, she argues:

[W]hat Humboldt appears to tell us is that the degree of "civility" of a society translates into its artistic and cultural manifestations [...] The Aztecs become barbaric because of their "incorrect" esthetics [sic], [as for] Humboldt, Coatli-

---

34 Klein, "A New Interpretation of the Aztec Statue Called Coatlicue," 243.
35 de León, "Coatlicue or How to Write the Dismembered Body," 283.
36 Klein, "A New Interpretation of the Aztec Statue Called Coatlicue," 229.
37 de León, "Coatlicue or How to Write the Dismembered Body," 262–64.

cue's body performs an "incorrect" esthetics because it does not present a mimetic or naturalist representation of the *female human body.*[38]

She continues: "This reveals that Humboldt, using his Eurocentric esthetic lens, could not understand Aztec ideology and representation of the human body through material culture."[39] What interests me in this debate is the question why "she" should need to have a human head at all, and why the absence of a human head should necessarily mean that "she" is decapitated? Coatlicue Mayor has eagle legs, "arms" formed by snakes, as well as a skirt made of serpents, which is decisive for the statue's association with Coatlicue. *Coatl* means "snake," *-i* is the generless third person possessive pronoun,[40] and *cuetli* means skirt. All these seem to suggest that this is not a representation of a human body, much less a "female human body."

Although Ann de León rightly points out that that the 19th-century European aesthetics that Humboldt had in mind "favored mimetic representation of the human body in art with correct proportion,"[41] she nevertheless curiously assumes that Coatlicue Mayor has a mutilated and decapitated body. For example, she states that "Coatlicue's decapitated head, [is] represented by two snakes joining profiles."[42]

Both de León and Klein have followed Justino Fernández's seminal essay on Coatlicue Mayor, which argues that the two snakes in lieu of a "decapitated head" represent two streams of blood.[43] If this were the case, then we might follow Baquedano and Graulich to interpret the snake reaching out from the ser-

---

38 Ibid., 266 emphasis mine.

39 de León, "Coatlicue or How to Write the Dismembered Body," 267.

40 James Lockhart, *Nahuatl as Written: Lessons in Older Written Nahuatl, with Copious Examples and Texts* (Stanford: Stanford University Press, 2001), 1.

41 de León, "Coatlicue or How to Write the Dismembered Body," 267.

42 Ibid., 280.

43 Justino Fernández, *Coatlicue: Estética del arte indígena antiguo* (México D.F.: Instituto de Investigaciones Estéticas, Universidad Nacional Autónoma de México, 1959).

pent-skirt on the lower part of the statue, between the two eagle legs, as menstruation.[44] This interpretation, however, is contradictory to Fernández's own theory elsewhere: "[T]his divinity [… is] also male, and for this reason a great serpent can be seen beneath the skirt."[45] Although Baquedano and Graulich seem to accept Fernández's theory that besides blood "the snake was also associated with the penis," they soon maintain that the two snakes between the statue's legs "stand for menstrual blood, for the cut throat and the female sex organ were regarded similarly since they were both sources of life."[46] The analogy between the "cut throat" and the "female sex organ" reminds one of the phallocentric idea that sees women as "naturally castrated" because of their allegedly dispossessed penis.

In these important studies that largely inspire my own interest in the issue, the familiar modern/colonial and heteronormative gender dichotomy has been highly operative, and although it is far from my intention to take the scholarship to task, I hope it is clear that modern/colonial categories and Eurocentric aesthetic judgment have little to say about the complexity of the statue. These theoretical apparatuses at best recycle gendered clichés regarding reproduction, generational conflict, or decapitation. What is alarming is perhaps not, or not only, the blunt Eurocentrism one finds in a Catholic friar's denomination of Huitzilopochtli as *demonio,* but rather in a benevolent gesture of "recognition." Ann de León, whose article astutely criticizes Eurocentrism in the receptions of Coatlicue Mayor, for example, suggests that "Fernández was indebted to the Avant-garde movements of the 20s and 30s [… that] had developed a new 'Western' aesthetics where the 'primitive' was viewed and evalu-

---

44 Elizabeth Baquedano and Michel Graulich, "Decapitation among the Aztecs: Mythology, Agriculture and Politics and Hunting," *Estudios de Cultura Náhuatl* 23 (1993): 163–77, at 169.

45 Justino Fernández, *A Guide to Mexican Art: From Its Beginnings to the Present,* trans. Joshua C. Taylor (Chicago: University of Chicago Press, 1969), 44.

46 Baquedano and Graulich, "Decapitation among the Aztecs," 169.

ated in a different way than in Humboldt's time."[47] Octavio Paz's short essay has similarly assumed this Western position of (aesthetic) judgment.[48] Why does Coatlicue Mayor or any non-Western art work have to wait for hundreds of years for the 20th-century Western vanguards — who were not only dealing with their own aesthetic and political problems, but were also largely indebted to so-called "primitive" art of the non-West — to be finally accepted? The locus of enunciation remains in the West, the epistemic zero point which judges the *other*'s art — once condemned as "primitive" and "monstrous," now a "masterpiece," as Paz calls it.

4.2 Translating Ometeotl, or the Gender Trouble of Nahua "Dualism"

Ometeotl, the supreme divinity in Nahua cosmology, has two gendered aspects: the feminine Omecihuatl and the masculine Ometecuhtli. They are also recognized as Tonacacihuatl and Tonacatecuhtli, Lady and Lord of Our Existence (*to-, "our"; nacatl, "that which grows from the earth and sustains life, i.e., maize"). Ometeotl, the divine duality, is so important that Miguel León-Portilla argues that all Nahua deities are different manifestations of Ometeotl,[49] a thesis accepted by Henry Nicholson.[50] Richard Haly however, strongly doubts the very existence of Ometeotl based on a theory that Nahua culture is

---

47 de León, "Coatlicue or How to Write the Dismembered Body," 280.

48 See Paz, "Diosa, demonia, obra maestra."

49 Miguel León-Portilla, *La filosofía nahuatl: Estudiada en sus fuentes* (México D.F.: Universidad Nacional Autonoma de México, 1956); Miguel León-Portilla, "Ometéotl, el supremo dios dual, y Tezcatlipoca 'dios principal,'" *Estudios de Cultura Náhuatl* 30 (1999): 133–52.

50 León-Portilla, *La filosofía nahuatl*; León-Portilla, "Ometéotl"; Henry B. Nicholson, "Religion in Pre-Hispanic Mexico," in *Handbook of Middle American Indians, Volumes 10 and 11: Archeology of Northern Mesoamerica*, eds. Gordon F. Ekholm and Ignacio Bernal (Austin: University of Texas Press, 1971), 10:395–446, at 409–10.

an oral tradition.[51] Ometeotl, or its correlating gendered aspects, often translated as Lady and Lord of Duality, Omecihuatl and Ometecuhtli, at first glance might seem similar to the colonial/ modern one: two genders, a heterosexual couple, lady and lord, woman and man. A second glance at how the divine triad has been translated in modern scholarship might further convince one that the Nahua *ometeotl* is no different from the colonial/ modern dualism. Before even beginning to talk about Omete- otl, we are confronted with at least three possible answers to the question: how many deities are there? Three, if one regards Ometeotl, Omecihuatl, and Ometecuhtli as individual, separate, and autonomous divine beings; two, if Omecihuatl and Ome- tecuhtli are regarded as the additive components of Ometeotl; one, if all three are seen as different aspects of one deity.

Deciding among these options determines how the three words, Nahua theology, and especially Nahua "dualism," which we will refer to as *ometeotl,* are understood and translated. Omecihuatl and Ometecuhtli are often unambiguously translat- ed as Goddess or God of Duality respectively, or as the feminine or masculine aspect of Ometeotl, the supreme one.[52] As I will show in the second part of this chapter, Omecihuatl and Om- etecuhtli do not exist independently from each other and *omete- otl* needs to be understood within the very cosmo-philosophical structure of Nahuatl that is reflected in its textual-visual system *tlacuilolli.* The Nahua duality principle works as follows: that Ometecuhtli takes up the masculine aspect is largely in relation to the fact that Omecihuatl takes up the feminine, and "[b]oth are in constant mutual interaction, flowing into each other."[53] Ometeotl themself has no gender — it is beyond gender.

---

51 Richard Haly, "Bare Bones: Rethinking Mesoamerican Divinity," *History of Religions* 31, no. 3 (1992): 269–304, at 269.

52 In this chapter I use the capitalized version "Ometeotl" to designate the di- vinity and the italicized version *"ometeotl"* to refer to the Nahua duality principle which is closely related to and also represented by, but not con- fined to the divine "triad" Ometeotl.

53 Sylvia Marcos, *Taken from the Lips: Gender and Eros in Mesoamerican Reli- gions* (Leiden: Brill, 2006), 36.

Unfortunately, when Ometeotl is translated into modern languages such as Spanish, English, and French as "dios," "god," or "dieu," Ometeotl is made a masculine deity pretending to be generic. Serge Gruzinski, investigating the "colonization of the imaginary," has produced masculinity for Ometeotl, a deity of duality, by rendering it "le Seigneur de la Dualité."[54] The "duality complex," as summarized by Nicholson, has become "the complex of Ometecuhtli (god of duality)" in Ortiz de Montellano and Schussheim's work on Aztec medicine.[55] The masculine aspect of Ometeotl, the masculine-gendered Ometecuhtli (remember that *tecuhtli* means "lord" in Nahuatl) is forced to take up the task of representing the whole duality principle, erasing both the genderless Ometeotl and the feminine-gendered Omecihuatl. What is more, the feminine aspect of Ometeotl, Omecihuatl, is often treated as the consort of Ometecuhtli. We read this asymmetrical representation of the Ometeotl triad by Bernadino de Sahagún as follows: "[T]he name of the God of heavens was Ometecuctli, and the name of his consort, the woman of the heavens, was Omecihuatl."[56] The feminine aspect of Ometeotl therefore becomes "other than the norm."[57] The phallocentric and dissymmetrical sexual difference, a problem local to the colonial/modern West, produced in the languages and cosmologies that condition or conceive such differences, has been transplanted onto the Nahua context, and quite literally separates and hierarchizes the two gendered aspects of

---

54 Serge Gruzinski, *La colonisation de l'imaginaire: Société indigènes et occidentalisation dans le Mexique espagnol XVIᵉ–XVIIIᵉ siècle* (Paris: Éditions Gallimard, 1988), 241.

55 Bernardo R. Ortiz de Montellano and Victoria Schussheim, *Medicina, salud y nutrición azteca* (México D.F.: Siglo Veintiuno, 2003), 63: "Complejo de Ometecuhtli (dios de la dualidad)."

56 Haly, "Bare Bones: Rethinking Mesoamerican Divinity," 279n39.

57 Braidotti contends, following Derrida, that "it can be argued that Western thought has a logic of binary oppositions that treats difference as that which is other-than the accepted norm" (*Nomadic Subjects: Embodiment and Sexual Difference in Contemporary Feminist Theory* [New York: Columbia University Press, 1994], 78).

Ometeotl.[58] This imposition of not only one's linguistic habits but also cosmological truths *and* problems onto the other in the process of translation, especially from an imperialist language to an indigenous one, is what I call the coloniality of translation.

The coloniality of translation operates on different levels, including the linguistic and the epistemic. On the linguistic level, the problem is already quite difficult to solve. In English, one might use "it," as when we refer to maize or an animal. The English "it," however, connotes a lack of full agency and "life" itself. As a divine being, Ometeotl is not an "it," not because Ometeotl might not be maize or an animal (in fact, Ometeotl as Tona-catecuhtli-Tonacacihuatl who sustain life, is maize), but because within the cosmology of the English language and its linguistic habits, the agentless and lifeless English "it" can hardly do justice to the divine Ometeotl. With Spanish, into which many Nahua texts were translated, the issue is even more complicated. Since compulsory masculine or feminine gendering is a grammatical feature of Spanish and many other European languages, Ometeotl has been coercively translated as "dios de la dualidad," the *male* god of duality.

These questions involving Ometeotl's "gender trouble," we should not forget, are posed to English or Spanish, not Nahuatl, a genderless language "written" in radically different ways than alphabetic, speech-recording languages like Spanish or English. Meanwhile, Ometeotl or any other divine beings in the Nahua universe constantly cross gender boundaries and animal–human–divine distinctions.[59] However, translating Ometeotl as "God of Duality" is *not* a choice without choice, even though in modern Spanish using the masculine to designate the generic is a common practice. Here we move to the second level of the

---

58 For detailed discussions on the complicity between modern colonialism and heteronormativity, see for example: Oyèrónkẹ́ Oyèwùmí, *The Invention of Women: Making an African Sense of Western Gender Discourses* (Minneapolis: University of Minnesota Press, 1997), and María Lugones, "Heterosexualism and the Colonial/Modern Gender System," *Hypatia* 22, no. 1 (2007): 186–209.

59 Sigal, *The Flower and the Scorpion,* 3.

coloniality of translation, that of the epistemic. Ometeotl's gen-der trouble is not confined by the particular characteristics of some languages such as Spanish and French. As we have seen in the previous chapter, Tlaltecuhtli, the deity of the earth, whose name is literally "*Lord* of the Earth," has been continuously translated as "Goddess of the Earth" in most modern receptions. Ometecuhtli, "Lord of Duality" might have shared the same fate as Tlaltecuhtli and become "Lady of Duality." However, this hypothetical "mistranslation" that emasculates Ome*tecuhtli,* or Ometeotl for that matter, would never happen.

In light of the consistent feminizing translation of Tlaltecuh-tli as "goddess," the translation of Ometeotl as a masculine god of duality cannot be said to be the mere result of the coercive features of the Spanish language. Rather, it points to the colo-niality of translation at the epistemic level. Although Nahua mythology "alludes to a set of powerful deities that asserted a feminine earth and a masculine sky,"[60] it is the colonial/mod-ern categorical logic underlying reception studies that has al-ready predefined the so-called "celestial" sphere as exclusively masculine and the "terrestrial" sphere as exclusively feminine. From the perspective of this strict gender division of heaven and earth, Ometeotl (and Omecihuatl/Ometecuhtli), dwelling in Omeyocan, or the Place of Duality, therefore belongs to the celestial sphere. Belonging to the heavenly sphere, Ometecuhtli can never share Tlaltecuhtli's fate of feminization.

The difference of the Nahua *ometeotl,* mapped onto the rela-tionship between heaven and earth, is that the gendered parts do not exist independent of each other. Deities are able "to change genders and identities in order to access relevant levels of the cosmos."[61] In fact, the celestial Ometeotl *in tlalxicco ónoc,* spreads from the navel of the *earth.*[62] Coatlicue has been "lowered" to the terrestrial sphere and has become fixed as one of the "earth

---

60 Ibid.
61 Ibid.
62 Miguel León-Portilla, *Aztec Thought and Culture: A Study of the Ancient Nahuatl Mind,* trans. Jack Emory Davis (Norman: University of Oklahoma Press, 1963), 32.

goddesses," despite being mother of the Moon (Coyolxauhqui), the Stars (Centzonhuitznahuac), and the Sun (Huitzilopochtli). Her daughter Coyolxauhqui has not been able to salvage herself from the constraint of the terrestrial, even though she is the deity of the moon. Meanwhile, Omecihuatl, Lady of Duality, who improperly dwells in Omeyocan at the celestial level, which in the colonial/modern mindset is reserved for the masculine deities, has been represented as playing so trivial a role that many studies and encyclopedias simply leave her out.

It should be clearer now how the modern translation of Nahua words and concepts into European languages has perpetuated the illusion of a universal applicability of local Western cosmology and neglected the conceptual inequivalence between the two worlds. This symbolic imposition, however, has been hardly successful. The intellectual limitations of Western cosmology with regard to comprehending the complex system of trans-gender and even trans-species articulations are exemplified in the case of Tlaltecuhtli. Although primarily a deity associated with feminine characteristics and represented in many occasions as a goddess, Tlaltecuhtli is also a masculine deity bearing a masculine title, *tecuhtli,* not to mention the zoomorphic and Tlaloc-faced representations.[63] That Tlaltecuhtli takes on multiple forms, concomitant with *tlacuilolli,* is in fact nothing strange.

If the decolonial is an "option" at odds with "missions" that seek to convert difference into homogeneity or into recognizable and thus controllable subjects, a decolonial methodology needs to understand the very modes of resistance that have *already* taken place. A decolonial approach is therefore more about learning to learn from indigenous modes of decolonization than it is about prescribing theories and methods of resistance. It also means learning to unlearn the concepts, assumptions, and the

---

63 For a comprehensive discussion of the different representations of Tlaltecuhtli as male, female, animal, and Tlaloc (rain god), see Eduardo Matos Moctezuma, "Tlaltecuhtli: Señor de la tierra," *Estudios de Cultura Náhuatl* 27 (1997): 15–40.

very language that we deploy to think and theorize in hetero-sexualist modernity/coloniality.

Before continuing our decolonial exploration of *ometeotl,* I will look briefly at a recent case in which the coloniality of knowledge is explicit. The erudite Nahua scholar Miguel León-Portilla wrote a book called *La filosofía nahua* already in 1959, when "the philosophical debate around decolonization was just at its inception."[64] His effort to bring Nahua thinking into the splendor of "philosophy" was soon criticized, and "major attacks [were] concerned [with] his 'imprudent' use of the term 'philosophy' to designate something that the Aztecs or Nahuatl-speaking people could have been engaged in."[65] This influential book was subsequently translated into English, as *Aztec Thought and Culture: A Study of the Ancient Nahuatl Mind* (1963), into French as *La pensée aztèque* (1985), and into German as *Das vorspanische Denken Mexikos: Die Nahuatl-Philosophie* (1970). Only the German version retained the term "philosophy" while insisting on Nahua philosophy as a form of "pre-Hispanic thinking." Mignolo uses the case regarding the "proper name" of "philosophy" used in the Nahua context to talk about "philosophy and the colonial difference." He contends,

> [León-Portilla] did not ask whether the Nahuatl [*sic*] had philosophy. He assumed that they did, but in doing so, he had to make an enormous effort to put the Nahuatls [*sic*] next to the Greeks and then defend his move to his ferocious critics — that is, to the "malaise" produced by the colonial difference.[66]

I have coined the word "cosmo-philosophy" to give an account of the *pensée aztèque.* I do so intentionally to scramble the neatness of terminologies such as "mythology," "cosmology," and

---

64 Walter Mignolo, "Philosophy and the Colonial Difference," in *Latin American Philosophy: Currents, Issues, Debates,* ed. Eduardo Mendieta (Bloomington: Indiana University Press, 2003), 80–86, at 82.

65 Ibid., 80.

66 Ibid., 85.

"philosophy," which are purportedly not the same thing in a modern Western context. This is not a compromise with coloni-al discourse, which assumes that the Nahuas had no philosophy or no capacity of producing something like philosophy, but an attempt to see colonial difference as a site of resistance and de-colonization. José Rabasa's insightful observation helps us here:

> [T]here [is not] any indication that they [the Nahuas] felt pressed to prove that Nahuatl was a language capable of do-ing history, literature, and philosophy, *as if these clear-cut distinctions were current in the European sixteenth century.*[67]

The clear compartmentalization of knowledge that separates thinking endeavors into properly named disciplines is not ques-tioned by Mignolo himself when he talks about "sixteenth-cen-tury Spanish philosophers." The decolonizing endeavor to de-link thought from modern categorical logic is not an easy task.[68]

4.3 Re-reading Coatlicue Mayor with/as *Ometeotl*

Omecihuatl and Ometecuhtli "give birth" to four gods. They are, from the eldest to the youngest, Tezcatlipoca in red, Yayauqui-Tezcatlipoca in black, Quetzalcoatl in white, and Huitzilopoch-tli in blue.[69] Many other creation myths exist in the exuberant Nahua cosmos, but one figure stands out: Coatlicue (the one with the *cuetli,* "skirt" of *coatl,* "snakes"). As we know from Sa-hagún's and Durán's ethnographical accounts reviewed above, and whose basic storylines are accepted by most modern stud-ies, Coatlicue gives birth to Huitzilopochtli.[70] The battle between Huitzilopochtli and his sister Coyolxauhqui, however, has dif-ferent interpretations. One version shows that Coyolxauhqui stands on her mother Coatlicue's side but is mistaken by her

---

67 Rabasa, "Thinking Europe in Indian Categories," 48.
68 Mignolo, "Philosophy and the Colonial Difference," 83.
69 León-Portilla, *La filosofía nahuatl,* 95.
70 Alfonso Caso, *El pueblo del sol* (México D.F.: Fondo de Cultura Económica, 1994), 23.

brother Huitzilopochtli; in another version the Sun God (Huitzilopochtli) sees the Moon Goddess (Coyolxauhqui) as a threat
and he kills her.[71] Nevertheless, the Coatlicue family represents
the whole universe with Coatlicue as the earth, Huitzilopochtli
the sun, Coyolxauhqui the moon, and Centzonhuitznahuac the
stars.[72] Coatlicue is also often referred to as a primordial mother
goddess and bears the name of Tonantzin, "Our Benevolent
Mother," which is also used for addressing Ometeotl-Omeci-
huatl.[73]

Another creation myth portrays the cosmic battle between
two often masculine-identified deities, Quetzalcoatl and Tezcatlipoca, and the often (wrongly) feminine-identified Tlaltecuhtli, discussed in the previous chapter. It tells that the cosmos was covered in water after the fourth sun.[74] Tlaltecuhtli,
who appears in this myth as a monster, swims in the cosmic
water and eats human cadavers. The two gods transform themselves into two giant snakes, dive into the sea, and cut Tlaltecuhtli in two. With the upper part, they are said to have made the
heavens and stars, and with the lower part the earth.[75] The reason why we bring up Tlaltecuhtli, the Earth Lord, is that they
are represented on the underside of the statue Coatlicue Mayor,
hidden from uninitiated viewers. Thus the two apparently unrelated creation myths are in fact synchronized on the statue
Coatlicue Mayor.[76]

---

71 Ann Bingham, *South and Meso-American Mythology A to Z* (New York:
    Facts on File, 2004), 33.

72 Ibid., 26.

73 León-Portilla, "Ometéotl."

74 The Nahuas designate cosmic eras with the symbol of "sun." According to
    the Aztec Calendar, the age in which the Aztec Empire lived is the "fifth
    sun" created after the death of the fourth "sun" (Caso, *El pueblo del sol*).

75 Michael E. Smith, *The Aztecs* (Oxford: Blackwell, 1996); Caso, *El pueblo del
    sol*; Bingham, *South and Meso-American Mythology A to Z.*

76 Luis Roberto Vera, *Coatlicue en Paz, la imagen sitiada: La diosa madre az-
    teca como imago mundi y el concepto binario de analogía/ironía en el acto de
    ver: Un estudio de los textos de Octavio Paz sobre arte* (Puebla: Benemérita
    Universidad Autónoma de Puebla, 2003); Fernández, *Coatlicue*; Iliana Go-
    doy, "Coatlicue: Visión holográfica," *Escritos: Revista del Centro de Ciencias
    del Lenguaje* 33 (2006): 79–92; León-Portilla, *La filosofía nahuatl.*

4.3.1 Ometeotl Manifested

Considering that Huitzilopochtli is born "twice," both to Omecihuatl and to Coatlicue, and that both Coatlicue and Omecihuatl
are referred to as Tonantzin, it is reasonable to hypothesize that,
if Omecihuatl and Coatlicue are not the same deity, they are at
least different manifestations of the same deity. Henry Nicholson
contends that the "great legion of deities was organized around
a few fundamental cult themes […]. [T]hey greatly overlapped
and no clear line can be drawn between them."⁷⁷ Omecihuatl
should be understood as the feminine *aspect* coexisting with,
but not *derivative* of, the duality deity Ometeotl, who does not
stand outside these manifestations. The Nahua concept of the
divine thus appears to be radically different from the Christian
doctrine of monotheism, but *also* from polytheism. Hunt aptly
summarizes that the Nahuas regard reality, nature, and experience as "nothing but multiple manifestations of a *single unity of
being*. God was *both* the one and the many. Thus the deities were
but his [*sic*] multiple personifications, his [*sic*] partial unfold-
ings into perceptible experiences."⁷⁸ Sylvia Marcos also explains
this pervasive divine presence in Nahua theology, different from
"the concept of an inert physical world ruled by a *deus ex machi-
na*," as follows:

[A] permanent interaction characterized the relations between the Nahuas and their divinities. The sacred domain
was not distant, it was a presence that suffused every element
of nature, every daily activity, every ceremonial action, and
every physical being: flora and fauna, the sun and moon and
starts, mountains, earth, water, fire were all divine presences.⁷⁹

If we accepted this, we may affirm that Omecihuatl ~~is~~ Ometeotl.
The Nahuas address Ometeotl as *tonantzin totohtzin* (our be-

---

77 Nicholson, "Religion in Pre-Hispanic Mexico," 408.
78 Eva Hunt, *The Transformation of the Hummingbird: Cultural Roots of a
    Zainacantecan Mythical Poem* (Ithaca: Cornell University Press, 1977), 55.
79 Marcos, *Taken from the Lips*, 36.

nevolent mother, our benevolent father). That is to say, Coatlicue, the *tonantzin,* ~~is~~ also Ometeotl. These correlations or un-
foldings in Nahuatl would be expressed as *omecihuatl ometeotl*
and *coatlicue ometeotl.* Furthermore, Ometeotl (and *ometeotl*)
manifest or are manifested in the Nahua pictorial "writing" system *tlacuilolli.*[80] This unique form of conveying knowledge challenges the familiar conceptual tools such as writing and painting
with which we as modern scholars make sense of the world. Pertaining strongly to the visual, *tlacuilolli* is not limited to the notion of art, "as something visual to be appreciated and enjoyed
but something separate from communication."[81] If we follow
Elizabeth Boone, who argues that in the Nahua pictorial writing
system *tlacuilolli* "the pictures *are* the texts," it is possible to read
not only the familiar book-like codices but also the statues and
calendar stones as more than just artistic representations, but as
"texts" or mediums that convey knowledge.[82] The earliest study
of Coatlicue Mayor and the calendar stone in the modern era,
by Antonio León y Gama, in fact, already places Coatlicue May-
or in the realm of writing by suggesting that "in the writings of
those Indians [...] there are still some figures whose hieroglyphs
encompass within themselves many allegorical significances to
be interpreted entirely."[83] Gordon Brotherston is one of the very
few who takes the calendar stone Piedra del Sol as *tlacuilolli.*[84]
In fact, as we have mentioned in the previous chapter, *icuiloa,*

---

80 Richard Haly claims that Ometeotl is an invention of ethnographers like
    León-Portilla who aims to make Nahua culture resemble Christendom. He
    analyzes how the so-called "oral tradition" of the indigenous Nahuas is only
    known to us through a mediated presence of the books in ethnography and
    the history of religions ("Bare Bones," 269). He further claims that there ex-
    ists no representation of Ometeotl (ibid., 278).
81 Boone, "Writing and Recording Knowledge," 3.
82 Ibid., 20.
83 Antonio de León y Gama, *Descripción histórica y cronológica de las dos pie-
    dras* (México D.F.: Imprenta de Don Felipe de Zúñiga y Ontiveros, 1792), 3.
84 Gordon Brotherston, "America and the Colonizer Question: Two Formative
    Statements from Early Mexico," in *Coloniality at Large: Latin America and
    the Postcolonial Debate,* eds. Mabel Moraña, Enrique Dussel, and Carlos A.
    Jáuregui (Durham: Duke University Press, 2008), 23–42.

the verbal root of *tlacuilolli,* connotes a wide range of activities besides writing and painting.[85] According to Marc Thouvenot, *icuiloa* also means to sculpt (on stone or wood), and "the action of sculpt — *icuiloa* — stones is not limited to small objects, but it is also used to refer to big works," such as palaces called "*tlacuilolli* of stones."[86]

As modern scholars, we need to rely on familiar concepts such as writing/text and painting/image to make sense of *tlacuilolli.* This unique form of conserving and conveying knowledge, however, is very different from a mere combination of "writing/text" and "painting/image." One needs to bear in mind that talking about *tlacuilolli* as "pictorial writing" or "writing/painting" is a form of translation and involves a certain level of coloniality that hides the "conceptual inequivalence" between the two cosmologies. At the same time, this emphasis on inequivalence does not mean that *tlacuilolli* is inscrutable.

Coatlicue Mayor conceived in *tlacuilolli* is more than a mere "representation" (both textual and visual) of a deity whose gender is subsequently fixed. It is, according to Roberto Vera, "both the syncretic expression of the binary thought that is the foundation of the Aztec metaphysics; and the multiple manifestations of masculinity and femininity."[87] Justino Fernández also comes to the conclusion that "the sculpture Coatlicue becomes much more than just the Earth Goddess or the Goddess of the Serpent Skirt. In effect, it symbolizes the earth, but also the sun, moon, spring, rain, light, life, death […] and the supreme creator: the dual principle."[88] That is to say, Ometeotl manifests himself and is manifested in Coatlicue Mayor following the duality principle.

---

85 Thouvenot, "Imágines y escritura entre los Nahuas del inicio del xvi."
86 Ibid., 174: "La acción de esculpir — icuiloa — piedras no se limitaba a objetos pequeños, pues se emplea también para referirse a obras grandes, como las construcciones. Así a los palacios, tecpancalli, se sesignaba como tlacuilolli de piedras."
87 Roberto Vera, *Coatlicue en Paz,* 12.
88 Fernández, *A Guide to Mexican Art,* 44.

In line with Nahua *ometeotl,* it is highly problematic to think of any independently existing "earth goddess" or "celestial god" without evoking any counterparts *already* within "him" or "her." I refer specifically to the feminine rendering of Coatlicue in studies that fix the genderless Nahua word as "Snakes-Her-Skirt."[89] The genderless possessive suffix -*i* has been fixed as feminine in this translation. The feminine identification of Coatlicue is by no means wrong, given that *cueitl* (or *cuetli*) is often used to designate femininity in *tlacuilolli* and Nahua rituals. The problem lies in the fixation of gender in the very instance of equating *i-cue* to "her skirt" and further equating the statue, a complex visual/textual/temporal system irreducible to either textual or visual elements or their sum, with a rather singular and *straight*-forward concept written in alphabets: "Coatlicue — Snakes-Her-Skirt."

4.3.2 The Manifold Duality/Divinity
Now, let us read the statue as a non-secular *tlacuilolli.*[90] The upper part of the statue, like the other parts, can be perceived in varying ways from different angles and perspectives. The dual principle, or *ometeotl,* according to Justino Fernández in his monograph dedicated to the study of Coatlicue Mayor, is located in the upper part of the statue.[91] This is Omeyocan, the "place of duality." From a holistic perspective, especially standing at a distance, one observes a face made of two beady eyes, a huge dentate mouth and a serpentine tongue divided in two halves stretching out of the half-open mouth. However, if one moves closer, another image emerges: two identical snakes, as seen in profile, facing each other. The frontal face we saw at first glance is made of two facing faces. Each eye and each half of the mouth now belong to the two different serpent heads that can be only seen in profile. This interpretation that sees two instead

89 Klein, "A New Interpretation of the Aztec Statue Called Coatlicue," 129.
90 I have deliberately not included any images in this book. This invites readers to reflect on the limits of the textual and its (linear) temporality, very different from the visual and *tlacuilolli,* the beyond-textual-and-visual medium that conveys knowledge and cosmo-philosophy.
91 Fernández, *Coatlicue,* 265.

of one head becomes more convincing if one goes around to the backside of the sculpture. From the backside we can observe an identical "one frontal face" made of two facing ones. This "one face" at the back mirrors the other "one face" at the front.

The simultaneous presence of two gendered aspects (Omeci- huatl, Ometecuhtli) and one genderless Ometeotl is perfectly incarnated in the upper part of the statue. We have argued pre- viously that Ometeotl is manifested in the two aspects sepa- rately and jointly. Each snake that forms the "head" is distinct yet identical — distinct because each one is a different snake, or gendered manifestation of Ometeotl in the myth — identical because they are both snakes mirroring simulating each other. Most importantly they are all (manifestations of) Ometeotl or *ometeotl*. We also note that on the level of Omeyocan (the up- per part of Coatlicue Mayor), the gendered aspects of Omete- otl are not separately discernible (if discernible at all), because neither of the two facing snakes can be considered to be the masculine or feminine aspect independently from the other, or separately gendered.

The sophisticated juxtaposition of the two snake heads seen from the profile with the two "one-faces" that are formed by the two snakes gives the duality principle a fourth dimension, coin- ciding with the creation myth of the four "sons" of Omecihuatl and Ometecuhtli, the four cardinal directions, the *nahui ollin* ("four movements"), and the four (preceding yet co-existing) cosmic eras. The two "one-faces" are in a mirroring relationship that can then be reduced to "one." That is to say, the two faces that we can see from the frontside and the backside of the statue are mirroring each other. Now we can start to appreciate the unfolding movement/*ollin* of Ometeotl. Ometeotl *inter*becomes the two aspects Omecihuatl and Ometecuhtli, which then un- fold into three/four and many that fold back, *simultaneously* with the unfolding process, into two/one, giving no chance for permanent polarizations.

Despite all this, the differentiation of how one might per- ceive the sculpture is certainly hypothetical and temporal. The boundary between the perspective that sees the "one face" and the perspective that sees the "two" facing profiles is uncertain. However, their mutual presence does not suggest that we are able to see *both* at once.

Eric Gombrich's classical study *Art and Illusion* opens with a case of a drawing which is both a rabbit and a duck. However, no matter how fast we switch between the two alternatives, we can only see either the rabbit or the duck at one time. This leads Gombrich to conclude, "we cannot experience alternative readings at the same time."[92] Earlier on the same page that discusses the duck-rabbit game of perception, the art historian accuses Egyptian art of having "adopted childish methods because Egyptian artists knew no better." It is not difficult to imagine Gombrich calling the Aztecs "primitives" as he does with other American "Indians."[93] But interestingly and perhaps unforeseen by Gombrich, his analysis of the duck-rabbit finds its best example in Nahua dualism. Ometeotl manifesting in Coatlicue Mayor moves beyond the confinement of the logic of "either… or" and its purported alternative: "both…and," but embodies what I call elsewhere the "transdualistic either… and."[94]

The frontal face, which is the assemblage of two distinct yet identical snake faces, exemplifies this complexity. This *one* that emerges out of two contradictory, yet complementary forces is only possible in a cosmology that does not polarize the world into separate entities. There is still the fourth dimension, which is the mirroring face on the backside of the statue. One needs to move in time and space so that this fourth dimension emerges and simultaneously folds back into the dualistic pair.

If we follow Ann de León's suggestion that "the front of Coatlicue represented the past, and her back the future," this physical shift from looking at the "past" (front) to the "future" (back) and then to the "past" again endorses the cyclical temporality of

---

92 Eric H. Gombrich, *Art and Illusion: A Study in the Psychology of Pictorial Representation* (London: Phaidon Press, 1984), 5.

93 Ibid., 85–86.

94 See Part I of this book and also my exploration of "either…and": Zairong Xiang, "Transdualism: Towards a Materio-Discursive Embodiment," *TSQ: Transgender Studies Quarterly* 5, no. 2 (2018): 425–42.

the Nahuas.[95] This movement that invokes the four dimensions invokes the Nahua cosmogony recorded in the calendar stone. In Coatlicue Mayor, we also see that each "arm" is formed by a snake, identical to the ones that form the "head" on the upper side. Being a symmetrical body, if the statue folds 90° inwards along the middle axis like closing an open book, the two snakes that form the "head" would overlap and become "one." The two snake "arms" would then face each other, forming exactly the same heads as in the upper part. Iliana Godoy, adopting a holographic analysis, suggests that Coatlicue Mayor enigmatically coincides with contemporary theories on the simultaneously folding and unfolding universe, through the movement we have just imagined by folding along the central axis.[96]

By turning 90°, one turns a quarter of a circle. Together with the central point, the unfolding statue forms a quincunx. The Piedra del Sol, housed with Coatlicue Mayor in the Sala Mexica of the Museo Nacional de Antropología, exemplifies the importance of the quincunx in Nahua cosmology. The sun stone encompasses four previous cosmic eras ("suns") and represents the Fifth Era as a conglomeration of these four suns. Coatlicue Mayor, folding and unfolding along the central axis, is linked with the sun stone through the idea of the quincunx, which conjures up the concept of duality. The lower part of the sun stone, with its two facing half-serpent, half-human faces, might also remind us of the facing snakes of Coatlicue Mayor's "head."

The fifth "sun" that the Piedra del Sol registers "is the synthesis and 'center' of the four 'earlier' ages. Each of the first four Suns forms one part or aspect of the contemporary Sun."[97] This temporality is considerably different from "cyclical time." The coexistence of "previous" eras in the current "sun" suggests the "ongoing presence of the past within the present, not as its precursor or source but as an ineradicable, integral part

---

95 de León, "Coatlicue or How to Write the Dismembered Body," 284.
96 Godoy, "Coatlicue," 85.
97 Wayne Elzey, "The Nahua Myth of the Suns: History and Cosmology in Pre-Hispanic Mexican Religions," *Numen* 23, no. 2 (1976): 114–35, at 125.

of the present."⁹⁸ The center of the four eras on the sun stone, where Tlatecuhtli, the deity of the earth, is present, is also where Coatlicue Mayor stands.⁹⁹ Carlos Navarrete and Doris Heyden argue that the Piedra del Sol was designed facing upwards rather than facing "us," as it is currently hung in the museum, like a European painting.¹⁰⁰ The connection between Coatlicue Mayor and the Piedra del Sol is only possible in a non-secular sense. What we need to remember is that these "statues," to which the secular vocabulary of modern research refers, were not inert art objects for the Nahuas to contemplate, and their synchronicity and multiplicity cannot be circumscribed (only) by a "profane" view. Secularism, Nelson Maldonado-Torres contends, "as its literal meaning conveys, became […] a call to leave the past behind and conform to the new standards of meaning and rationality." It also "inverts and then properly modernizes the imperial dimension found in the radical dichotomy between the sacred and the profane."¹⁰¹

---

98 Mieke Bal, "Postmodern Theology as Cultural Analysis," in *A Mieke Bal Reader* (Chicago: University of Chicago Press, 2006), 391–414, at 392.

99 Conventionally, as the name of the calendar stone shows, the deity that appears in the center has been identified as Tonatiuh, (deity of) the sun, a thesis that has since been contested. Klein, for example, argues against this identification, after showing the divine functions and the related artistic representations of Tonatiuh, which are incompatible with the one allegedly present in the center of the sun stone. Like the other four "suns" represented around it, the fifth cosmic era or "sun" would also be "at the navel of the female earth goddess [*sic*] Tlaltecuhtli." She argues that it is then more appropriate to identify the deity present at the center as Tlaltecuhtli with her/his "connotations of earth, death, darkness, and cyclic completion" (Cecelia F. Klein, "The Identity of the Central Deity on the Aztec Calendar Stone," *The Art Bulletin* 58, no. 1 [1976]: 1–12, at 2–3). For an overview of the debate on the identification of the central figure of the calendar stone, see David Stuart, "The Face of the Calendar Stone: A New Interpretation," *Maya Decipherment: Ideas on Ancient Maya Writing and Iconography,* June 13, 2016, https://decipherment.wordpress.com/2016/06/13/the-face-of-the-calendar-stone-a-new-interpretation/.

100 Carlos Navarrete and Doris Heyden, "La cara central de la Piedra del Sol: Una hipotesis," *Estudios de Cultura Náhuatl* 11 (1974): 355–76, at 373–74.

101 Nelson Maldonado-Torres, "Secularism and Religion in the Modern/Colonial World-System: From Secular Postcoloniality to Postsecular Transmo-

The pervasive, divine presence is exemplified by the inner logic between the two seemingly unrelated "stones." The abstract coherence between Coatlicue Mayor and the Piedra del Sol is maintained through the idea of the quincunx and "cyclical time."[102] If this is accepted, Coatlicue Mayor cannot be an inert sculpture, an artistic representation, or a "written/painted" record of a mythical figure, but needs to be viewed as a vibrating divine presence that dynamically (dis)closes a (secret) linkage that synchronizes all other existences in the Nahua cosmos.[103]

In the context of Spanish iconoclasm during the post-*Conquista* period, it is precisely the irrepressible photographicality of the Nahua language that both haunted the Spanish authority and enabled indigenous counter-colonial strategies through ghost invocation.[104]

In the *Vuelta a "El laberinto de la soledad"* published on the 25th anniversary of the first publication of *El laberinto de la soledad* in 1950,[105] Octavio Paz reveals the motifs behind his influential essay: "One of the central ideas of the book is that there is a Mexico buried but alive. It is better to say: inside of

---

dernity," in *Coloniality at Large: Latin America and the Postcolonial Debate* (Durham: Duke University Press, 2008), 360–87, at 362–69.

102 One can also imagine that Coatlicue Mayor is symbolically standing on the Aztec Calendar Stone whose central deity, Tlaltecuhtli, is also the center of Coatlicue Mayor hidden underneath, facing/in the earth.

103 One might also find in this projection a similarity to the idea of photographicality, a synchronic concept in star-reading, history, language, and translation developed by Eduardo Cadava via Walter Benjamin: "Benjamin not only associates stars with a photographic language that focuses on the relations between light and darkness, past and present, life and earth, reading and writing, and knowledge and representation-motifs that all belong to the history of photographic phenomena — but he also links them to the possibility of mimesis in general" (Eduardo Cadava, *Words of Light: Theses on the Photography of History* [Princeton: Princeton University Press, 1997], 26).

104 See Rabasa, *Tell Me the Story of How I Conquered You.*

105 I am quoting from the Colección Heteroclásica that published Octavio Paz, *El laberinto de la soledad, Postdata/Vuelta a "El laberinto de la soledad* (Madrid: Fondo de Cultura Económica, 2007). "Vuelta a 'El laberinto de la soledad'," an interview with Claude Fell, was first published in *Plural* 50 (November 1975).

the Mexicans, men and women, there is a universe of hidden images, desires and impulses."[106]

The *vuelta* or return, the return of the "dead," the repressed or the buried, haunted the Spaniards during the *Conquista*. The so-called "dead" are the *enterrados pero vivos,* buried but alive, just like the fate of Coatlicue Mayor. Yet the past, invoked through hidden worship of the ineffaceable indigenous world, is alive until today. Returning to Bullock's witness account at the beginning of the chapter, we read his lament: "notwithstanding the extreme diligence of the Spanish clergy for three hundred years, there still remains some taint of heathen superstition among the descendants of the original inhabitants."[107] This continued pagan practice that Bullock condemns paradoxically enables the pagan natives to look back. This persistence proves precisely that the indigenous people "refuse to recognize the Spanish conquest as liberation from magic, superstition, and Satan."[108] Paz romanticizes the *Conquista* and suggests that the arrival of the Spaniards appears to be a liberation for the people subjugated by the Aztecs.[109] Even if he was partially right, the so-called "liberation" was only just a temporary illusion. The *conquistadores* who imposed European ideologies did not seek to liberate the subaltern *pueblos,* but to subjugate all of them, both Aztecs and their rivals. The surviving indigenous people did not accept that imposition. "Even today, when indigenous peoples in Mexico demand the recognition of their juridical institutions, the recognition they seek is not of how they approximate European systems of law."[110]

In his insightful close reading of the relationship between *tlacuilolli* and the introduction of the alphabetic writing system

---

106 Paz, *El laberinto de la soledad,* 289: "una de las ideas ejes del libro es que hay un México enterrado pero vivo. Mejor dicho: hay en los mexicanos, hombres y mujeres, un universo de imágenes, deseos e impulsos sepultados."

107 Bullock, *Six Months' Residence and Travels in Mexico,* 341–42.

108 Rabasa, "Thinking Europe in Indian Categories," 68.

109 Paz, *El laberinto de la soledad,* 102: "la llegada de los españoles parece una liberación a los pueblos sometidos por los aztecas."

110 Rabasa, "Thinking Europe in Indian Categories," 71.

in the "New World," José Rabasa complicates the issue of the "tyranny of the alphabet."[111] He suggests rather that the adoption of alphabetic writing with its mimetic function "does not stand in place of the pictorial version, but rather reproduces speech," at least in the early post-*Conquista* years.[112] The most important aspect of this mimetic function of the alphabet is that it is compatible with the (photo)graphical *tlacuilolli,* as Cadava has theorized with the help of Benjamin.[113] Alphabetic writing and *tlacuilolli* together serve the natives as a counter-colonial strategy that "inscribes the dead for their invocation as ghosts, as revenants that reading and performance [of both alphabetic and pictorial *texts*] bring about."[114] The Spanish religious and lay authorities "could never anticipate Indian understandings of writing and reading for invoking the dead."[115] When one starts to *read* the statue that returns home from the burial grounds of Eurocentric condemnation and modern scholarship's secularization, one would allow oneself to be enchanted by "her" vibrating and symphonic coherence that temporarily dissolves life and death, masculinity and femininity, future and past, yet simultaneously keeps them apart.

If our analysis is in the right direction, we can have a last glance at Coatlicue Mayor. However, this is a "glance" perpetually denied. Tlaltecuhtli, the deity of the earth, the same one that dwells at the center of the fifth "sun" represented by the sun stone, is found surprisingly on the underside of Coatlicue Mayor, a mysterious space that grants no direct access, at least to the uninitiated viewers, if human at all. If the statue were just an artistic representation, why would the Nahua artist(s) have bothered to "represent" Tlaltecuhtli painstakingly at a place that in fact no one except for the sculptor(s) would ever see?

Coatlicue Mayor stands in the quincunx center of the universe, the navel of the earth, where Ometeotl *in tlalxicco ónoc*

---

111 Ibid., 65.
112 Ibid., 54.
113 Cadava, *Words of Light.*
114 Rabasa, "Thinking Europe in Indian Categories," 54.
115 Ibid.

("spreads out on the navel of the earth"). This is also where Tlaltecuhtli stands. Underneath Coatlicue Mayor, "in the breast [of
Tlaltecuhtli], the quincunx is situated in the center of the cent-
ers, at the cross of the celestial paths, those of the underworld
and the four poles of the universe."[116] The "statue" enables the
idea of an emergent third dimension from the juxtaposition of
the complementary duals. It simultaneously multiplies to the
fourth and fifth possibilities *ad infinitum,* and is (un)folding
into the unity with Ometeotl and as *ometeotl,* standing in the
center of the universe, which is also where Tlaltecuhtli dwells.

Therefore let us stop here, where a whole dimension of
Coatlicue Mayor is literally hidden from us. This inaccessible
source and origin secure some secrets of the Nahua cosmo-
philosophy. *Tlacuilolli,* far beyond simply "art and writing" or
"pictorial writing" (although it conveys both translatable meanings), is a radically different form of knowledge that retains a
space for the irreducible conceptual inequivalence[117] that resists
the colonial imposition and universalization of its cosmology
(including its problematic, hierarchical dualism). The modern
scholar's desire to scrutinize everything is denied, even if simply
by the material inaccessibility that the Museo Nacional de Antropología decides to preserve. Instead of exposing the underside of Coatlicue Mayor, the museum has found a special way
to (re)present Tlaltecuhtli without presenting them: a replica.
Although it would have been technically possible to show the
underside of the statue through a mirror box, as the museum

---

116 Matos Moctezuma, "Tlaltecuhtli," 23–24: "en el pecho el quincunce […] se
    sitúa en el centro de centros, en el cruce de caminos celestes y del infra-
    mundo y de los cuatro rumbos del universo."
117 In his *Introduction to Classical Nahuatl,* Richard Andrews succinctly criti-
    cizes the fallacy of conceptual equivalence: "the failure to recognize the dif-
    ference between these two audiences (that of the original text and that of the
    translation) rests on a naïve faith in 'equivalence' which holds that mean-
    ing and thoughts are universal (or nearly so) — which is true if one means
    by 'meaning' and 'thought' the high-generality concepts, the common-
    denominator abstractions shared by every language-using Homo sapiens"
    (Richard Andrews, *Introduction to Classical Nahuatl* [Norman: University
    of Oklahoma Press, 2003], 18).

does with other statues, such as Ehecatl's, they chose not to do so. This replica is and is not Tlaltecuhtli. In a similar way in which we have relied on "pictorial writing" or "writing/painting" to understand *tlacuilolli,* the replica of Tlaltecuhtli standing besides Coatlicue Mayor is a form of translation. It defies a naïve cultural relativism that denies translatability and therefore risks perpetuating a colonialist stereotype of the inscrutable other. But it also marks the limit of what is translatable and therefore what the colonial/modern knowledge is capable of comprehending, destroying, and appropriating.

Tlaltecuhtli, now standing at the center/origin of the Nahua universe, beneath the *ometeotl* Coatlicue Mayor in the form of *tlacuilolli,* cannot be bothered with validation from colonial/modern knowledge. It continuously opens to dimensions that remain closed to us.

Acknowledgments

This book grew out of my PhD thesis and would not have been possible without the support, help, and love from many people. First and foremost, I would like to thank my PhD supervisors Pascale Amiot and Ingrid Hotz-Davies for their intellectual guidance and unconditional support in this unconventional project. My greatest gratitude goes to Ingrid, who continues to be my attentive and critical reader beyond the PhD program. This book was written in transit thanks to the utterly unorthodox experience with the Erasmus Mundus Joint Doctorate (EMJD) *Cultural Studies in Literary Interzones,* which has funded my research stays in Bergamo, Perpignan, Mexico City, and Tübingen. I'd like to express my special thanks to Didier Girard for encouraging me to move beyond and explore broader cultural landscapes. As always, I share all my trivial achievements with Sun Jianqiu, who encouraged and recommended me to the EMJD programme. I am indebted to Liu Yiqing and Gao Fengfeng, who allowed me to audit their MA seminars on Biblical literature when I was a Bachelor's student in Beijing.

Friends and colleagues have read and commented on the manuscript in different occasions and formats. These critical minds have greatly refined my thoughts and sharpen my mind: Delfina Cabrera, Karen Cordero, Rebecca Hahn, Milisava Petkovic, Christian Abes, Ann Heilmann, and my fellow colleagues at the ICI Berlin from 2014–2016. Despite the book's flaws and shortcomings, Caio Yurgel, Rosa Barotsi, Claire Nioche, James Burton, James Miller, and Catherine Keller have tirelessly encouraged me in trusting its uniqueness and have given this project undeserved attention and indispensable input.

Intellectual labor is never just a matter of thinking. The emotional care and hospitality of friends have granted me luxurious tranquility, and their loyalty and trust have maintained my sanity: Gabriel Toro, He Ying, Zhang Xiao, Gero Bauer, Zheng Jingwei, Totzalan Lezama, Jordan Rodriguez, Walid El-Houri. I thank my MA program and the friends of GEMMA-Woman's and Gender Studies for making me a feminist. 謝謝爸爸媽媽愛護和支持我，從不給我施加任何壓力並任由我選擇自己不同的生活方式，做自己喜歡的事情。謝謝貴陽和蒙自的家人對我一如既往的關愛。 Debo muchas gracias a mi familia española, Toro, por darme un verdadero hogar en Europa. It is impossible to name the multitude of all the generous hands along the way. I share this work with them, all those named and unnamed graces.

Last but not least, I'd like to wholeheartedly thank my publishers at punctum books for their commitment, patience, and generous support in the realization of this book, especially to Vincent W.J. van Gerven Oei for painstakingly and thoughtfully enlightening these pages.

Tübingen/Berlin
October 2018

Bibliography

Alter, Robert. *Genesis: Translation and Commentary.* London: W.W. Norton & Company Inc., 1996.

Althaus-Reid, Marcella. *Indecent Theology: Theological Perversions in Sex, Gender and Politics.* London: Routledge, 2000.

Anderson, Perry. *The Origins of Postmodernity.* New York: Verso, 1998.

Andrews, Richard. *Introduction to Classical Nahuatl.* Norman: University of Oklahoma Press, 2003.

Auerbach, Eric. *Mimesis: The Representation of Reality in Western Literature.* Princeton: Princeton University Press, 2003.

Bachelard, Gaston. *Le nouvel esprit scientifique.* Paris: PUF, 1995.

Bahrani, Zainab. *Women of Babylon: Gender and Representation in Mesopotamia.* London: Routledge, 2001.

Bal, Mieke. "Postmodern Theology as Cultural Analysis." In *A Mieke Bal Reader,* 391–414. Chicago: University of Chicago Press, 2006.

Bandstra, Barry L. *Reading the Old Testament: An Introduction to the Hebrew Bible.* Belmont: Wadsworth Publishing Company, 1995.

Baquedano, Elizabeth, and Michel Graulich. "Decapitation among the Aztecs: Mythology, Agriculture and Politics and Hunting." *Estudios de Cultura Náhuatl* 23 (1993): 163–77.

Barton, George A. "Tiamat." *Journal of American Oriental Society* 15 (1893): 1–27.

Bauman, Whitney. *Theology, Creation, and Environmental Ethics: From Creatio Ex Nihilo to Terra Nullius.* London: Routledge, 2009.

Benjamin, Walter. "Theses on the Philosophy of History." In *Illuminations: Essays and Reflections,* translated by Harry Zohn, edited by Hannah Arendt, 253–64. New York: Schocken Books, 1969.

Bersani, Leo. "Is the Rectum a Grave?" In *Is the Rectum a Grave? And Other Essays,* 3–30. Chicago: University of Chicago Press, 2010.

Bhabha, Homi K. *The Location of Culture.* London: Routledge, 1994.

Bierhorst, John. *Cantares Mexicanos: Songs of the Aztecs.* Stanford: Stanford University Press, 1985.

Bingham, Ann. *South and Meso-American Mythology A to Z.* New York: Facts on File, 2004.

Black, Jeremy, and Anthony Green. *Gods, Demons and Symbols of Ancient Mesopotamia: An Illustrated Dictionary.* London: British Museum Press, 1992.

Boone, Elizabeth Hill. "Aztec Pictorial Histories: Records without Words." In *Writing without Words: Alternative Literacies in Mesoamerica and the Andes,* edited by Elizabeth Hill Boone and Walter Mignolo, 50–76. Durham: Duke University Press, 1994.

———. "The 'Coatlicues' at the Templo Mayor." *Ancient Mesoamerica* 10, no. 2 (1999): 189–206.

———. "Writing and Recording Knowledge." In *Writing without Words: Alternative Literacies in Mesoamerica and the Andes,* edited by Elizabeth Hill Boone and Walter Mignolo, 3–26. Durham: Duke University Press, 1994.

Braidotti, Rosi. *Nomadic Subjects: Embodiment and Sexual Difference in Contemporary Feminist Theory.* New York: Columbia University Press, 1994.

Bredbeck, Gregory W. *Sodomy and Interpretation.* Ithaca: Cornell University Press, 1991.

Brotherston, Gordon. "America and the Colonizer Question: Two Formative Statements from Early Mexico." In *Coloniality at Large: Latin America and the Postcolonial Debate,* edited by Mabel Moraña, Enrique Dussel, and Carlos A. Jáuregui, 23–42. Durham: Duke University Press, 2008.

———. "Towards a Grammatology of America: Lévi-Strauss, Derrida and the Native New World Text." In *Literature, Politics and Theory: Papers from the Essex Conference, 1976-1984,* edited by Francis Barker, Peter Hulme, Margaret Iversen, and Diana Loxley, 190–209. London: Methuen & Co. Ltd, 1986.

Budge, E.A. Wallis. *The Babylonian Legends of the Creation and the Fight between Bel and the Dragon (As Told by Assyrian Tablets from Nineveh).* London: The British Museum, 1921.

Bullock, William. *Six Months' Residence and Travels in Mexico.* London: John Murray, 1824.

Burkhart, Louise M. "Pious Performances: Christian Pageantry and Native Identity in Early Colonial Mexico." In *Native Tradition in the Postconquest World,* edited by Elizabeth Hill Boone and Tom Cummins, 361–81. Washington, DC: Dumbarton Oaks, 1998.

Butler, Judith. "Against Proper Objects. Introduction." *differences: A Journal of Feminist Cultural Studie*s 6, nos. 2–3 (1994): 1–26.

———. *Bodies That Matter: On the Discursive Limits of "Sex."* London: Routledge, 1993.

———. *Gender Trouble: Feminism and the Subversion of Identity.* London: Routledge, 1999.

Cadava, Eduardo. *Words of Light: Theses on the Photography of History.* Princeton: Princeton University Press, 1997.

Campos, Haroldo de. *Galáxias* [1963–1976]. São Paolo: Editora 34, 2004.

———. *Galáxias.* Translated by Odile Cisneros with Suzanne Jill Levine. http://www.artsrn.ualberta.ca/galaxias/index.html.

Caso, Alfonso. *El pueblo del sol.* México D.F.: Fondo de Cultura Económica, 1994.

———. *The Aztecs: People of the Sun.* Translated by Lowell Dunham. Norman: University of Oklahoma Press, 1958.

Castro-Kláren, Sara. "Posting Letters: Writing in the Andes and the Paradoxes of the Postcolonial Debate." In *Coloniality at Large: Latin America and the Postcolonial Debate,* edited by Mabel Moraña, Enrique Dussel, and Carlos A. Jáuregui, 130–57. Durham: Duke University Press, 2008.

Chernow, Barbara A., and George A. Vallasi, eds. *The Columbia Encyclopedia.* Fifth Edition. New York: Columbia University Press, 1993.

Chow, Rey. *The Protestant Ethnic and the Spirit of Capitalism.* New York: Columbia University Press, 2002.

———. *Writing Diaspora: Tactics of Intervention in Contemporary Cultural Studies.* Bloomington: Indiana University Press, 1993.

Cixous, Hélène. "Castration or Decapitation?" Translated by Annette Kuhn. *Signs: Journal of Women in Culture and Society* 7, no. 1 (1981): 41–55. https://www.jstor.org/stable/3173505.

———. "Le sexe ou la tête." *Les Cahiers du GRIF* 13 (1976): 5–15.

——— and Catherine Clément. *La jeune née.* Paris: Union Générale d'Éditions, 1975.

Cohen, Jeffrey J. "Monster Culture (Seven Theses)." In *Monster Theory: Reading Culture,* edited by Jeffrey J. Cohen, 3–25. Minneapolis: University of Minnesota Press, 1996.

———, ed. *Monster Theory: Reading Culture.* Minneapolis: University of Minnesota Press, 1996.

Collins, Patricia H. *Black Feminist Thought: Knowledge, Consciousness, and the Politics of Empowerment.* New York: Routledge, 2000.

"Compare the Two Speeches." *The Sojourner Truth Project.* https://www.thesojournertruthproject.com/compare-the-speeches/.

Corcoran, Cecilia M. "Finding the Goddess in the Central Highlands of Mexico." *Feminist Theology* 8, no. 24 (2000): 61–81. DOI: 10.1177/096673500000002410.

Coronil, Fernando. "Beyond Occidentalism towards Post-Imperial Geohistorical Categorie." *Transformations: Comparative Studies of Social Transformations,* Working Paper 72 (May 1992): 1–29.

———. "Elephants in the Americas? Latin American Postcolonial Studies and Global Decolonization." In *Coloniality at Large: Latin America and the Postcolonial Debate,* edited by Mabel Moraña, Enrique Dussel, and Carlos A. Jáuregui, 396–416. Durham: Duke University Press, 2008.

Crais, Clifton, and Pamela Scully. *Sara Baartman and the Hottentot Venus: A Ghost Story and a Biography.* Princeton: Princeton University Press, 2009.

Crenshaw, Kimberle. "Demarginalizing the Intersection of Race and Sex: A Black Feminist Critique of Antidiscrimination Doctrine, Feminist Theory and Antiracist Politics." *University of Chicago Legal Forum* (1989): art. 8. https://chicagounbound.uchicago.edu/uclf/vol1989/iss1/8.

———. "Mapping the Margins: Intersectionality, Identity Politics, and Violence against Women of Color." *Stanford Law Review* 43, no. 6 (1991): 1241–99. DOI: 10.2307/1229039.

Cupitt, Don. *Creation Out of Nothing.* London: SCM Press Ltd., 1990.

Cusicanqui, Silvia Rivera. "*Ch'ixinakax Utxiwa:* A Reflection on the Practices and Discourses of Decolonization." *South Atlantic Quarterly* 111, no. 1 (2012): 95–109. DOI: 10.1215/00382876-1472612.

Dalley, Stephanie. *Myths from Mesopotamia: Creation, The Flood, Gilgamesh, and Others.* Oxford: Oxford University Press, 2008.

Day, John. *God's Conflict with the Dragon and the Sea.* Cambridge: University of Cambridge Oriental Publications, 1985.

DeFrancis, John. *The Chinese Language: Fact and Fantasy.* Honolulu: University of Hawai'i Press, 1984.

Delany, Samuel R. *The Motion of Light in Water: Sex and Science Fiction Writing in the East Village.* Minneapolis: University of Minneapolis Press, 2004.

Derrida, Jacques. *Of Grammatology.* Translated by Gayatri Chakravorty Spivak. Baltimore: Johns Hopkins University Press, 1997.

Ducille, Ann. "On Canons: Anxious History and the Rise of Black Feminist Literary Studies." In *The Cambridge Companion to Feminist Literary Theory,* edited by Ellen Rooney, 29–52. Cambridge: Cambridge University Press, 2006.

Durán, Diego. *Historia de las Indias de Nueva España y Islas de Tierra Firme, Tomo I.* 1867; rpt. Alicante: Biblioteca Virtual Miguel de Cervantes, 2005. http://www.cervantesvirtual.com/nd/ark:/59851/bmck0706.

Dussel, Enrique. *Politics of Liberation: A Critical World History.* Translated by Thia Cooper. London: SCM Press Ltd, 2011.

Elzey, Wayne. "The Nahua Myth of the Suns: History and Cosmology in Pre-Hispanic Mexican Religions." *Numen* 23, no. 2 (1976): 114–35. DOI: 10.2307/3269663.

Eng, David L. *The Feeling of Kinship: Queer Liberalism and the Racialization of Intimacy.* Durham: Duke University Press, 2010.

Étiemble, René. *L'Europe chinoise I: De l'empire romain à Leibniz.* Paris: Gallimard, 1988.

Evans, Paul S. "Creation, Progress and Calling: Genesis 1-11 as Social Commentary." *McMaster Journal of Theology and Ministry* 13 (2011): 67–100.

Fausto-Sterling, Anne. "The Five Sexes: Why Male and Female Are Not Enough." *The Sciences* (March/April 1993): 20–25.

Fenollosa, Ernest. *The Chinese Written Character as a Medium for Poetry.* San Francisco: City Lights Books, 1969.

Fernández, Justino. *A Guide to Mexican Art: From Its Beginnings to the Present.* Translated by Joshua C. Taylor. Chicago: University of Chicago Press, 1969.

————. *Coatlicue: Estética del arte indígena antiguo.* México D.F.: Instituto de Investigaciones Estéticas, Universidad Nacional Autónoma de México, 1959.

Fewell, Danna Nolan, and David M. Gunn. *Gender, Power & Promise: The Subject of the Bible's First Story.* Nashville: Abingdon, 1993.

Foucault, Michel. "Le vrai sexe." In *Dits et écrits IV, 1980–1988,* texte no. 287. Paris: Gallimard, 1994.

Freeman, Elizabeth. *Time Binds: Queer Temporality, Queer Histories.* Durham: Duke University Press, 2010.

Frymer-Kensky, Tikva. *In the Wake of the Goddesses: Women, Culture and the Biblical Transformation of Pagan Myth.* New York: The Free Press, 1992.

Gabilondo, Joseba. "Introduction to 'The Hispanic Atlantic.'" *Arizona Journal of Hispanic Cultural Studies* 5 (2001): 91–113. DOI: 10.1353/hcs.2011.0060.

Gallop, Jane. *The Daughter's Seduction: Feminism and Psychoanalysis.* Ithaca: Cornell University Press, 1982.

Gelb, Ignace J. *A Study of Writing.* Chicago: University of Chicago Press, 1974.

———— et al., eds. *The Assyrian Dictionary of the Oriental Institute of the University of Chicago, Volume 2: B.* Chicago: The Oriental Institute and J.J. Augustin Verlagsbuchhandlung, 1965.

Ghose, Indira. *Women Travellers in Colonial India: The Power of the Female Gaze.* Delhi: Oxford University Press, 1998.

"Goddess Tiamat." *Journeying to the Goddess.* July 20, 2012. https://journeyingtothegoddess.wordpress.com/2012/07/30/goddess-tiamat/.

Godoy, Iliana. "Coatlicue: Visión holográfica." *Escritos: Revista del Centro de Ciencias del Lenguaje* 33 (2006): 79–92.

Gombrich, Eric H. *Art and Illusion: A Study in the Psychology of Pictorial Representation.* London: Phaidon Press, 1984.

Gómez-Barris, Macarena. *The Extractive Zone: Social Ecologies and Decolonial Perspectives.* Durham: Duke University Press, 2017.

Graulich, Michel. "Aztec Human Sacrifice as Expiation." *History of Religions* 39, no. 4 (2000): 352–71. https://www.jstor.org/stable/3176544.

Greenberg, Julie. "Definitional Dilemmas: Male or Female? Black or White? The Law's Failure to Recognize Intersexuals and Multiracials." In *Gender Nonconformity, Race, and Sexuality: Charting the Connections,* edited by Toni Lester, 102–24. Madison: University of Wisconsin Press, 2002.

Griffin, Susan. *Woman and Nature: The Roaring inside Her.* New York: Harper & Row, 1978.

Gruzinski, Serge. *La colonisation de l'imaginaire: Sociétés indigènes et occidentalisation dans le Mexique espagnol XVIᵉ-XVIIIᵉ siècle.* Paris: Éditions Gallimard, 1988.

Halberstam, Judith. *Skin Shows: Gothic Horror and the Technology of Monsters.* Durham: Duke University Press, 1995.

Haly, Richard. "Bare Bones: Rethinking Mesoamerican Divinity." *History of Religions* 31, no. 3 (1992): 269–304. https://www.jstor.org/stable/1062864.

Haritaworn, Jin. *Queer Lovers and Hateful Others: Regenerating Violent Times and Places.* London: Pluto Press, 2015.

Harris, Rivkah. "The Conflict of Generations in Ancient Mesopotamian Myths." *Comparative Studies in Society and History* 34, no. 4 (1992): 621–35. https://www.jstor.org/stable/179349.

Heidel, Alexander. "The Meaning of *Mummu* in Akkadian Literature." *Journal of Near Eastern Studies* 7, no. 2 (1948): 98–105. DOI: 10.1086/370863.

Hertz, J.H., ed. *The Pentateuch and Haftorahs: Hebrew Text with English Translation and Commentary.* London: Soncino Press, 1988.

Hornsby, Teresa J., and Ken Stone. *Bible Trouble: Queer Reading at the Boundaries of Biblical Scholarship.* Atlanta: Society of Biblical Literature, 2011.

Huddart, David. *Homi K. Bhabha.* London: Routledge, 2006.

Humboldt, Alexander von. *Vues de Cordillères et monuments des peuples indigènes de l'Amérique.* Paris: Librairie Grecque–Latine–Allemande, 1816.

Hunt, Eva. *The Transformation of the Hummingbird: Cultural Roots of a Zainacantecan Mythical Poem.* Ithaca: Cornell University Press, 1977.

Hurowitz, Victor Avigdor. "Alliterative Allusions, Rebus Writing, and Paronomastic Punishment: Some Aspects of Word Play in Akkadian Literature." In *Puns and Pundits: Word Play in the Hebrew Bible and Ancient Near Eastern Literature,* edited by Scott B Noegel, 63–113. Bethesda: CDL Press, 2000.

Instituto Nacional de Antropología e Historia. "Se cumplen 10 años del descubirmiento del monolitode la diosa Tlaltecuhtli." October 1, 2016. http://www.inah.gob.mx/boletines/5623-se-cumplen-10-anos-del-descubrimiento-del-monolito-de-la-diosa-tlaltecuhtli.

Irigaray, Luce. "Ce sexe qui n'en est pas un." *Les Cahiers du GRIF* 5, no. 1 (1974): 54–58.

———. *Speculum de l'autre femme.* Paris: Éditions de Minuit, 1974.

Jacobsen, Thorkild. "Sumerian Mythology: A Review Article." *Journal of Near Eastern Studies* 5, no. 2 (1946): 128–52. DOI: 10.1086/370777.

———. *The Treasures of Darkness.* New Haven: Yale University Press, 1976.

Janku, Andrea. "'Gutenberg in Shanghai. Chinese Print Capitalism, 1876-1937' by Christopher A. Reed [Book Review]." *The China Quarterly* 182 (2005): 443–45.

"Johannes Gutenberg." *Encyclopedia Brittanica.* https://www.britannica.com/biography/Johannes-Gutenberg.

Jonghe, M. Édouard de, ed. "Histoyre du Mechique, manuscrit français inédit du XVIᵉ siècle." *Journal de la Société des Américanistes, nouvelle série* 2 (1905): 1–41.

Keller, Catherine. *Face of the Deep: A Theology of Becoming.* London: Routledge, 2003.

———— and Laurel C. Schneider, eds. *Polydoxy: Theology of Multiplicity and Relation.* New York: Routledge, 2011.

Kheel, Marti. "From Heroic to Holistic Ethics: The Ecofeminist Challenge." In *Ecofeminism: Women, Animals, Nature,* edited by Greta Gaard, 243–71. Philadelphia: Temple University Press, 1993.

Kimmel, Michael. "Toward a Pedagogy of the Oppressor." *Tikkun* 17, no. 6 (2002): 42. http://www.tikkun.org/article.php/nov2002_kimmel.

Kimmich, Dorothee "'Interzones': Spaces of a Fuzzy Cultural Logic," in *Charting the Interzone,* 42–49. EMJD Interzones Official Website, 2010. http://wwwdata.unibg.it/dati/bacheca/676/54572.pdf.

King, Leonard William. *The Seven Tablets of Creation.* London: Luzac and Co., 1902.

Klein, Cecelia F. "A New Interpretation of the Aztec Statue Called Coatlicue, 'Snakes-Her-Skirt'." *Ethnohistory* 55, no. 2 (2008): 229–50. DOI: 10.1215/00141801-2007-062.

————. "None of the Above: Gender Ambiguity in Nahua Ideology." In *Gender in Pre-Hispanic America: A Symposium at Dumbarton Oaks,* edited by Cecelia F. Klein, 183–254. Washington, DC: Dumbarton Oaks, 2001.

————. "The Identity of the Central Deity on the Aztec Calendar Stone." *The Art Bulletin* 58, no. 1 (1976): 1–12. DOI: 10.2307/3049459.

Knapp, Bettina Liebowitz. *Women in Myth.* New York: State University of New York, 1997.

Kosofsky Sedgwick, Eve. *Tendencies.* London: Routledge, 1994.

Kramer, Samuel Noah. *Sumerian Mythology: A Study of Spiritual and Literary Achievement in the Third Millennium B.C.* Philadelphia: University of Pennsylvania Press, 1972.

————. "The Babylonian Genesis; The Story of Creation by Alexander Heidel." *Journal of American Oriental Society* 63, no. 1 (1943): 69–73.

Kristeva, Julia. *Etrangers à nous-mêmes.* Paris: Librairie Arthème Fayard, 1988.

————. *Pouvoirs de l'horreur: Essai sur l'abjection.* Paris: Seuil, 1980.

Lacadena, Alonso. "Regional Scribal Traditions: Methodological Implications for the Decipherment of Nahuatl Writing." *The PARI Journal* 8, no. 4 (2008): 1–22.

Laiou, Angeliki E. "Many Faces of Medieval Colonization." In *Native Traditions in the Postconquest World,* edited by Elizabeth Hill Boone and Tom Cummins, 13–30. Washington, DC: Dumbarton Oaks, 1998.

Laqueur, Thomas. *Making Sex: Body and Gender from the Greeks to Freud.* Cambridge: Harvard University Press, 1990.

Las Casas, Bartolomé de. *Historia de las Indias, Tomo I.* Madrid: Imprenta de Miguel Ginesta, 1875. http://bib.cervantesvirtual.com/servlet/SirveObras/p244/12033856617830495876213/index.htm.

Leick, Gwendolyn. *A Dictionary of Ancient Near Eastern Mythology.* London: Routledge, 1991.

León, Ann de. "Coatlicue or How to Write the Dismembered Body." *Modern Language Notes* 125 (2010): 259–86. DOI: 10.1353/mln.0.0243.

León-Portilla, Miguel. *Aztec Thought and Culture: A Study of the Ancient Nahuatl Mind.* Translated by Jack Emory Davis. Norman: University of Oklahoma Press, 1963.

————. "El destino de las lenguas indígenas de México." In *De historiografía lingüística e historia de las lenguas,* edited by Ignacio Guzmán Betancourt, Pilar Máynez, and Ascensión H. de León-Portilla, 51–70. Mexico D.F.: Siglo XXI, 2004.

————. *La filosofía nahuatl: Estudiada en sus fuentes.* México D.F.: Universidad Nacional Autonoma de México, 1956.

————. "Ometéotl, el supremo dios dual, y Tezcatlipoca 'dios principal.'" *Estudios de Cultura Náhuatl* 30 (1999): 133–52.

León y Gama, Antonio de. *Descripción histórica y cronológica de las dos piedras.* México D.F.: Imprenta de Don Felipe de Zúñiga y Ontiveros, 1792.

Levenson, Jon D. *Creation and the Persistence of Evil.* San Francisco: Harper & Row Publishers, 1988.

"Ley General de Derechos Lingüísticos de Los Pueblos Indígenas," 2003. https://www.inali.gob.mx/pdf/ley-GDLPI.pdf.

Lockhart, James. *Nahuatl as Written: Lessons in Older Written Nahuatl, with Copious Examples and Texts.* Stanford: Stanford University Press, 2001.

Loo, Peter L. van der. "Voicing the Painted Image: A Suggestion for Reading the Reverse of the Codex Cospi." In *Writing without Words: Alternative Literacies in Mesoamerica and the Andes,* edited by Elizabeth Hill Boone and Walter Mignolo, 77–86. Durham: Duke University Press, 1994.

López Austin, Alfredo. "La verticalidad del cosmos." *Estudios de Cultura Náhuatl* 52 (2016): 119–50.

López de Palacios, Juan. *Requerimiento.* 1513. https://antropologiacbcdotcom.files.wordpress.com/2014/08/lopez-de-palacios-rubio-requerimiento.pdf.

López Luján, Leonardo, and Vida Mercado. "Dos esculturas de Mictlantecuhtli encontradas en el recinto sagrado de México-Tenochtilan." *Estudios de Cultura Náhuatl* 26 (1996): 41–68.

"Los dioses de los Mexicas." *ABC Punto Radio.* April 29, 2012. http://www.ivoox.com/dioses-mexicas-audios-mp3_rf_1195682_1.html.

Lu, Yan. *Re-Understanding Japan: Chinese Perspectives, 1895–1945.* Honolulu: University of Hawai'i Press, 2004.

Lugones, María. "Heterosexualism and the Colonial/Modern Gender System." *Hypatia* 22, no. 1 (2007): 186–209.

———. "Toward a Decolonial Feminism." *Hypatia* 25, no. 4 (2010): 742–59. https://www.jstor.org/stable/4640051.

Maldonado-Torres, Nelson. "Secularism and Religion in the Modern/Colonial World-System: From Secular Postcoloniality to Postsecular Transmodernity." In *Coloniality at Large: Latin America and the Postcolonial Debate*, edited by Mabel Moraña, Enrique Dussel, and Carlos A. Jáuregui, 360–87. Durham: Duke University Press, 2008.

Marcos, Sylvia. "Mesoamerican Women's Indigenous Spirituality: Decolonizing Religious Beliefs." *Journal of Feminist Studies in Religion* 25, no. 2 (2009): 25–45. DOI: 10.2979/fsr.2009.25.2.25.

———. *Taken from the Lips: Gender and Eros in Mesoamerican Religions.* Leiden: Brill, 2006.

Martinés, José Luis. *El "Códice florentino" y la "Historia general" de Sahagún.* México D.F.: Archivo General de la Nación, 1989.

Massad, Joseph Andoni, ed. *Desiring Arabs.* Chicago: University of Chicago Press, 2008.

Matos Moctezuma, Eduardo. *Las piedras negadas: De la Coatlicue al Templo Mayor.* México D.F.: Consejo Nacional para la Cultura y las Artes, 1998.

———. "Tlaltecuhtli: Señor de la tierra." *Estudios de Cultura Náhuatl* 27 (1997): 15–40.

———. *Vida y muerte en el Templo Mayor.* México D.F.: Editorial Océano, 1986.

——— and Leonardo López Luján. "La diosa Tlaltecuhtli de la Casa de las Ajaracas y el rey Ahuítzotl." *Arqueología Mexicana,* https://arqueologiamexicana.mx/mexico-antiguo/la-diosa-tlaltecuhtli-de-la-casa-de-las-ajaracas-y-el-rey-ahuitzotl.

McClintock, Anne. *Imperial Leather: Race, Gender and Sexuality in the Colonial Contest.* New York: Routledge, 1995.

Meyers, Carol. "Contesting the Notion of Patriarchy: Anthropology and the Theorizing of Gender in Ancient Israel." In *A Question of Sex? Gender and Difference in the Hebrew Bible and Beyond,* edited by Deborah W. Rooke, 84–105. Sheffield: Sheffield Phoenix Press, 2007.

Michalowski, Piotr. "Presence at the Creation." In *Lingering Over Words: Studies in Ancient Near Eastern Literature in Honor of William L. Moran,* edited by P. Steinkeller, 381–96. Atlanta: Scholars Press, 1990.

Mignolo, Walter. *The Darker Side of the Renaissance: Literacy, Territoriality and Colonization.* Ann Arbor: University of Michigan Press, 1995.

———. *The Darker Side of Western Modernity: Global Futures, Decolonial Options.* Durham: Duke University Press, 2011.

———. *The Idea of Latin America.* Oxford: Blackwell, 2005.

———. "Philosophy and the Colonial Difference." In *Latin American Philosophy: Currents, Issues, Debates,* edited by Eduardo Mendieta, 80–86. Bloomington: Indiana University Press, 2003.

———. "Writing and Recorded Knowledge in Colonial and Postcolonial Situations." In *Writing without Words: Alternative Literacies in Mesoamerica and the Andes,* edited by Elizabeth Hill Boone and Walter Mignolo, 293–313. Durham: Duke University Press, 1994.

Mikulska Dąbrowska, Katarzyna. "El concepto de Ilhuicatl en la cosmovisión nahua." *Revista Española de Antropología Americana* 38, no. 2 (2008): 151–71.

Mittman, Asa Simon, and Peter J. Dandle, eds. *The Ashgate Research Companion to Monsters and the Monstrous.* London: Routledge, 2012.

Mobley, Gregory. *The Return of the Chaos Monsters: And Other Backstories of the Bible.* Grand Rapids: Wm. B. Eerdmans Publishing Co., 2012.

Moi, Toril. *Sexual/Textual Politics: Feminist Literary Thought.* Second Edition. London: Routledge, 2002.

Morin, Edgar. *Introduction à la pensée complexe.* Paris: ESF Editeur, 1990.

Munitz, Milton K., ed. *Theories of the Universe: From Babylonian Myth to Modern Science.* New York: The Free Press, 1965.

Muñoz, José Esteban. *Cruising Utopia: The Then and There of Queer Futurity.* New York: New York University Press, 2009.

Murison, Ross G. "The Serpent in the Old Testament." *The American Journal of Semitic Langauges and Literatures* 21, no. 2 (1905): 115–30. DOI: 10.1086/369534.

Murthy, K. Krishna. *A Dictionary of Buddhist Terms and Terminologies.* New Delhi: Sundeep Prakashan, 1999.

Muss-Arnolt, W. "The Babylonian Account of Creation." *The Biblical World* 3, no. 1 (1894): 17–27. https://www.jstor.org/stable/3135405.

Nancy, Jean-Luc. *Être singulier pluriel.* Paris: Galilée, 1996.

Navarrete, Carlos, and Doris Heyden. "La cara central de la Piedra del Sol: Una hipotesis." *Estudios de Cultura Náhuatl* 11 (1974): 355–76.

Nguyen, Hoang Tan. *A View from the Bottom: Asian American Masculinity and Sexual Representation.* Durham: Duke University Press, 2014.

Nicholson, Henry B. "Religion in Pre-Hispanic Mexico." In *Handbook of Middle American Indians, Volumes 10 and 11: Archaeology of Norhern Mesoamerica,* eds. Gordon F. Ekholm and Ignacio Bernal, 10:395–446. Austin: University of Texas Press, 1971.

Nietzsche, Friedrich. *Beyond Good and Evil.* Translated by Helen Zimmern. Madison: Cricket House Books, 2012.

Noegel, Scott B, ed. *Puns and Pundits: Word Play in the Hebrew Bible and Ancient Near Eastern Literature.* Bethesda: CDL Press, 2000.

O'Brien, Julia M., ed. *The Oxford Encyclopedia of the Bible and Gender Studies.* Oxford: Oxford University Press, 2014.

O'Gorman, Edmundo. *La invención de América: El universalismo de la cultura occidental.* México D.F.: Universidad Nacional Autónoma de México, 1958.

Online Oxford English Dictionary, http://www.oed.com/.

Ortiz de Montellano, Bernardo R., and Victoria Schussheim. *Medicina, salud y nutrición azteca.* México D.F.: Siglo Veintiuno, 2003.

Oshima, Takayoshi. "The Babylonian God Marduk." In T*he Babylonian World,* edited by Gwendolyn Leick, 348–60. New York: Routledge, 2007.

"Ostasien." *Gutenberg-Museum Mainz.* http://www.gutenberg-museum.de/122.0.html

Otzen, Benedikt, Hans Gottlieb, and Knud Jeppesen. *Myths in the Old Testament.* London: SCM Press Ltd, 1980.

Oyèwùmí, Oyèrónkẹ́. *The Invention of Women: Making an African Sense of Western Gender Discourses.* Minneapolis: University of Minnesota Press, 1997.

Painter, Nell I. "Representing Truth: Sojourner Truth's Knowing and Becoming Known." *The Journal of American History* 81 no. 2 (1994): 461–92. DOI: 10.2307/2081168.

———. "Sojourner Truth in Life and Memory: Writing the Biography of an American Exotic." *Gender & History* 2, no. 1 (1990): 3–16. DOI: 10.1111/j.1468-0424.1990.tb00073.x.

Panabière, Louis. *Cité aigle, ville serpent.* Perpignan: Presses Universitaires de Perpignan, 1993.

Pappe, Ilan. *The Ethnic Cleansing of Palestine.* London: Oneworld Publications, 2006.

Paz, Octavio. "Diosa, demonia, obra maestra." In *México en la obra de Octavio Paz III: Los privilegios de la vista,* 39–58. México D.F.: Fondo de Cultura Económica, 1977.

———. *El laberinto de la soledad, Postdata/Vuelta a "El laberinto de la soledad."* Madrid: Fondo de Cultura Económica, 2007.

Preciado, Beatriz. "Terror anal." In *El deseo homosexual de Guy Hocquenghem,* 133–72. Santa Cruz de Tenerife: Editorial Melusina, 2009.

Puar, Jasbir K. "'I Would Rather Be a Cyborg than a Goddess': Intersectionality, Assemblage, and Affective Politics." *Transversal Texts by EIPCP — European Institute for Progressive Cultural Policies,* January 2011. http://eipcp.net/transversal/0811/puar/en/.

Qian, Zhongshu. *Limited Views: Essays on Ideas and Letters.* Translated by Ronald Egan. Cambridge: Harvard University Asia Center/University Press, 1998.

———. 管錐編 [*Limited Views*]. Vol. 1. Beijing: Sanlian Shudian Press, 2007.

Quijano, Aníbal. "Colonialidad del poder y clasificación social." *Journal of World-Systems Research* 6, no. 2 (2000): 342–86.

———. "Coloniality and Modernity/Rationality." *Cultural Studies* 21, nos. 2–3 (2007): 168–78. DOI: 10.1080/09502380601164353.

Rabasa, José. *Tell Me the Story of How I Conquered You: Elsewheres and Ethnosuicide in the Colonial Mesoamerican World.* Austin: University of Texas Press, 2011.

———. "Thinking Europe in Indian Categories, Or, 'Tell Me the Story of How I Conquered You.'" In *Coloniality at Large: Latin America and the Postcolonial Debate,* edited by Mabel Moraña, Enrique Dussel, and Carlos A. Jáuregui, 43–76. Durham: Duke University Press, 2008.

———. *Without History: Subaltern Studies, the Zapatista Insurgency, and the Specter of History.* Pittsburgh: University of Pittsburgh Press, 2010.

Raitt, Jill. "'Vagina Dentata' and the 'Immaculatus Uterus Divini Fontis.'" *Journal of the American Academy of Religion* 48, no. 3 (2011): 415–31. https://www.jstor.org/stable/1462869.

Rich, Adrienne. "Disloyal to Civilization: Feminism, Racism, Gynephobia." In *On Lies, Secrets, and Silence,* 275–310. New York: W.W. Norton & Company Inc., 1978.

Ricoeur, Paul. *Philosophie de la volonté: Finitude et culpabilité 2,2: La symbolique du mal.* Paris: Aubier, 1960.

Roberto Vera, Luis. *Coatlicue en Paz, la imagen sitiada: La diosa madre azteca como imago mundi y el concepto binario de analogía/ironía en el acto de ver: Un estudio de los textos de Octavio Paz sobre arte.* Puebla: Benemérita Universidad Autónoma de Puebla, 2003.

Rodríguez, Ana Mónica. "El hueco central de Tlaltecuhtli, misterio a debatir cuando se muestre al público." *La Jornada.* March 23, 2010. http://www.jornada.unam.mx/2010/03/23/cultura/a05n1cul.

Rohrlich, Ruby. "State Formation in Sumer and the Subjugation of Women." *Feminist Studies* 6, no. 1 (1980): 76–102. DOI: 10.2307/3177651.

Rorty, Richard. *Consequences of Pragmatism.* Minneapolis: University of Minnesota Press, 1982.

Roth, Martha T. *Law Collections from Mesopotamia and Asia Minor.* Atlanta: Scholars Press, 1995.

Rubin, Gayle. "Thinking Sex: Notes for a Radical Theory of the Politics of Sexuality." In *Pleasure and Danger: Exploring*

Female Sexuality, edited by Carole S. Vance, 276–319. Boston: Routledge & Kegan Paul, 1984.

Sahagún, Bernardino de. *Historia general de las cosas de Nueva España.* México D.F.: Imprenta del Ciudadano Alejandro Valdés, 1829.

Said, Edward W. *Orientalism.* London: Routledge & Kegan Paul, 1978.

Santos, Boaventura de Sousa. *Epistemologies of the South: Justice against Epistemicide.* New York: Routledge, 2016.

Shang, Wei. "Writing and Speech: Rethinking the Issue of Vernaculars in Early Modern China." In *Rethinking East Asian Languages, Vernaculars, and Literacies, 1000–1919,* edited by Benjamin A. Elman, 254–301. Leiden; Boston: Brill, 2014.

Sharp, Christina. *Monstrous Intimacies: Making Post-Slavery Subjects.* Durham: Duke University Press, 2010.

Showalter, Elaine. *Sexual Anarchy: Gender and Culture at the Fin de Siècle.* London: Bloomsbury, 1991.

Sigal, Pete. "Imagining Cihuacoatl: Masculine Rituals, Nahua Goddesses and the Texts of the Tlacuilos." *Gender & History* 22, no. 3 (2010): 538–63. DOI: 10.1111/j.1468-0424.2010.01610.x.

———. "Latin America and the Challenge of Globalizing the History of Sexuality." *American Historical Review* 114 (2009): 1340–53. DOI: 10.1086/ahr.114.5.1340.

———. "Queer Nahuatl: Sahagún's Faggots and Sodomites, Lesbians and Hermaphrodites." *Ethnohistory* 54, no. 1 (2007): 9–34. DOI: 10.1215/00141801-2006-038.

———. *The Flower and the Scorpion: Sexuality and Ritual in Early Nahua Culture.* Durham: Duke University Press, 2011.

Smith, Dinitia. "Has History Been Too Generous to Gutenberg?" *New York Times.* January 27, 2001. http://www.nytimes.com/2001/01/27/arts/27PRIN.html.

Smith, Michael E. *The Aztecs.* Oxford: Blackwell, 1996.

"Sojourner Truth: 'Ain't I a Woman?' December 1851." *Modern History Sourcebook.* https://sourcebooks.fordham.edu/halsall/mod/sojtruth-woman.asp.

Spelman, Elizabeth V. *Inessential Woman: Problems of Exclusion in Feminist Thought.* London: The Women's Press, 1988.

Spielrein, Sabrina. "Destruction as the Cause of Coming into Being." *Journal of Analytical Psychology* 39, no. 2 (1994): 155–86.

Spivak, Gayatri Chakravorty. *Outside in the Teaching Machine.* New York: Routledge, 1993.

———. "Translator's Preface." In Jacques Derrida, *Of Grammatology,* ix–lxxxvii. Baltimore: Johns Hopkins University Press, 1997.

Stephen, Arata. "The Occidental Tourist: *Dracula* and the Anxiety of Reverse Colonization." *Victorian Studies* 33, no. 4 (1990): 621–46. https://www.jstor.org/stable/3827794.

Stryker, Susan, and Stephen Whittle, eds. *The Transgender Studies Reader.* London: Routledge, 2006.

Stuart, David "The Face of the Calendar Stone: A New Interpretation." *Maya Decipherment: Ideas on Ancient Maya Writing and and Iconography.* June 13, 2016. https://decipherment.wordpress.com/2016/06/13/the-face-of-the-calendar-stone-a-new-interpretation/.

Talon, Philippe. *The Standard Babylonian Creation Myth Enūma Eliš.* Helsinki: Neo-Assyrian Text Corpus Project, 2005.

Taylor, Mark C. *Erring: A Postmodern A/Theology.* Chicago: University of Chicago Press, 1984.

"The Complete Jewish Bible with Rashi Commentary." *Chabad.* http://www.chabad.org/library/bible_cdo/aid/8165/jewish/Chapter-1.htm.

Thomas, Calvin. *Straight with a Twist: Queer Theory and the Subject of Heterosexuality.* Chicago: University of Illinois Press, 2000.

Thomas, Nicholas. *Colonialism's Culture: Anthropology, Travel and Government.* Princeton: Princeton University Press, 1994.

Thouvenot, Marc. "Imágenes y escritura entre los nahuas del inicio del XVI." *Estudios de Cultura Náhuatl* 41 (2010): 169–77.

"Tiamat: Lady of Primeval Chaos, the Great Mother of the Gods of Babylon." *Gateways to Babylon.* http://www.gatewaystobabylon.com/gods/ladies/ladytiamat.html.

Tlostanova, Madina, and Walter Mignolo. *Learning to Unlearn: Decolonial Reflections from Eurasia and the Americas.* Columbus: Ohio State University Press, 2012.

Todorov, Tzvetan. *La conquête de l'Amérique: La question de l'autre.* Paris: Éditions du Seuil, 1982.

Tong, Rosemarie. *Feminist Thought: A More Comprehensive Introduction.* Third Edition. Boulder: Westview Press, 2009.

Truth, Sojourner. "Ain't I a Woman?" *Sojourner Truth.* http://www.sojournertruth.org/Library/Speeches/AintIAWoman.htm.

Tsumura, David Toshio. *The Earth and the Waters in Genesis 1 and 2: A Linguistic Investigation.* Sheffield: Sheffield Academic Press, 1989.

Udofia, O.E. "Imperialism in Africa: A Case of Multinational Corporations." *Journal of Black Studies* 14, no. 3 (1984): 353–68. DOI: 10.1177/002193478401400305.

Warlock Asylum. "The Worship of Tiamat in Ancient History." *Warlock Asylum International News.* September 17, 2010. https://warlockasyluminternationalnews.com/2010/09/17/the-worship-of-tiamat-in-ancient-history/.

Watney, Simon. *Policing Desire: Pornography, AIDS and the Media.* London: Comedia, 1987.

Wittig, Monique. "One Is Not Born a Woman (1981)." In *The Straight Mind and Other Essays,* 9–20. Boston: Beacon Press, 1992.

———. "The Straight Mind." In *The Straight Mind and Other Essays,* 21–32. Boston: Beacon Press, 1980.

Xiang, Zairong. "'*adam* Is Not Man': Queer Body before Genesis 2:22 (and After)." In *Unsettling Science and Religion: Contributions and Questions from Queer Studies,* edited by Whitney Bauman and Lisa Stenmark, 183–97. Lanham: Lexington Books, 2018.

———. "Transdualism: Towards a Materio-Discursive Embodiment." *TSQ: Transgender Studies Quarterly* 5, no. 2 (2018): 425–42.

Zhang, Longxi. *The Tao and the Logos: Literary Hermeneutics, East and West.* Durham: Duke University Press, 1992.

Zsolnay, Ilona, ed. *Being a Man: Negotiating Ancient Constructs of Masculinity.* London; New York: Routledge, 2017.

Manuscripts

Códice florentino, http://www.wdl.org/en/item/10612/zoom/#group=1&page=37&zoom=1.250682300324051&centerX=0.35689399306587916&centerY=1.0281884961394223.

Films

Almodóvar, Pedro, dir. *Entre tinieblas.* 1988. http://www.imdb.com/title/tt0085496/.

Lee, Ang, dir. *Life of Pi.* 2012. https://www.imdb.com/title/tt0454876/.

Made in the USA
Middletown, DE
19 February 2021

34042241R00149